UK Business and Financial Cycles Since 1660

Nicholas Dimsdale · Ryland Thomas

UK Business and Financial Cycles Since 1660

Volume I: A Narrative Overview

palgrave
macmillan

Nicholas Dimsdale
University of Oxford
Oxford, Oxfordshire, UK

Ryland Thomas
Bank of England
London, UK

ISBN 978-3-030-26345-4 ISBN 978-3-030-26346-1 (eBook)
https://doi.org/10.1007/978-3-030-26346-1

Cover credit: Heritage Image Partnership Ltd/Alamy Stock Photo

This Palgrave Macmillan imprint is published by the registered company Springer Nature Switzerland AG
The registered company address is: Gewerbestrasse 11, 6330 Cham, Switzerland

The views expressed here represent those of the authors and do not represent the views of the Bank of England or its policy committees.

The original version of the book was revised: Post publication corrections have been updated. The correction to the book is available at https://doi.org/10.1007/978-3-030-26346-1_8

Acknowledgements

We would like to thank many colleagues for their help and support in writing this book. In particular, we are grateful to Jason Lennard and Sally Srinivasan for reading the manuscript and making many helpful suggestions and changes. We are also both grateful to Jagjit Chadha who kindly allowed us to draw from many joint pieces of work and for permission to access the library and archive at the National Institute of Economic and Social Research which provided many nuggets of information and sources of inspiration. We are also very grateful to Steve Broadberry, Solomos Solomou and Martin Weale for their help and advice on the GDP data and their insights on historical UK business cycles from their previous work on which we have drawn heavily. We are also very grateful to Olly Bush, Nick Crafts, John Gent, Terry Mills and Ranald Michie for kindly providing us with data from their previous work. At the Bank of England we would also like to thank James Talbot and Fergal Shortall for their support and backing for this project. Finally, we would like to thank our families for their help, support and understanding throughout the writing of this book, in particular Nadia, Collette, Harry, Amy, Archie and Suzi.

Contents

List of Figures

List of Tables

1
Introduction

In 2008 the UK economy suffered its deepest recession since the 1930s. The recession had several defining characteristics: it took place simultaneously with a global recession; the exchange rate depreciated sharply; and the fiscal deficit increased markedly. Perhaps more importantly the financial sector was arguably both the source and propagator of the crisis and epitomised the potential link between the business and credit cycles. However deflation was avoided in part due to a concerted effort by policymakers around the world to loosen monetary policy in response to the downturn. Many of the features of what has been called the "Great Recession" had been observed before, others had not. The main aim of this book is to place these recent events in a much longer historical context using the plethora of data available to researchers of the UK's economic history going back to the late C17th.

The time of writing (2019) is a propitious time for reviewing historical business and credit cycles. The last major historical review of economic cycles in the UK is almost 50 years old.[1] But the results of an

[1]We are thinking here of Aldcroft and Fearon (1972). Other studies that focus on particular periods or recessions are Dimsdale (1990), Solomou (1994), Dow (1998), Chadha and Nolan (2002), Broadberry and van Leeuwen (2010) and Morys (2014).

N. Dimsdale and R. Thomas,
UK Business and Financial Cycles Since 1660,
https://doi.org/10.1007/978-3-030-26346-1_1

enormous research effort since then means there is now an extensive range of macroeconomic and financial data reaching back as far as the late C17th that allows an updated review to be compiled. This in turn allows the narrative of those cycles to be reconsidered in the light of recent events and informed by the latest research. This book is the first of two volumes that intends to make a contribution to that review. Its aim is to compile an up-to-date overview of the key historical data and techniques available for analysing cyclical phenomena and to review the key features of historical recessions and recoveries, drawing on the extensive literature on the United Kingdom's economic history. This first volume reviews the evidence on the UK business cycle with a focus on cyclical fluctuations in output in the short-to-medium term. A second volume will focus on monetary and credit cycles, which many argue are of a longer duration. That volume will examine their interaction with business cycle fluctuations.

A further contribution of this book is to link analysis of the latest data with an updated narrative of the cycle based on contemporary and secondary sources. Most of the data used in this volume come from the Bank of England's Millennium dataset which was compiled by the authors using the latest research into historical UK statistics. That dataset is provided free online on the Bank of England's website alongside this publication.[2] Previous narratives based on earlier analyses of the data may (or may not) need revising as a result of recent research. It is also possible to review those narrative accounts through the lens of more modern concepts of the business cycle and its drivers. In particular, a recent feature of the literature since the Great Recession has been a focus on the intertwined nature of business and credit cycles. And a key question is whether they are separate but interlinked phenomena or are they one and the same. It is also important to recognise that many of the earlier narratives of business cycle were undertaken by those who were closer to the events they were writing about and had a better understanding of the institutions and infrastructure underpinning

[2] https://www.bankofengland.co.uk/-/media/boe/files/statistics/research-datasets/a-millennium-of-macroeconomic-data-for-the-uk.xlsx.

the economy at the time. As a result it is important to review theories of the business cycle as they developed over time and also consider institutional change so that old and new perspectives can be joined.

The book is primarily an overview and aimed at undergraduate students of the UK's economic history who want an introduction to the subject. But we also hope it will be of use to graduate students and economic historians as a reference guide to business cycles in the UK. The chronological narrative of business cycles in the UK we hope will also be of interest to the general reader.

The book is structured as follows. Chapter 2 provides a short review of theories of the economic cycle and how they developed. This does not pretend to be comprehensive and focuses on some of the key concepts and ideas from the vast literature on the subject. Our focus is the business cycle but many of these theories involve money and credit in both the impulse and propagation of the cycle.

Chapter 3 then considers the range of metrics for evaluating both business and credit cycles and their interaction. The statistical techniques used here are familiar to many economists and again we do not pretend to be exhaustive. We merely wish to summarise some of the key properties of the techniques available. The emphasis will be on univariate analysis of the business cycle using a single indicator such as GDP which has been the focus of much of the literature, although many of the features carry through to a multivariate analysis.

Chapter 4 then discusses the new national accounts data that have become available which allow us to review the basic chronology of UK economic cycles using a set of standard metrics. We argue that the second half of C17th provides the best starting place for an analysis of business cycles in the UK given developments in trade, banking, financial markets and the fiscal power of the state. Symptomatic of this, Crafts and Mills (2017) show the 1660s as the period when per capita incomes begin to take off and exhibit sustained positive growth over the subsequent three centuries (Chart 1.1), albeit coming to a plateau in the wake of the Great Recession in 2008.

Chapter 5 then brings together the results of Chapters 3 and 4 to provide a summary of business cycle metrics under the different

Chart 1.1 Trend and cycles in GDP per capita 1270–2018 (*Source* Thomas and Dimsdale [2017] based on the method of Crafts and Mills [2017])

approaches. As we show, the range of different business cycle estimates you can derive from the available techniques is very wide and depends almost entirely on the judgements and priors made by the investigator—what you put in is what you get out. In our view a statistical approach to the cycle is incomplete and will never be definitive given the judgements embodied in the choices that have to be made to de-trend data and extract cycles. This means supporting econometric analysis with a narrative approach to the cycle.

Chapter 6 then focuses on that alternative analysis—a simple narrative approach to the cycle linked as far as possible to the metrics developed in Chapter 5. It reviews the standard historical narrative of previous studies and re-evaluates them in the light of new data and research. It provides a complete chronology of the key cycles in the UK since 1660 and considers some of the key drivers of UK business cycles, including the role of external factors, and monetary and fiscal policies. The aim of the updated narrative is to highlight potential new research areas. Our hope is that these can be investigated in more detail and with more sophisticated techniques by other researchers who possess knowledge and skills that are greater than our own.

References

Aldcroft, D., & Fearon, P. (1972). *British Economic Fluctuations, 1790–1939*. Basingstoke: Macmillan.

Broadberry, S., & van Leeuwen, B. (2010). *British Economic Growth and the Business Cycle, 1700–1870: Annual Estimates* (CAGE Online Working Paper Series 20).

Chadha, J., & Nolan, C. (2002). A Long View of the UK Business Cycle. *National Institute Economic Review, 182*(1), 72–89.

Crafts, N., & Mills, T. (2017). Six Centuries of British Economic Growth: A Time-Series Perspective. *European Review of Economic History, 21*(2), 141–158.

Dimsdale, N. (1990). Money, Interest and Cycles in Britain Since 1830. *Greek Economic Review, 12*(Supplement), 153–196.

Dow, J. (1998). *Major Recessions, Britain and the World, 1920–1995*. Oxford: Oxford University Press.

Morys, M. (2014). Cycles and Depressions. In R. Floud, J. Humphries, & P. Johnson (Eds.), *The Cambridge Economic History of Modern Britain: Volume II. 1870 to the Present*. Cambridge: Cambridge University Press.

Solomou, S. (1994). Economic Fluctuations. In R. Floud & D. McCloskey (Eds.), *The Economic History of Britain since 1700 Volume 2: 1860–1939* (pp. 1870–1913). Cambridge: Cambridge University Press.

Thomas, R., & Dimsdale, N. (2017). *A Millennium of UK Macroeconomic Data*. Bank of England OBRA Dataset.

2

Business, Monetary and Credit Cycles in Theory

The literature on business cycles is vast and that on monetary and credit cycles ever growing. That means any summary of business and credit cycle theory is unlikely to be comprehensive and will always be to some extent superficial. It is also a fact that different theories of the cycle often have a number of common elements, so making fine distinctions between them is difficult. Many theories of the business cycle also imply a monetary or credit cycle of some form, for example those that involve overoptimistic expectations and fixed investment in need of long-term finance. To the extent the two cycles are distinct many have argued that business cycle downturns following a boom in money and credit tend to be larger (Jordà et al. 2013). So in many theories the business, monetary and credit cycles are closely intertwined and difficult to separate. Nevertheless it is necessary to attempt a summary of some of the key theories behind business, monetary and credit cycles in order to provide context.

The original version of this chapter was revised: Typographical and grammatical corrections were incorporated. The correction to this chapter is available at https://doi.org/10.1007/978-3-030-26346-1_8

N. Dimsdale and R. Thomas,
UK Business and Financial Cycles Since 1660,
https://doi.org/10.1007/978-3-030-26346-1_2

2.1 Business Cycle Definition

As discussed in Harding and Pagan (2006) there are different forms of behaviour that can be classed as "cyclical". Often researchers use very different definitions of the cycle and this can lead to confusion when comparing results across empirical studies.

We might start with the definition of the business cycle by Burns and Mitchell (1946) who were pioneers in the precise measurement of the business cycle at the National Bureau of Economic Research (NBER):

> Business cycles are a type of fluctuation found in the aggregate economic activity of nations that organize their work mainly in business enterprises: a cycle consists of expansions occurring at about the same time in many economic activities, followed by similarly general recessions, contractions, and revivals which merge into the expansion phase of the next cycle; this sequence of changes is recurrent but not periodic.

They also had a view on the duration of such cycles:

> In duration business cycles vary from more than one year to ten or twelve years; they are not divisible into shorter cycles of similar character with amplitudes approximating their own.

Today business cycles are typically described as medium-term fluctuations lasting around 2–8 years based on subsequent analysis of US data in the post-war period.

Lucas (1975) offered a narrower, more precise definition of the economic cycle

> real output undergoes serially correlated movements about trend which are not explainable by movement in the availability of factors of production.

Serial correlation means that today's output fluctuation depends to some extent on previous period's fluctuations. So Lucas's definition would suggest that the cycle is simply the serially correlated component of what is left over after removing the trend from output, and that the trend is driven by full employment of the available factors of production.

This shows it is important to be clear about the definition of the cycle. Burns and Mitchell largely think of the cycle in terms of identifying expansions and contractions in the *level of activity*. This is often called *classical* cycle analysis. Lucas on the other hand articulates cycles in terms of the movement of *output relative to trend*. So a cycle is envisaged as a period of above trend growth followed by a period of below trend growth. This type of cycle is typically known as a *growth* cycle to distinguish it from the classical Burns and Mitchell definition. We return to this distinction in Chapter 3 when we discuss the different methods of deriving metrics on the business cycle.

2.2 Impulse and Propagation of Business Cycles

It was the Norwegian economist Ragnar Frisch who emphasised the distinction between impulse and propagation (Frisch 1933). Economic shocks to the supply and demand of commodities are the *impulses* that disturb the economy away from a steady growth path or equilibrium position. And various lags, adjustment costs and other *propagation* mechanisms, both within and across sectors and industries, are what cause the movement in output following the impulse to be persistent and "cyclical" in nature. This view lends itself more to the growth cycle view than the classic cycle view but both are compatible for example if contractions in output in a classical cycle are largely the result of negative shocks to demand or a financial crisis.

Theories of the cycle that are based on frequent random impulses to the economy are normally described as stochastic models of the cycle. Alternative theories of such cycles then place different weight on the nature of the impulses that lead to fluctuations—for example whether the shocks are real or monetary—and also often differ on the nature of the propagation mechanism.

However in extreme cases the cycle may not involve random shocks and can be completely deterministic where the cycle occurs endogenously. For example, the famous cobweb theory where supply is a function of previous period's prices can lead to endogenous "periodic" cycles without the need for shocks. Such deterministic cycles are often characterised by sinusoidal waves where the cycle persists forever in a regular pattern but in principal can also be chaotic or degenerate. The simplest form of deterministic cycle is a cosine wave

$$c_t = r^t a \cos(bt)$$

where $r^t a$ is the amplitude of the cycle which is damped if $r < 1$. b is the frequency of the cycle and the period of the cycle q is the number of time periods it takes to complete a cycle, which is given by

$$q = 2\pi / b$$

This deterministic cycle is shown in Fig. 2.1. One can of course combine the idea so that there can be stochastic cycles which are also periodic. In other words cycles are driven by shocks but have fundamental periodic cycles within the propagation mechanism. So a stochastic

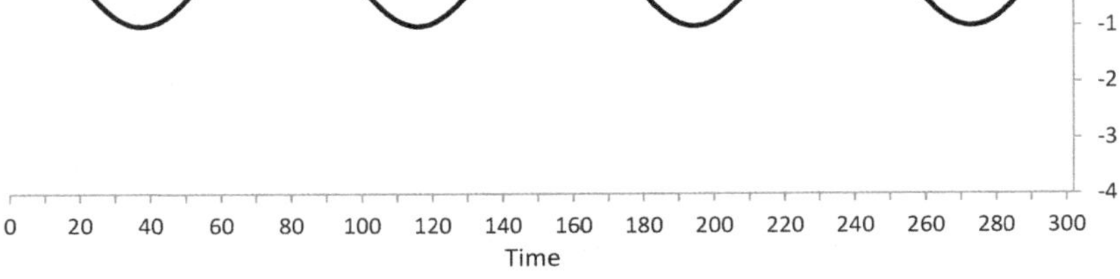

Fig. 2.1 Deterministic periodic cycle

"periodic" cycle will imply that a single shock in itself will generate a subsequent cycle that could in principle last forever—a "rocking horse" cycle is the name given to it by Frisch—taking the form of a sinusoidal wave although as discussed this may be damped with the amplitude of the cycle generated diminishing over time. In a stochastic periodic cycle what we then observe as the economic cycle is in fact a series of overlapping waves driven by positive and negative shocks. The cycles arising from each shock may be damped but new shocks give the overall cycle new "energy" in the words of Frisch.

This discussion suggests it is important to be clear what is meant by a cycle. It is possible for a "cycle" in the sense of Lucas to be generated by successive positive and negative shocks working through persistent mechanisms that generate serially correlated movements in output. Each shock in itself does not lead to a cycle but rather a persistent movement away from trend, possibly "hump-shaped", that then dissipates to zero over time asymptotically rather than causing a persistent movement in output in the opposite direction further out in time. But because positive shocks to output are followed by negative shocks to output this generates what might look like a cycle over time. For example we might have the simple autoregressive or AR(1) model:

$$c_t = \theta c_{t-1} + v_t$$

Figure 2.2 shows how a sequence of "white noise" shocks (zero mean and unit variance) generated by this process can look similar to a stochastic version of the periodic cycle shown in Fig. 2.1 even though the inherent propagation mechanisms are different.

We evaluate these differences later when we discuss econometric models of the cycle. However it is worth noting at this point that given the difficulty in defining what a cycle is, many prefer to be agnostic and talk about economic "fluctuations" as discussed in Ashton's (1959) classic work[1] on C18th England.

[1]Ashton (1959, p. 2).

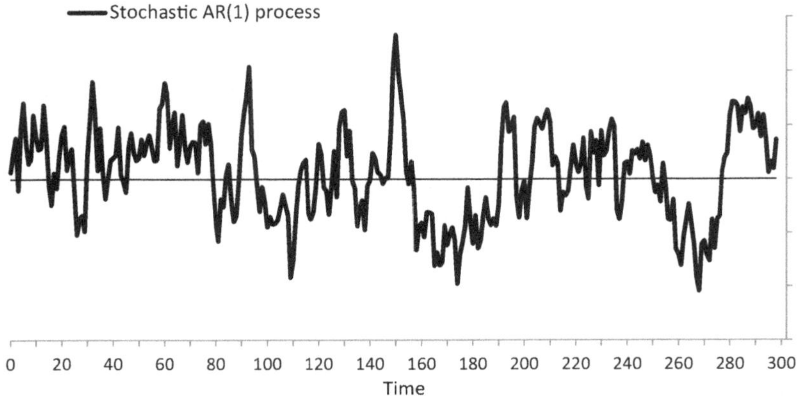

Fig. 2.2 Serially-correlated AR(1) cycle

2.3 Classical Theories of the Business Cycle

Today business cycles are described as medium-term fluctuations lasting around 2–8 years. However the early pioneers of business cycle analysis were interested in a wide range of short, medium and long-term fluctuations in output. So business cycle theory encompassed a number of different concepts and ideas. Interest in business and credit cycles began during the C18th and C19th following the development of market-based industrial economies and the periodic booms, downturns and financial crises that went with them. This analysis reached its peak in the first half of the C20th as the economic data required to analyse such cycles was more readily available. By the time of Schumpeter's two-volume analysis in 1939 (Schumpeter 1939) business cycles were classified into different types of cycle, largely based on their periodicity and typically named after their originator.

The "Kitchin" inventory cycle of 2–5 years

The articulation of the classic inventory cycle is usually attributed to Kitchin (1923) although the role of inventories had been identified earlier. This theory is typically associated with unexpected shifts in consumer demand. A fall in demand initially leads to some fall in output and or prices, but is partly absorbed in the short run by companies building up stocks. However at some point in the future, if the fall in demand is persistent then eventually firms will want to destock this adds to the fall in output or, if expenditure picks up may delay a recovery in output. So the output response to shifts in demand takes the form of a short cycle.

The Juglar cycle of 7–11 years

The classical medium-term business cycle was identified by Juglar in the C19th. Juglar's study (Juglar 1862) was largely empirical but the Juglar cycle is typically associated with movements in fixed investment spending, the source of which might be expectations of future demand or in response to technological shocks. Juglar was the first to consider different phases of the cycle in terms of boom, slump and recovery.

The Kuznets cycle of 15–25 years

Simon Kuznets identified a longer cycle in 1930 (Kuznets 1930). He ascribed these swings to movements in building and infrastructure investment which he associated with large scale movements in immigration and population. The driver of these cycles has often been argued to be shifts in land prices that follow large scale migration movements which develop incentives for business and infrastructure development. The movements in migration themselves are the results of divergent real wages in developing parts of the world that prompts shifts in labour.

The Kondratieff long technological cycle of 45–60 years

Cycles of even longer duration were identified by Kondratieff in the 1920s. Kondratieff's study (see Kondratieff and Stolper 1935 for the English translation) was largely empirical and sought to identify the various characteristics of such cycles, such as the fact that innovations tended to cluster in downswings and their application in upswings. Most interpretations of these very long cycles are that they represent waves of technological development and innovation that often take time for their full benefits to work through. Schumpeter developed a particular theory behind Kondratieff waves with the idea of clustered innovations driving investment and productivity (Schumpeter 1939; Mensch 1979).

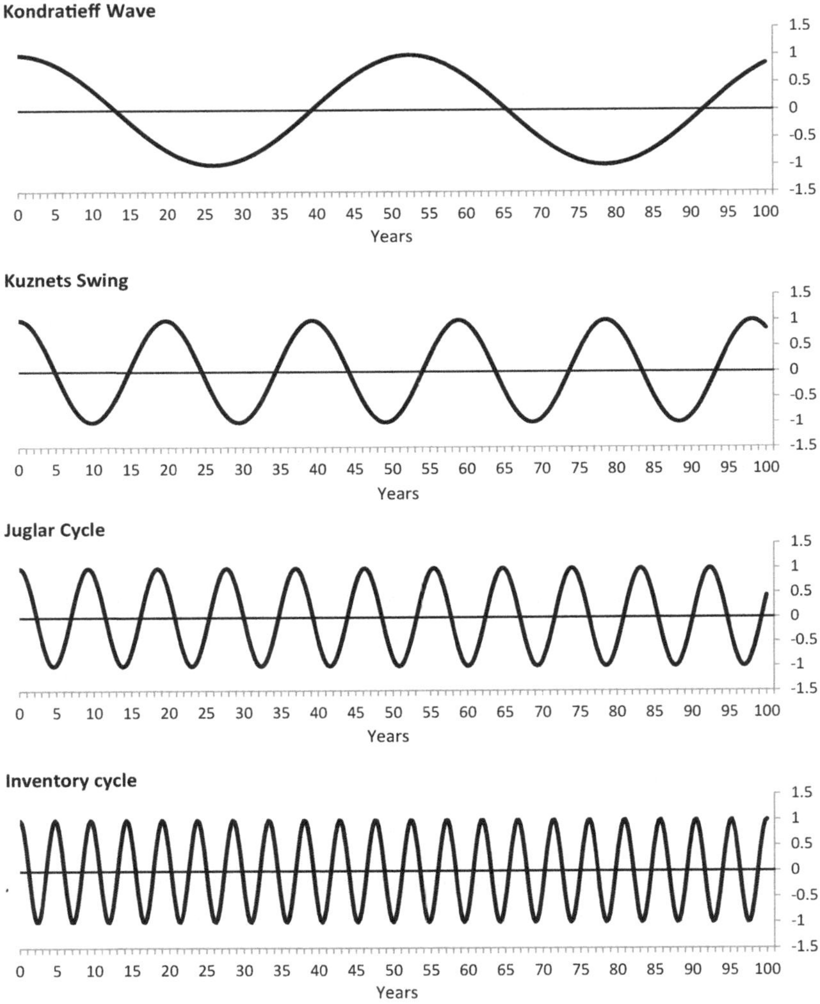

Fig. 2.3 Stylised representation of the classical business cycles dichotomy

A more modern interpretation of this idea is the idea of General Purpose Technologies or GPTs (David 1990) which represent major innovations that have widespread uses which get fulfilled over time. Steam, electricity and information and communications technology (ICT) are examples of

GPTs. Some of these theories argue that the diffusion of a new GPT will initially generate a productivity slowdown in the early phase of the diffusion process, and are only followed by productivity acceleration later. However the evidence supporting the Kondratieff wave as a result of technological improvements and GPTs more generally is mixed. Solomou (1994) however argues that long swings may result from institutional changes, for example the introduction of a gold standard or monetary union.

The different cycles are summarised in Fig. 2.3 using simple deterministic periodic cycles to represent each theory. Schumpeter in his work suggested that the overall cyclical pattern observed was a composite of the different periodic cycles. So for example a Kondratieff wave could consist of two Kuznets swings, which in turn could contain two to three Juglar cycles.

Alongside these classic empirically-based studies which tended to focus on real shocks driving the cycle, other theories of the cycle were being expounded in which money and credit placed a central role.

2.4 Classical Monetary and Credit Cycles

Wicksell (1898) and Austrian Business Cycle theorists such as Hayek (1929 [1933]), von Mises (1934) and Lachmann (1956) were the first to explicitly include money and credit into a narrative about cycles. Wicksell introduced the idea of the natural rate of interest—the rate of interest that would equate planned investment with planned saving in a closed economy (r^* in Fig. 2.4). He showed how, in a monetary economy, the market rate of interest could easily differ from that natural rate setting in motion an unstable cumulative process of higher inflation and lower real interest rates. Shocks to investment and saving might change the natural rate of interest but market rates, pinned down by monetary factors in the short run, might not. He argued that a positive gap between planned investment and planned saving at the market rate of interest could only be filled by money and credit creation by the banking system (over and above any change in the demand for money) which holds the interest rate below the natural rate. This money creation finances an increase in nominal spending, which pushes up output

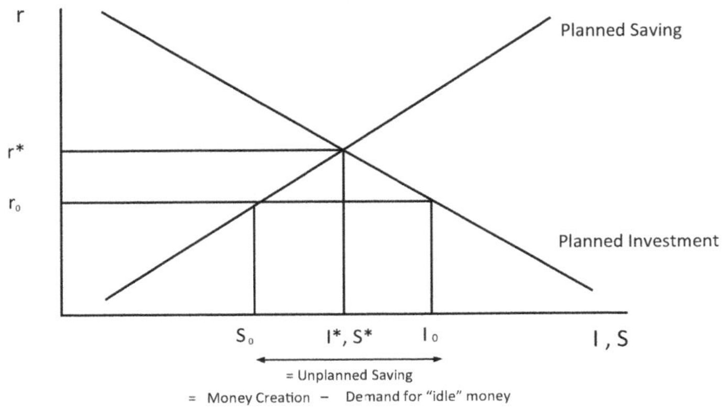

Fig. 2.4 The Wicksellian natural rate and the monetary cycle

and inflation. One could think of the money received by the recipients of the higher level of spending as representing, in the first instance, "unplanned saving" that plugs the gap between investment and spending plans (Fig. 2.4). The resulting adjustment leads to an ever-increasing spiral of higher inflation and lower real interest rates unless market rates are brought in line with the natural rate.

The Austrians developed a similar line of thought but developed it into an explicit theory of cycles during the early C20th. Much of the emphasis of the theory is on monetary policy as the cause of the boost to credit creation by the banking system. This falsely informs producers of a time preference alteration. Consumer time preferences are deemed to be the signals for producers to allocate their production over time. High saving supposedly indicates a preference for future consumption and low current consumption. In an upswing in the cycle expansionary monetary policy, which reduces interest rates relative to the time preference of consumers, distorts that signal. It increases margins on investment, especially for loans with long-term capital structure and results in ill-informed investors favouring long-term investment into their production process, referred to as "malinvestment". This is accommodated by high credit growth and broad money creation. The effect of increased spending by firms does filter through to an increase in demand; however, this is not sufficient to meet the output expectations on which the finance of the long-term loans depends. As firms begin to default, banks scale back credit and demand repayments resulting in a credit crunch, possible recession and a readjustment period.

Austrian business cycle theory does not cover the exact details of the bust phase, simply that it is inevitable. Von Mises, for example, argued that the ensuing credit crunch involves consumers adjusting their balance of saving and investment; and that the recession is caused by the absorption of losses during the period of monetary boom. The recovery from recession comes as economic activity refocuses on more accurate, sustainable consumer desires. It is acknowledged that the boom can be artificially maintained providing that credit continues to expand. The exact time-frame over which a typical cycle occurs, depends on for how long monetary policy remains loose. However, the longer the credit-fuelled boom continues for, the longer and more severe the readjustment period.

A similar monetary theory of the cycle was developed by the British economist Ralph Hawtrey. He too argued that the trade cycle is driven by changes credit and money creation by the banking system. Hawtrey's theoretical cycle begins with a rise in credit encouraging firms to increase expenditure while credit is typically cheap following a downturn. The increased expenditure filters through to consumers, meaning an increase in household income. Household's increase spending on consumption as their incomes rise, causing a depletion of firms inventories (some of which they are assumed to have paid for with the newly issued, cheap credit). The shortage means prices begin to rise and firms seek further credit to buy factors of production at the new, higher prices. This cycle causes inflation and a growing money supply. Periods of boom come to a sudden and violent halt when banks suspend credit expansion. A slowdown in credit on the other hand sparks a contractionary spiral in the equivalent opposite fashion.

The main feature of these monetary theories is that they view the money supply as endogenous and driven by the decisions of the banking system. The shock that causes banks to increase or decrease credit can be due to monetary policy to the extent it is set different to the natural rate. But more generally any shock to demand and supply that effects the natural rate of interest can set this process in motion if not perfectly offset by policy or market interest rates. This can include animal spirits and overoptimistic expectations by households and firms or by changes in the lending behaviour of the banking system.

2.5 Modern Theories of the Business Cycle

The experience of the Great Depression of the 1930s and the Keynesian revolution in response to it reset the business cycle research agenda. In particular the role of macroeconomic stabilisation policy to control the cycle and avoid unnecessary swings in output and unemployment came to the forefront. Different views about the drivers of economic cycles and the friction that led to movements in output and unemployment would then determine whether policymakers could do anything to alleviate fluctuations. For example, macroeconomic stabilisation policy offered a way of ending the business cycle completely to the extent cycles reflected shifts in expectations and demand which could be offset by fiscal and monetary policy. Others put more weight on the idea that shocks were fundamentally supply-side driven and that there was little policy could do other than to put in place structural policies that could counter such forces in the longer term. Overall many of the classic theories discussed earlier were reformulated or articulated in a slightly different way to reflect the emphasis on frictions and the role of policy in alleviating them.

2.5.1 The Post-WW2 Keynesian Multiplier-Accelerator View of the Cycle

The Keynesian view of the cycle that emerged in the writings of Keynes and his followers closely resembles some of the ideas in the Kitchin and Juglar cycles. Shocks to aggregate demand, either from consumption, government spending and exports or shifts in investment due to "animal spirits" lead to an initial increase in output and income because wages and prices are sticky and output is demand-determined. The Keynesian multiplier however would imply that the initial increase in output will lead to future rounds of spending given a non-zero propensity to consumer out of income. If this process is characterised as a lagged relationship between consumption this period and income in the previous period this in itself would imply the response of output to a change in demand will be spread out over several periods. In addition there is the relationship between both inventory and fixed investment with the change in demand and output arising from the desire to restore stock-GDP/sales ratios. These relationships then imply persistent cyclical fluctuations in output and employment. Take the following simple model embodying a propensity to consume out of lagged income, an accelerator term in investment and a stock cycle.

$$Y_t = C_t + \Delta S_t + I_t + \mathrm{NX}_t$$

$$C_t = \pi Y_{t-1}$$

$$I_t = \theta(C_t - C_{t-1})$$

$$\Delta S_t = S_t - S_{t-1}$$

$$S_t = \sigma Y_{t-1}$$

where Y is GDP, C is consumption, S is the level of stocks or inventories, I is fixed investment and NX is net exports (exports—imports).

A shock to net exports (NX) of £100mn and values of $\pi = 0.8$, $\theta = 1$ and $\sigma = 0.2$ in this model will lead to the cycles shown in Fig. 2.2. The multiplier effect will lead to a gradual increase in GDP to £500mn given the marginal propensity to consumer, π, out of each round of income is 0.8, giving a total multiplier of 5 ($=1/(1-0.8)$). Adding an accelerator effect where investment is a function of the change in output leads to a damped cyclical impact over and above the multiplier effect given the value of θ. Adding a simple stockbuilding element where stocks are a function of lagged output leads to a regular cycle pattern around the Keynesian multiplier impact of £500mn under the parameters calibrated above. In general the model above will lead to a second

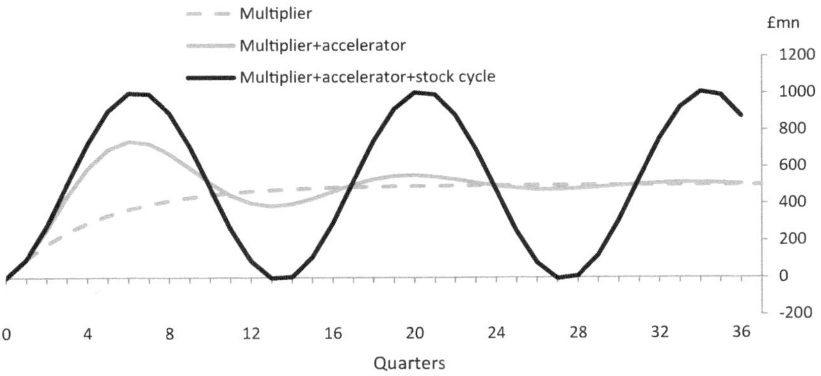

Fig. 2.5 The multiplier-accelerator and stock cycles

order autoregressive or "AR(2)" process for output which can generate damped or unstable cycles under different parameter values as will be discussed later. Figure 2.5 illustrates.

The existence of such cycles suggests a role for macroeconomic stabilisation policy to offset such fluctuations. In the post-war period fiscal policy—either government spending or tax changes—were argued to be the most effective tools to offset such fluctuations. It was recognised however that if stabilisation policy was implemented in a laggardly fashion it could augment rather than offset the business cycle. Moreover fiscal and monetary policies themselves could end up being the drivers of such cycles if they were used in a pro-active fashion to try and boost the economy. For example during the 1950s, 60s and 70s UK governments attempted several times to use fiscal policy to break out of what was perceived to be poor productivity performance compared to other competitor countries. These attempts were based on overoptimistic expectations of how such movements in demand could lead to increases in the economy's supply capacity.

2.5.2 Monetarist and New Classical Monetary Cycles

The emphasis on aggregate demand shocks and sticky wages and prices as a source of fluctuations faced criticism in the 1970s from both monetarists and the new classical macroeconomic revolution (see Hoover 1988).

Monetarists such as Milton Friedman and later new classical economists such as Lucas (1973) placed more emphasis on monetary shocks (unexpected movements in the money supply) as a source of disturbances and placed more weight on the role of expectations and uncertainty about relative price movements rather than sticky prices as the reason such disturbances cause temporary movements in output away from trend. For example, Friedman is usually associated with the idea of adaptive inflation expectations. In Friedman's story an increase in the money supply and nominal spending would lead in the first instance to an unexpected increase in inflation given flexible goods prices. The actual real wage faced by firms would fall incipiently causing firms to demand more workers. This would then start to bid up nominal wages. However because this increase in nominal wages would be perceived as a rise in real wages by workers with adaptive inflation expectations, they would then be prepared to supply more labour in response. The resulting increase in nominal wages would therefore end up being less than the increase in prices, leading to an equilibrium fall in the real wage and higher output and employment.

Friedman and Schwartz (1963, 1982) in their monetary history volumes on the United States and UK used this approach to re-evaluate the role of monetary disturbances in historical economic cycles. Famously they argued that the Great Depression in the United States was mainly the result of the fall in the broad money supply arising from the large number of bank failures. The blame for this was firmly squared at the Federal Reserve for not acting as a lender of last resort.[2]

The new classical monetary approach to business cycles (Lucas 1973, 1975) placed more emphasis on microfounded models and rational expectations. In this case monetary shocks would only cause a very temporary disturbance to output to the extent agents have imperfect information and confuse a change in the general level of prices with a

[2]Often the fall in the money supply is attributed to a fall in the monetary base mentioned in Friedman's (1968) presidential address. Although there was a fall in the monetary base in 1928–1930, the large fall of 33% in M2 between 1930 and 1933 is mainly due to a fall in deposits relative to commercial bank reserves. For a discussion of this see Nelson (2018).

relative price change that causes them to supply more labour or output. However, persistent cycles could be generated if shocks to the money stock were serially correlated and by the added persistence implied by the impact on investment and the capital stock which would ultimately need to be unwound if the money supply shock was neutral on output. These mechanisms are discussed further in Hoover (1988). This results in the Lucas "surprise" supply curve linking output to surprise changes in prices and money. If money growth is assumed to be serially correlated this can be solved out to generate a second order difference equation in output which once simulated produces a persistent response to a monetary shock.

The main issue with the monetary disturbances approach is the articulation of what counts as a monetary disturbance in practice and why they might be serially correlated. Typically the literature uses an exogenous money supply process as a pedagogical device to articulate the theory. In practice the nature of an underlying monetary shock will differ according to the policy regime and the financial structure of the economy. For example, under a gold standard a monetary shock might be associated with a gold discovery at the world level. However for an individual country the money supply is endogenous and would respond to any shock that caused balance of payments to move into deficit. Many of these shocks would be real shocks, e.g. a deficit caused by a poor harvest or some other real shock. Similar issues apply to the fiat money economies of the C20th where many countries implemented monetary policy via setting short-term interest rates. The money supply will endogenously respond to the interest rate rule of the policymaker. Therefore monetary shocks are really deviations from the expected policy rule of the monetary authorities and the persistence of the implied money supply process will depend on the persistence of the interest rate rule and the variables it reacts to. Furthermore there is the distinction between shocks to narrow and broad money. Should shocks to the banking system's willingness to supply credit be thought of as a monetary shock in this framework or a real shock? And if so how does this relate to the Austrian School and Hawtrey narratives for the business cycle discussed earlier which put money creation by banks at the heart of the process. These issues were taken up by many economists in the 1970s and 1980s as the monetary and fiscal authorities in many countries grappled with monetary targets at the same time as they were liberalising the banking and financial system. This forced the development of a greater understanding of the financial nexus between the central bank, the government and the commercial banking system (see Goodhart and Needham (2017) for an excellent exposition of how this developed in the UK). The most prominent and articulate advocate of how this system has led to broad money cycles in the UK and other countries has been Congdon (1992, 2005) who emphasises the link between broad money, asset prices and nominal spending and how this can explain the business cycles observed since 1970s. Many central banks also emphasise the need to take into account the money creating power of the banking system and the role of monetary and macroprudential policy in ensuring this does not endanger monetary and financial stability (see Mcleay et al. 2014; Jakab and Kumhof 2018).

2.5.3 New Keynesian Business Cycles

The New Keynesian approach to the business cycle developed in the mid-1980s and to some extent represents a synthesis of earlier ideas. The new classical emphasis on microfoundations and rational expectations was combined with an articulation of the key wage and price frictions that ultimately lay behind cyclical movements in output. Imperfect competition was the key to explaining why output was demand-determined. Given prices exceed marginal cost in equilibrium then if prices are sticky in the short run it would be profitable for producers to expand output in the face of a demand shock.

A key feature of the New-Keynesian model was the "divine coincidence". If the economy is hit by either shocks to aggregate demand or supply then stabilising output around trend—where "trend" is strictly the level of output consistent with flexible prices—is also consistent with stabilising inflation. Given the key welfare loss in the model arises from the relative price distortions implied by sticky prices, then stabilising the output gap and inflation was also the optimal prescription for monetary policy. Only shocks to mark-ups, or other distortions that cause potential supply to move from its "efficient" level, would lead to a trade-off between stabilising output and inflation, and therefore a case for allowing output to move way from its flexible price level. Although this idea had been implicit in earlier descriptions of the cycle the implications for the interpretation of cycles was clear. In the absence of large trade-off inducing shocks then any persistent cycle that emerged must be the result of sub-optimal stabilisation policy. These results can be tempered if other frictions or policy preferences are brought into the mix. For example the perfect stabilisation of output around trend might lead to considerable instrument volatility if the immediate effect of policy was quite small and only came through with a lag. Such volatility in interest rates or distortionary tax rates might have additional welfare implications that might mean it was optimal for policy not to stabilise output fully, at least in the absence of additional policy instruments.

2.5.4 Real Business Cycles

The new classical revolution in economics also produced an alternative theory of business cycles where technology and other supply shocks play a prominent role as the key drivers of business cycles. The movements in real output and employment following such shocks are also equilibrium movements and do not rely on sticky wages and prices. This approach became known as the real business cycle (RBC) theory and was first articulated in the well-known paper by Kydland and Prescott (1982) and developed further in papers such as Long and Plosser (1983) and King and Plosser (1984). The papers showed how key features of the business cycle could be replicated in relatively simple models with capital accumulation and random shocks to technology. Shocks to technology were defined as unexpected shifts in output not explained by movements in capital and labour inputs—and known as the "Solow residual" after Solow (1957). RBC theory also had definitive predictions for how other variables moved over the cycle. For example real product wages should move pro-cyclically with shifts in the marginal product of labour. As King and Plosser (1984) argued money and credit can be brought into the picture as endogenous reactors to the output and expenditure movements generated by such cycles. Other real rigidities were then brought in to explain why, in the data, employment moved by more and real wages by less than the simple canonical RBC model would predict.

The key issue again is how the technology shocks identified by the theory should be interpreted in practice. Should they be taken literally as random shocks to knowledge or technical progress or are they just indicative of supply shocks more generally, that are observationally equivalent to shifts in output relative to capital and labour inputs. For example, oil price or import price shocks might show up as a fall in output relative to inputs of capital and labour.[3] A key implication however of RBC analysis is that the cycle and trend of a series are likely to be related phenomena i.e. permanent and cyclical movements in output arise from the same underlying technology shocks.

Although supply movements are likely to be driven by shocks to technical progress or the supply of factor inputs, some models predict that demand shocks, if they are persistent and not offset by policy, may also have permanent effects on supply. For example, some of those made unemployed in a downturn may find it increasingly difficult to get a job as the duration of their unemployment status increases. So persistent demand shocks may lead to an increase in the share of the long-term unemployed and may increase the equilibrium or "natural rate" of unemployment. Such models are said to exhibit "hysteresis" (see Blanchard and Summers 1986; Layard and Nickell 1986).

2.5.5 Financial and Credit Cycles

The role of financial factors and credit have long played a part in the theory of business cycles, as we have seen with the discussion of the Austrians' and Hawtrey's theories of the cycle. The issue is whether credit and finance are an intrinsic part of the business cycle or whether a distinct credit or financial cycle exists independently of the business cycle,

[3] Oil/import price increases will lower oil/imported inputs which will cause gross output to fall if there is some substitutability between oil and other factor inputs.

but with the two interacting at key turning points. Below we focus on some of the modern theories of the financial cycle, starting with Minsky (1986) and Kindleberger (1978) before moving on to the recent analysis especially by Claudio Borio and others at the Bank for International Settlements (BIS).

Minsky's "Financial Instability Hypothesis" focuses on the build-up of speculative (and ultimately unstable) credit granted in the upswing of an economic cycle. During stages of stable economic growth, when firms have predictable cash flows that easily cover the financing of credit, they take on liabilities that they can only afford given continued economic prosperity. A point comes where the over-leveraged economy can no longer service its debt, credit will tighten and there will be a downswing or recession until the general economic situation is more robust and then a recovery can begin. Minsky stated

> Every disaster, financial or otherwise, is compounded out of initial displacements or shocks, structural characteristics of the system, and human error. (Minsky 1986)

Minsky sees credit cycles as part of the DNA of a deregulated financial system. The build-up of instability during times of economic boom is inevitable and will recur in a cyclical fashion. The explanation offered as to the reason behind a bust is an "unusual" event or, what has become termed a "Minsky moment", that exposes the shortcomings in the system. Minsky argues that these events receive the majority of the blame for the bust or it is blamed on a simple human error that we can easily correct in the future; whereas, in reality it is the nature of a deregulated financial system. Minsky calls for tighter regulation and discusses the possibility of allowing small, perhaps local crises to happen in order to keep balance sheets stable in the long-term.

Kindleberger's most influential work, *Manias, Panics and Crashes: A History of Financial Crises*, was published in 1978, but re-printed after the dot-com bubble because of its renewed resonance. From the title, manias are described as the result of overly bullish expectations, driven by increased credit creation and resulting in speculative bubbles. The panic stage is characterised by a general movement by agents into money or liquid assets and away from real or financial assets as they realise the increasing likelihood of a crisis. The crash then comes as banks cease to lend at all and there is a fire sale of assets which forces down prices. It is not until assets become sufficiently affordable and agents begin to return to illiquid assets that a recovery can begin. A central bank or equivalent lender of last resort can convince people that liquidity will be available to meet demand (at some price) in exchange for (or secured on) illiquid assets.

A key concept that Kindleberger refers to is that of "displacement", a process by which an event or series of events cause a change in economic activity. With regard to displacement, Kindleberger argues that consistently positive events can create a sentiment of overconfidence that can be more dangerous than a negative shock such as poor harvests or war. He reaches the conclusion (in agreement with Minsky) that by the time the cycle has reached its peak, it is too late for policymakers. Automatic stabilisers need to be in place to prevent the stage of mania being reached, otherwise once mania is in progress, a bust is almost inevitable.

The relative popularity of Minsky's and Kindleberger's theories has grown significantly since the subprime mortgage crisis and ensuing global recession. In the modern literature, credit (bank and non-bank) is the focus of attention in the analysis of financial cycles and their impact on residential and commercial property prices (e.g. Mian and Sufi 2014). A key turning point in the history of credit cycles is often argued to be the extensive financial deregulation during the 1970s and 1980s which has led to increasing levels of private sector debt burdens most of it secured on property. An extremely influential body of work by Jordà et al. (2016) and Knoll et al. (2017) has examined credit and house prices in developed economies since 1870. They emphasise the break in the behaviour of credit from the 1970s onwards noting the "hockey stick" profile in private sector debt ratios over this period. Minsky's work has also been the basis of modern post-Keynesian analysis of the credit and financial cycle (see Keen 2013; Lavoie 2014).

A variety of methods are used to gauge the state of the credit cycle in the modern literature. Aikman et al. (2013) use the ratio of credit to GDP to demonstrate the credit cycle. Whereas, Drehman et al. (2012) look at credit to the private non-financial sector, the ratio of credit to

GDP, equity prices, residential property prices and an index of aggregate asset prices (this includes residential property, commercial property and equity prices). They do however, conclude that equity prices are an unreliable measure of the financial system and disregard them in the analysis.

One general conclusion made is that there is a stark contrast in the duration of financial cycles and business cycles. Drehman et al. (2012) find that, on average, medium-term business cycles last between 7 and 10 years; whereas, they find medium-term financial cycles to last between 10 and 20 years depending on the degree of regulation in the economy. In addition, they find the amplitude of financial cycles to be greater than business cycles:

> On average, the standard deviation of the frequency-based financial cycle is more than seven times larger than that for the cycle in output at business cycle frequencies. Even when compared to the medium-term cycle in output, the standard deviation is two and a half times larger. (Drehman et al. 2012)

A key debate here is whether macro and micro prudential policies, such as setting capital requirements for financial institutions, can act to dampen financial cycles or at least make the financial sector more resilient to shocks, so that a downturn in the economy is not also associated with a financial crisis and the financial system can keep on providing credit.

2.6 Summary—Impulse, Propagation and Policy Response

Bringing this together we can summarise what theory suggests are likely to be the key impulses that generate business cycles and some of the important propagation mechanisms. Theory would also suggest various policies should be able to act as a stabilising mechanism to dampen cycles if set appropriately but may act as a destabilising force if not. So those policies arguably need to be added to the taxonomy of impulses and propagation mechanisms suggested by Frisch. This taxonomy is summarised in Table 2.1.

Table 2.1 Impulse, propagation and policy stabilisation

Shocks hitting the economy
• **Aggregate supply shocks**. This could take the form of shocks originating in particular sectors of the economy such as the impact of harvests on agricultural output or technological progress in high tech sectors such as information and communication technology. These can then have broader impact on the aggregate if these sectors are an input into other sectors. Alternatively shocks to supply could involve shocks to the supply of factors of production such as a shift in labour market participation or hours worked
• **Domestic demand shocks** arising from changing consumer preferences or a change in the underlying behaviour of government and its preference for higher or lower taxes and government spending.
• **World demand shocks** reflecting demand for UK products from overseas. Wars and other trade disruptions are likely to be a key source of shocks to the demand for exports
• For a small open economy **terms of trade shocks** are likely to be important disturbances to both the demand and supply side of the economy reflecting changes to the relative prices of important exported and imported commodities such as oil. Again wars may be an important source of these shocks if they result in shortages of key raw materials and supplies
• **Shocks to expectations or "News shocks".** These shocks reflect "animal spirits" and expected increases in expected future productivity and income. These may raise demand even if expectations are overoptimistic and not subsequently validated. That lack of validation may then cause a crash
• **Shocks to uncertainty** may cause households and companies to reduce or delay consumption and investment spending directly. It could however lead to a temporary increase in demand if there is uncertainty about future supplies and stocks are built up in advance. Uncertainty may also affect demand indirectly by affecting risk premia in financial markets which alters the cost of finance for companies and households
• **Shocks originating in the banking system** arising from its willingness to extend credit to the economy will also have an impact on the economy via loan and deposit rates and the broader effects from increasing the money supply

(continued)

Table 2.1 (continued)

Key propagation mechanisms
• **Nominal rigidities** cause movements in nominal spending to affect output in the short run rather than prices. In the simplest case this reflects costs of changing prices "menu costs" or it could relate to sticky "information". Nominal rigidities are what leads output to move away from "trend" although trend has a specific meaning relating to the level of output that would prevail under flexible prices
• **Real rigidities** imply that shocks will amplify the impact of demand and technology shocks on output and employment and there will be less impact on real wages and other relative prices. They may also affect the degree of nominal rigidity by affecting the incentives of firms facing menu costs to change their price
• Various **adjustment costs** are likely to mean that movements in output are persistent or serially correlated in the sense meant by Lucas. For example a combination of capital and investment adjustments costs may imply "hump-shaped" responses of demand to particular shocks which may look like a periodic cycle if positive and negative shocks follow each other
• **Expectations** themselves can act as a propagation mechanism. For example adaptive inflation expectations can lead to destabilising output movements through Wicksell's famous spiral of ever-increasing or decreasing real interest rates. Learning mechanisms may also lead to persistence in outcomes

(continued)

Table 2.1 (continued)

Policy as a stabilisation mechanism
• Prior to modern monetary policy frameworks being developed, **monetary standards** such as the classical gold standard were argued to act as a stabilising mechanism through the price-specie mechanism, where gold flows would move between deficit and surplus countries to restore balance via spending and prices, possibly supported by the behaviour of central banks where they existed
• **Modern day monetary frameworks** envisage central banks following a policy rule of some kind which seeks to stabilise inflation and output. In response to demand shocks optimal policy typically involves stabilising demand around potential and attempting to remove the cycle. However some shocks may imply a trade-off between stabilising inflation and stabilising output
• **Macroprudential policies** may also be used to help mitigate risks building up in particular sectors and make the financial system resilient to shocks
• **Fiscal policy** may also be used for stabilisation purposes and aggregate demand management. For example automatic stabilisers such as unemployment benefits may kick in during a recession to cushion demand, or the government may choose to cut taxes in order to stabilise unemployment. However fiscal policy is subject to implementation and impact lags and may act to destabilise the economy if they are insufficiently nimble. If aggregate demand stabilisation is left to monetary policy, fiscal policy may still provide an important role in stabilising the government's debt and ensure that monetary policy is supported by fiscal actions and does not lead to movements in risk premia or inflation expectations that might undermine the role of monetary policy

References

Aikman, D., Haldane, A., & Nelson, B. (2013). Curbing the Credit Cycle. *Economic Journal, 125*(585), 1072–1109.

Ashton, T. (1959). *Economic Fluctuations in England 1700–1800*. Oxford: Clarendon Press.

Blanchard, O., & Summers, L. (1986). Hysteresis and the European Unemployment Problem. *NBER Macroeconomics Annual, 1*, 15–90.

Burns, A., & Mitchell, W. (1946). *Measuring Business Cycles*. New York: NBER.

Congdon, T. (1992). *Reflections on Monetarism*. Oxford: Clarendon Press.

Congdon, T. (2005). *Money and Asset Prices in Boom and Bust* (IEA Hobart Paper No. 153). London.

David, P. (1990). The Dynamo and the Computer: An Historical Perspective on the Productivity Paradox. *American Economic Review, 80*(2), 355–361.

Drehman, M., Borio, C., & Tsatsaronis, K. (2012). *Characterising the Financial Cycle: Don't Lose Sight of the Medium Term* (BIS Working Paper 380).

Friedman, M. (1968). The Role of Monetary Policy: Presidential Address Delivered at the 80th Annual Meeting of the American Economic Association. American Economic Review 58(1): 1–17.

Friedman, M., & Schwartz, A. (1963). *A Monetary History of the United States, 1867–1960*. Princeton: Princeton University Press.

Friedman, M., & Schwartz, A. (1982). *Monetary Trends in the United States and the United Kingdom*. Chicago: University of Chicago Press for the NBER.

Frisch, R. (1933). Propagation Problems and Impulse Problems in Dynamic Economics. In K. Koch (Ed.), *Economic Essays in Honour of Gustav Cassel*. London: Allen & Unwin.

Goodhart, C. A. E., & Needham, D. J. (2017). Historical Reasons for the Focus on Broad Monetary Aggregates in Post-World War II Britain and the 'Seven Years War' with the IMF. *Financial History Review, 24*(3), 331–356.

Harding, D., & Pagan, A. (2006). A Suggested Framework for Classifying the Modes of Cycle Research. *Journal of Applied Econometrics, 20*, 151–159.

Hayek, F. (1929 [1933]). *Monetary Theory and the Trade Cycle*. New York: Harcourt Brace.

Hoover, K. (1988). *The New Classcical Macroeconomics*. Oxford: Basil Blackwell.

Jakab, Z., & Kumhof, M. (2018). *Banks are Not Intermediaries of Loanable Funds—Facts, Theory and Evidence* (Bank of England Working Paper No. 761).

Jordà, Ò., Schularick, M., & Taylor, A. (2013). When Credit Bites Back. *Journal of Money, Credit and Banking, 45*(s2), 3–28.

Jordà, Ò., Schularick, M., & Taylor, A. (2016). The Great Mortgaging: Housing Finance, Crises, and Business Cycles. *Economic Policy, 31*(85), 107–115.

Juglar, C. (1862). *Des Crises commerciales et leur retour periodique en France, en Angleterre, et aux Etats-Unis*. Paris: Guillaumin.

Keen, S. (2013). A Monetary Minsky Model of the Great Moderation and the Great Recession. *Journal of Economic Behavior & Organization, 86,* 221–235.

Kindleberger, C. (1978). *Manias, Panics, and Crashes: A History of Financial Crises*. New York: Basic Books.

King, R., & Plosser, C. (1984). Money, Credit, and Prices in a Real Business Cycle. *The American Economic Review, 74*(3), 363–380.

Kitchin, J. (1923). Cycles and Trends in Economic Factors. *Review of Economics and Statistics, 5*(1), 10–16.

Knoll, K., Schularick, M., & Steger, T. (2017). No Price Like Home: Global House Prices, 1870–2012. *American Economic Review, 107*(2), 331–353.

Kondratieff, N. D., & Stolper, W. F. (1935). The Long Waves in Economic Life. *The Review of Economics and Statistics, 17*(6), 105.

Kuznets, S. (1930). *Secular Movements in Production and Prices: Their Nature and Their Bearing Upon Cyclical Fluctuations*. Boston: Houghton Mifflin.

Kydland, F., & Prescott, E. (1982). Time to Build and Aggregate Fluctuations. *Econometrica, 50*(6), 1345–1370.

Lachmann, L. (1956). *Capital and Its Structure*. London: Bell & Sons.

Lavoie, M. (2014). *Post-Keynesian Economics: New Foundations*. Cheltenham: Edward Elgar.

Layard, R., & Nickell, S. (1986). *Unemployment in Britain. Economica 53*(210(S)): S121–S169.

Long, J., & Plosser, C. (1983). Real Business Cycles. *Journal of Political Economy, 91*(1), 39–69.

Lucas, R. (1973). Some International Evidence on Output-Inflation Tradeoffs. *American Economic Review, 63*(3), 326–334.

Lucas, R. (1975). An Equilibrium Model of the Business Cycle. *Journal of Political Economy, 83*(6), 1113–1144.

McLeay, M., Radia, A., & Thomas, R. (2014). Money Creation in the Modern Economy. *Bank of England Quarterly Bulletin, 54*(1), 14–27.

Mensch, G. (1979). *Stalemate in Technology: Innovations Overcome the Depression*. Cambridge, MA: Ballinger Publishing.

Mian, A., & Sufi, A. (2014). *House of Debt*. Chicago: Chicago University Press.

Minsky, H. (1986). *Stabilizing an Unstable Economy*. London: Yale University Press.

Nelson, E. (2018). Seven Fallacies Concerning Milton Friedman's "The Role of Monetary Policy". *Journal of Money, Credit and Banking*. Early View.

Schumpeter, J. (1939). *Business Cycles: A Theoretical, Historical, and Statistical Analysis of the Capitalist Process*. New York: McGraw-Hill.

Solomou, S. (1994). Economic Fluctuations. In R. Floud & D. McCloskey (Eds.), *The Economic History of Britain Since 1700 Volume 2: 1860–1939* (pp. 1870–1913). Cambridge: Cambridge University Press.

Solow, R. (1957). Technical Change and the Aggregate Production Function. *The Review of Economics and Statistics, 39*(3): 312–320.

von Mises, L. (1934). *The Theory of Money and Credit*. London: Jonathan Cape.

Wicksell, K. (1898). *Interest and Prices*, Reprinted 1965. New York: Augustus Kelley.

3

Statistical and Econometric Analysis of the Cycle

A vast (and daunting) array of statistical and econometric techniques are available to the researcher for deriving business cycle metrics. Again doing justice to this literature is incredibly difficult but it is useful to cover the broad approaches adopted and how they relate to the theoretical models discussed in the previous chapter.

3.1 Aggregated or Disaggregated Data

In this section we draw heavily on the discussion in Chadha et al. (2019) to which the reader is directed for more detail. As Chadha et al. (2019) note there are two key issues with regard to business cycle determination.

The first issue is whether one should look at many disaggregated series to analyse the business cycle or whether a single aggregate measure of output such as GDP should be analysed. Many classic analyses of business cycle dating in the United Kingdom typically used a wide variety of series. Burns

The original version of this chapter was revised: Typographical and grammatical corrections were incorporated. The correction to this chapter is available at https://doi.org/10.1007/978-3-030-26346-1_8

N. Dimsdale and R. Thomas,
UK Business and Financial Cycles Since 1660,
https://doi.org/10.1007/978-3-030-26346-1_3

and Mitchell's (1946) chronology of the UK business cycle up until 1938, from 1792 on annual basis and from 1848 on a monthly basis, was based on 141 time series covering not only production indices and activity series, but also commodity prices, asset prices, interest rates and money and credit series. A number of chronologies followed in this tradition such as Ashton (1959) for the C18th, Gayer et al. (1953) for the period 1792–1848, and Rostow (1972) who covered the years from 1788 to 1914.

The obvious problem is that the range of indicators may provide conflicting answers to key turning points in the business cycle. Burns and Mitchell (1946) note that "*there were cases in which the turning points were widely scattered, and others in which they were concentrated around two separate dates.*" Their approach was to derive "specific cycles" in each time series and then combined and "weighted" to determine the "reference cycle" for the overall economy. As noted by Romer (1994) there was a large degree of subjective judgement involved in weighting together different series and the method used was left relatively vague.

At that time, aggregate measures of economic activity, such as real GDP, were still in their infancy, particularly given the focus on not only the C20th, but also the C19th. So in this sense Burns and Mitchell like other researchers had no other choice than to use a range of indicators. As Harding and Pagan (2002) point out this is indeed what Burns and Mitchell would have used had it been available:

> Aggregate [economic] activity can be given a definite meaning and made conceptually measurable by identifying it with gross national product.
>
> Unfortunately, no satisfactory series of any of these types is available by months or quarters for periods approximating those we seek to cover. (Burns and Mitchell 1946)

Given the increasing availability of national accounts data, later business cycle chronologies tended to use aggregate measures of economic activity such as GDP to identify turning points. In the post-WW2 period, the Central Statistical Office (CSO 1993), now the Office for National Statistics (ONS), maintained a quarterly "reference chronology", covering from 1958 to 1992, based on turning points in real GDP. The Organisation for Economic Co-operation and Development (OECD 2019) continue to produce a set of turning points for the

United Kingdom using (de-trended) real GDP and a version of the Bry and Boschan (1971) algorithm we discuss later. This chronology extends back to 1955 on a monthly basis. And leading research institutes, such as the Centre for Economic Policy Research (CEPR 2019) and National Bureau of Economic Research (NBER 2019), focus on real GDP (and some its components) and employment.

Focusing on an aggregate measure of economic activity, such as real GDP, clearly has advantages. As we discuss in Chapter 4 real GDP can be measured in three different ways. On the expenditure side, it combines together consumption, investment and government spending by domestic residents plus net spending by overseas residents on exports (exports minus imports) using their share in total expenditure to weight them together. On the output side, it combines the production of the agricultural, industrial and services sectors weighted by their respective shares in the value added they contribute to the economy. These components are, in turn, aggregates of many more sub-components. And on the income side, GDP can be measured as the sum of employment earning and profits delated by the GDP deflator to give a measure of real output. So GDP weights together many different indicators of activity according to their overall importance in the economy.

However there remain issues with using GDP as a sole representative indicator. First, as we go back in time GDP data may only exist at an annual frequency when precise business cycle dating requires quarterly or monthly data especially if that dating is ultimately used to inform monthly and quarterly policy decisions. This can be ameliorated by using monthly and quarterly indicators to interpolate or "temporally disaggregate" aggregate measures of GDP using methods such as those suggested by Chow and Lin (1971). So in some sense this is just a method that combines the aggregate and disaggregated approaches but in a way that is constrained to match the aggregate annual data.

Second, there may be reasons why GDP or output is not the best summary measure for business cycle analysis. Output might be the best measure for assessing inflationary pressures but it may not provide the best measure of social welfare in the economy. Unemployment, GDP per person or productivity may be better indicators of overall welfare. Here of course one can adopt Burns and Mitchell's approach which establishes a reference cycle based on GDP and then specific cycles for other variables of interest can then be benchmarked against that.

Thirdly one might not consider cycles to be important for welfare unless it is broadly spread across different sectors. Zarnowitz (1985), building on Lucas' definition of the cycle, argues that business cycles represent expansions and contractions that consist of recurrent serially correlated and *cross-correlated movement in many economic variables.* So the dispersion of cyclical or serially correlated movements across many activities is more important than one narrowly concentrated in a few industries or sectors.

Finally each of the three approaches to measuring GDP themselves often provide conflicting answers. For example, in the UK the output, income and expenditure measures suggest a different profile for the slowdown in productivity at the end of the C19th and the start of the C20th. Therefore, it is not clear that focusing on an aggregate measure of economic activity gets around the issue of measurement error. Often the only thing that can be done is to average the estimates from the three approaches. However, using *balanced* estimates of real GDP would help to ameliorate this problem, where estimates from the three approaches are weighted together based on a subjective assessment of the reliability of its underlying components (Sefton and Weale 1995). The subjective element of course remains important.

We discuss the availability of GDP data and the importance of some of these issues in the UK in Chapter 4.

3.2 Classical Versus Growth Cycles—To De-trend or Not to De-trend?

The second issue is whether business cycle metrics should be derived from the level of activity—the classic cycle—or whether it should be applied to de-trended data and generate "growth cycles". Burns and Mitchell (1946) were clear they were interested in expansions and contractions in the level of activity and this methodology is currently still used by the NBER Business Cycle Dating Committee which meets to determine the chronology of US business cycles. However as Romer (1994) discusses the NBER chronology appears to have shifted over time. Prior to 1927 the dating appears to be based on de-trended data and this can have significant impact on business cycle chronology and metrics. For example, Romer (1994) shows how this shift in procedure is largely behind the result that US recessions appear to get shorter over time and generates an alternative chronology prior to 1927 based on an algorithm that closely matches the NBER dating of post-war US cycles.

So which method is to be preferred? Harding and Pagan (2002) are quite clear "there is no need to perform a de-trending operation to analyse the business cycle". They note the wide variety of de-trending methods available to researchers each of which might produce a different chronology and metrics. A number of recent chronologies published by researchers such as Romer (1994), Davis (2006), Berge and Jordà (2013), and Jordà et al. (2013) follow their approach and prefer to base them on data in levels. This is also true of the modern chronologies published by the CEPR and NBER.

However some researchers are interested in business cycles for analysing the degree of inflationary pressure in the economy and de-trended measures of output or "output gaps" are a key ingredient in Phillips curve analysis that links inflation to activity. More generally policymakers may be interested in ironing out inefficiencies in the economy. Growth cycles tend to be correlated with fluctuations in unemployment and monetary and fiscal policy might be set to offset those movements. So in this respect growth cycles are a more useful concept to analyse for policymakers. However one has to be careful to de-trend output in the right way. As discussed earlier, the correct concept of trend for the New Keynesian model is the level of output that would prevail under flexible prices and it is not clear any of the statistical methods of de-trending output do this effectively as we will see.

The metrics one derives from the classic and growth cycle are different in a number of respects. First, classic cycles tend to have much longer expansion phases than compared with contraction phases. Typically in many countries recessions have been short and sharp and so the metrics for the two phases appear highly asymmetric. Growth cycles on the other hand tend to be more symmetric as the contraction phase applies to any period where growth is below the estimated trend and not just to absolute falls in activity.

Also as Romer (1994) notes, growth cycles based on de-trended output tend to have peaks that appear earlier than classic cycles and troughs that appear later, if the profile of output is relatively smooth. This is because output, although increasing, may slow relative to trend before it falls in absolute terms. Similarly contractions in growth cycles will persist beyond the period of falling output until output growth returns to trend.

As a result of these differences it is important to decide on which metrics are important for the purposes to which business cycle measurement is being put. Classical cycles are more judgement-free and so in some sense the business cycles facts that will emerge will be firmer. That means they may be more useful for comparing turning points across time such as in Romer's analysis. But classical cycles may be less useful in themselves for policy purposes when judgements about trend inevitably have to be made.

We discuss methods of deriving business cycle metrics under both methods in the next two sections.

3.3 Methods of Determining Turning Points in Classic Cycles

The classic approach to chronicling the business cycle is to identify turning points such as peaks and troughs. This then defines two phases. The *expansion phase* is the period following the trough of the cycle to the next peak. The *contraction* phase is then the period following the peak to the trough. The full cycle is then the combined expansion and contraction phase. There are two general approaches to detecting turning points in classic cycles. The first takes what is effectively a graphical approach supported by algorithms to censor and refine the turning points obtained. The second involves applying a statistical model to the data.

3.3.1 The Graphic or Algorithmic Approach

Under the simplest algorithmic approach a set of candidate peaks, P_t, and troughs, T_t, can be identified by looking at changes or the first difference in the level of output. A peak period P is defined if output is lower both before and after that period. A trough is defined if output is higher either side of that period.

$$P_t = 1 \text{ if } y_t \geq y_{t-1} \text{ and } y_t > y_{t+1}$$
$$T_t = 1 \text{ if } y_t \leq y_{t-1} \text{ and } y_t < y_{t+1}$$

Figure 3.1 shows this graphically for the case of a smooth cycle.

It may seem odd that the analysis of a classical cycle's turning points is based on the change or growth of output, given the distinction made earlier with growth cycles. But as stressed by Harding and Pagan (2002), the rules above are not about locating a cycle in the growth rate they are just an input into the dating process of the classical cycle in levels.

For annual data the application of this dating rule is relatively straightforward and this process may then be sufficient with no further iterations unless the changes are very small and there are "flat points" at

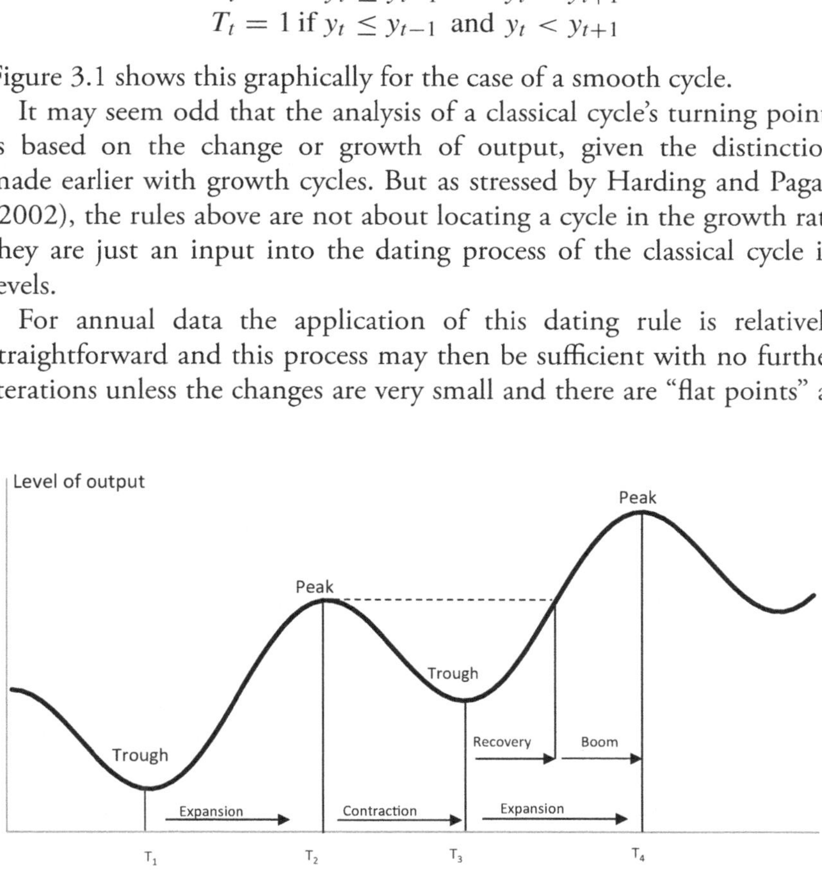

Fig. 3.1 Classical business cycle dating

peaks or troughs where one has to decide whether output has peaked or troughed at the start or end of the flat point.

For monthly and quarterly data one might want also to place some restrictions on the length of the cycles given volatility and measurement error in the data. And, when those rules are in place certain other features then hold such as making sure peaks and troughs alternate. This process requires an explicit algorithmic procedure to implement. The most popular algorithm is that developed by Bry and Boschan (1971). They specify a set of rules that apply to monthly seasonally adjusted series:

- First a contraction or expansion phase must have a duration of no less than 5 months. This is the source of the popular idiom known as a "technical" recession which involves two consecutive quarters of negative growth.
- Second a full cycle, on both a Peak-to-Peak and Trough-to-Trough basis must have a duration of at least 15 months.

However further censoring rules may then apply to the data. For example a two-quarter contraction maybe succeeded by a quarter of growth, which in turn is followed by a quarter or quarters of decline. Such "double-dip" recessions are common. This raises the question of whether the contraction should be dated up to the earlier or later trough. A metric that can be used is the absolute output gain in the intervening quarter of growth. If it is larger (smaller) than the absolute output loss in the subsequent quarter or quarters of decline, we select the earlier (later) trough as marking the end of the contraction.

A further issue is the notion of the *recovery* phase of the cycle which forms part of the expansion phase. Figure 3.1 demonstrates this in the expansion between time periods T_3 and T_4. The recovery point is where, following a period of contraction, output recovers to reach its previous peak, beyond that is the "boom" period. However it may be the case that output may not have returned to its previous peak by the time the next contraction occurs. The recovery is "interrupted". This then leads to issues of how to treat "mini" peaks and troughs that occur in between the previous trough and the recovery point.

3.3.2 The Statistical Approach—Markov-Switching Methods

Another way to detect business cycle turning points is through an explicit statistical model of the data and then using the estimated parameters of the model to try and obtain a business cycle chronology based on the probability of being at a particular turning point. A popular method of doing this is the Markov-switching approach developed by Hamilton (1989). This approach is well able to capture the asymmetry observed in the data that troughs are shorter and sharper than expansions and assumes no prior knowledge of turning points (unlike the earlier method of Neftci 1982).

Under this approach mean or underlying growth in the economy is in one of two states (S): a high-growth or expansion state ($S=1$), or a low-growth/contraction state where $S=0$. And the economy randomly switches between these two unobserved states. By specifying the statistical model underlying this switching one can try and determine from the data which state the economy is in. Using a simple autoregressive or AR(2) process for output we can show an example of this approach:

$$y_t = y_{t-1} + \mu_{st} + \phi(y_{t-1} - y_{t-2} - \mu_{st-1}) + v_t$$

where μ_{st} is the mean growth rate that switches between states:

$$\mu_{st} = \alpha_0 + \alpha_1 S_t$$

The probability P of being in one state or the other follows a first-order Markov process. This defines the probability of being in a particular state conditional on the existing state:

$$P\left[S_t = 1 | S_{t-1} = 1\right] = p$$

$$P\left[S_t = 0 | S_{t-1} = 1\right] = 1 - p$$

$$P\left[S_t = 0 | S_{t-1} = 0\right] = q$$

$$P\left[S_t = 0|S_{t-1} = 1\right] = 1 - q$$

Hamilton then develops an approach for estimating the parameters of this statistical model. Which state an economy is in at any particular time remains unobservable in the Hamilton framework. The probability of being in a particular state at a particular time can be calculated based on the estimated parameters of the model and the evolving path of the process. The key metric for determining a turning point is through evaluating the conditional probability based on the observed movements of output at that point $P[S_t = 1|y_t, y_{t-1}, y_{t-2}]$ which Hamilton's filtering process determines. He augments this with a smoothing procedure using future values of y to ensure the path of probabilities remains smooth. One then needs to set a benchmark probability to determine whether the economy is one state or another. Hamilton (1989) suggests using the rule that a quarter is part of a low-growth, or recessionary, period if the smoothed conditional probability $P[S_t = 1|y_{t+2}, y_{t+1}, y_t, y_{t-1}, y_{t-2}] < 0.5$.

3.4 Methods of De-trending—Growth Cycles

The basic method to determine metrics for growth cycles is to remove both the trend and irregular (white noise) components from a series to leave the cyclical component(s). There are three popular and related procedures for de-trending a series on a univariate basis, which are then often extended to a multivariate basis where common trends and cycles between variables can be identified. These three methods are discussed in turn but can be shown to derive from a more general model and as a result the implicit restrictions in the three models can be identified and discussed.

Essentially a series can be decomposed into a trend component (τ) a cyclical component (c) and a white noise component ω where $\omega_t = N(0, \sigma_\omega)$ is normally distributed and may contain measurement error in the data. For quarterly and monthly data an additional seasonal component (s) can be added

$$y_t = \tau_t + c_t + \omega_t + s_t$$

Many of the differences between de-trending methods depend on how the trend and cyclical components are specified and the extent to which the trend and cycle are assumed to be correlated.

3.4.1 The Unobserved Components Model

The Unobserved Components (UC) model was popularised by Harvey (1989) and Harvey and Jaeger (1993). In this model the trend and the cyclical components are assumed to be uncorrelated phenomena that are driven by different "shocks" or stochastic processes.

The trend component itself is typically written as a random walk with drift.

$$\tau_t = \tau_{t-1} + \mu_t + \epsilon_t$$

which can be written as:

$$\tau_t = \mu t + \sum_{j=0}^{t} \varepsilon_{t-j}$$

where the trend has both a stochastic and deterministic trend component. The term μt represents the deterministic component of the trend which grows at a constant "drift" rate μ whereas $\sum_{j=0}^{t} \epsilon_{t-j}$ represents the "stochastic trend" based on the cumulative effect of "permanent" shocks that affect the trend level of output and other variables in economy. Again those permanent shocks have a distribution: $\varepsilon_t = N(0, \sigma_\varepsilon)$.

However this model can be generalised further where the drift term itself can be stochastic. This means there can be "shocks" to both the trend growth rate and trend level of output. This is known as the "local linear trends" model.

$$\mu_t = \mu_{t-1} + \eta_t$$

where again the error term is a mean-zero normally distributed variable, $\eta_t = N\left(0, \sigma_\eta\right)$

Another way of modelling the trends is as a sequence of one-off deterministic regime shifts in either the level or deterministic trend component:

$$\tau_t = \mu + \mu * D_t + \tau_{t-1}$$

$$\tau_t = \mu t + \mu * \sum_{i=0}^{t} D_{t-i}$$

where D is a vector of impact dummy variables and $\sum_{i=0}^{t} D_{t-i}$ a vector of one-zero step-dummies. D can also be specified so there are one-off shifts in the slope of the deterministic trend. This is known as a "linear segmented trend" model (see Perron and Wada [2009] and Crafts and Mills [2017]). Essentially this involves determining separate growth regimes with a different trend growth rate. The timing of regimes can either be determined statistically or by assumption based on known features of the economy or using natural breakpoints such as wars.

In the UC model the cyclical component is typically written as an autoregressive moving average model or "ARMA" model driven by a different set of shocks υ_t. In this case

$$\Psi(L)c_t = \Phi(L)\,\upsilon_t$$

where υ_t is a set of shocks $\upsilon_t = N(0, \sigma_\upsilon)$ which generate dynamic or cyclical (serially correlated) effects through the distributed lag matrices $\Psi(L)$ and $\Phi(L)$. So for example $\Phi(L)\upsilon_t$ is a distributed lag of current and past cyclical shocks $= \Phi_0\upsilon_t + \Phi_1\upsilon_{t-1} + \ldots$

The simplest model of the cycle that can generate serially correlated movements and periodic cycles is the stationary AR(2) model discussed earlier when discussing the multiplier-accelerator model.

$$c_t = \psi_1 c_{t-1} + \psi_2 c_{t-2} + \upsilon_t$$

The nature of the cycle generated depends on the roots (z) of this second order difference equation.

$$z_1, z_2 = \frac{-\psi_1 \pm \sqrt{\psi_1^2 + 4\psi_2}}{2}$$

If the roots are real

$$\psi_1^2 + 4\psi_2 > 0$$

then the impact of a shock υ_t will gradually and asymptotically tend to zero. In this case a "cycle" may only be observed because the shock process is white noise and negative shocks are likely to follow positive shocks. But this would be in line with the Lucas definition of the cycle which refers to serially-correlated movements around a trend.

If on the other hand the roots are complex

$$\psi_1^2 + 4\psi_2 < 0$$

then a shock υ_t will generate a periodic cycle of its own with periodicity or length of cycle given by

$$k = \frac{2\pi}{\cos^{-1}\left[\psi_1/(2\sqrt{-\psi_2})\right]}$$

In this case what we observe as the cycle will be a mixture of overlapping waves responding to positive and negative shocks as discussed in Chapter 2.

An alternative approach is where the cyclical component can be set up explicitly as a trigonometric function where the cycle can be expressed as a mixture of sine and cosine waves dependent on two parameters α and β with a given frequency λ

$$c_t = \alpha \cos \lambda t + \beta \sin \lambda t$$

$$c_t^* = -\alpha \sin \lambda t + \beta \cos \lambda \tau$$

which are combined recursively to produce a time-varying stochastic cycle given by

$$\begin{bmatrix} c_t \\ c_t^* \end{bmatrix} = \rho \begin{bmatrix} \cos \lambda & \sin \lambda \\ -\sin \lambda & \cos \lambda \end{bmatrix} \begin{bmatrix} c_{t-1} \\ c_{t-1}^* \end{bmatrix} + \begin{bmatrix} \upsilon_t \\ \upsilon_t^* \end{bmatrix}$$

where ρ is a damping factor < 1 to ensure the process is stationary. This is effectively an ARMA(2) model which reduces to a simple AR(1) process if $\lambda = 0$ or π. But in general, this framework assumes the cycles are periodic by definition.

A satisfactory description of cyclical movements may require more than one cyclical component operating at different frequencies, for example a business cycle frequency of 2–8 years and a credit cycle component of 8–20 years. Simultaneous estimation of these different cyclical components can be achieved within the UC framework. So in principle c_t can be set up as a set of N trigonometric cycles.

$$c_t = \sum_{j=1}^{N} c_{j,t}$$

The parameters of the model are typically estimated using the Kalman Filter and a key restriction in the "standard" UC model is that the covariance between the unobserved shocks driving the cycle and the shocks driving the trend is zero.

$$\mathrm{Cov}(\varepsilon_t \upsilon_t) = 0$$

Many applications of the UC model with this restriction trend to produce a relatively smooth trend component and relatively large cyclical components.

3.4.2 The Beveridge-Nelson Decomposition

The Beveridge-Nelson (1981) decomposition (BN) starts from a similar underlying specification to the UC model. The trend component is typically set up in the same way but in this case the cyclical component is a moving average process resulting from the same stochastic source as the trend. In this case:

$$y_t = \tau_t + c_t$$

$$\tau_t = \tau_{t-1} + \mu_t + \varphi(1)\epsilon_t$$

$$c_t = \tilde{\varphi}(L)\epsilon_t$$

So the trend and cycle are perfectly and (negatively) correlated in this model. Decompositions using this approach typically produce more variable trends and much smaller cyclical components. We will see this is very evident in the UK data. Morley et al. (2003) show that the Beveridge and Nelson (1981) decomposition is in fact equivalent to that of the trend-cycle decomposition from a general UC model that allows for correlation between the shocks driving the trend and cycle. In other words the standard UC model employed by many researchers effectively imposes what in many cases is a testable zero correlation restriction on the shocks driving trend and cycle. Morley et al. (2003) show this zero correlation restriction can be rejected for US quarterly data. Once the restriction of a zero correlation between the shocks driving trend and cycle is relaxed the UC and BN models are essentially the same. As Grant and Chan (2017) discuss both methods in this case will in general deliver cycles that exhibit what many business cycle researchers find unpalatable—cycles that are noisy and small in amplitude.

3.4.3 HP and Band-Pass Filters—Non-parametric Methods

An alternative approach to deriving trends and cycles is to use a non-parametric filtering approach. In this case the specification of the trend and cycle components are not determined a priori and then estimated but rather are derived by meeting some other a priori criteria. One well known non-parametric method is the Hodrick-Prescott or HP filter. The Hodrick-Prescott decomposition is based on the smoothing problem initiated by Bohlmann (1899) and Whittaker (1923). The trend is the solution to the following problem

$$\min_{\tau}\left[\sum_{t=1}^{T}(y_t-\tau_t)^2+\lambda\sum_{t=1}^{T}\left(\Delta^2\tau_t\right)^2\right]$$

where λ is a fixed constant that penalises variability in the trend component. The larger the value of λ, the smoother is the associated HP trend. Hodrick and Prescott (1980, 1997) highlight that λ may be viewed as the noise-to-signal ratio under certain restrictive conditions. They then suggest setting λ = 1600 for US quarterly data and 100 for annual data. Grant and Chan (2017) show that a general unobserved component with a more flexible specification for the trend and which allows for correlation between trend and cycle components nests the HP filter as a special case. Harvey and Jaeger (1993) show that the HP filter is the optimal linear estimator of the trend in the basic UC model

$$y_t = \tau_t + \nu_t$$

$$\tau_t = \tau_{t-1} + \mu_t + \epsilon_t$$

$$\mu_t = \mu_{t-1} + \eta_t$$

$$\lambda = \frac{\sigma_\nu}{\sigma_\eta}$$

Notice, however, that this rationalisation has the following assumptions: (i) the series is integrated of order 2; (ii) the cyclical component is a white noise process; and (iii) that the chosen value of the parameter λ corresponds to the ratio of the variance of the irregular component to the variance of the innovation in the trend component. This is one reason why HP filters may produce spurious cycles if the smoothing parameter chosen or other implied restrictions are different to that implied by the unrestricted estimates of the UC model. As an example of the HP filter producing spurious cycles Harvey and Jaeger (1993) and Harding and Pagan (2005) show that if output follows a random walk, which would be interpreted in the UC framework as a pure stochastic trend, and one applies the standard HP filter to data generated from the random walk process one will generate what looks like a cycle with significant serial correlation.

Band-pass filters are another popular way of non-parametric de-trending but take a slightly different approach to the HP filter. The band-pass filter essentially takes a two-sided weighted moving average of the data where the weights are chosen so that cycles in a particular band, given by a specified lower and upper bound, are allowed through and the remaining cycles are filtered out. Essentially for business cycle analysis a business cycle band of 2–8 years is typically chosen. Baxter and King (1995) and Christiano and Fitzgerald (1999) both provide approximations to the ideal band-pass filter. These filters have also been argued to generate spurious cycles (e.g. Benati 2001). Because the band-pass filter is both a low pass and a high pass filter, it leads to cycles that are typically smoother than the HP filter, which acts only as a high pass filter and does not cut off higher frequency movements below say two years.

A feature of both types of filters is whether the filter is "one-sided" or "two-sided". A one-sided filter only uses information up to time t when assessing the state of the cycle at time t. A two-sided filter however uses both past and future observations to assess the state at any given moment in time. For the purposes of developing forecasting models, e.g. Phillips curve models that use the output gap to forecast inflation, a one-sided filter is a more appropriate method to de-trend output. This is because when carrying out forecasts in real time future information about the time series is unavailable, so one needs to construct a model based on what forecast information set that will be available at the time. For the purposes of retrospectively analysing business cycles however a two-sided filter is more appropriate as it takes into account all the information we have about the time series although there will still be an issue about the end point of the series where the filter will be missing the information about future values.

References

Ashton, T. (1959). *Economic Fluctuations in England 1700–1800*. Oxford: Clarendon Press.

Baxter, M., & King, R. (1995). *Measuring Business Cycles: Approximate Band-Pass Filters for Economic Time Series* (NBER Working Paper 5022).

Benati, L. (2001). *Band-Pass Filtering, Cointegration, and Business Cycle Analysis* (Bank of England Working Paper 142).

Berge, T., & Jorda, O. (2013). A Chronology of Turning Points in Economic Activity: Spain, 1850–2011. *SERIEs, Journal of the Spanish Economic Association, 4*(1), 1–34.

Beveridge, S., & Nelson, C. (1981). A New Approach to Decomposition of Economic Time Series into Permanent and Transitory Components with Particular Attention to Measurement of the 'Business Cycle'. *Journal of Monetary Economics, 7*(2), 151–174.

Bohlmann, G. (1899). Ein ausgleichungsproblem. *Nachrichten Gesellschaft Wissenschaften Gottingen. Mathematisch-Physikalische Klasse, 1899*, 260–271.

Bry, G., & Boschan, C. (1971). *Cyclical Analysis of Time Series: Selected Procedures and Computer Programs*. New York: NBER.

Burns, A., & Mitchell, W. (1946). *Measuring Business Cycles*. New York: NBER.

Central Statistical Office. (1993). A Review of CSO Cyclical Indicators. *Economic Trends, 477*, 99–107.

Centre for Economic Policy Research. (2019). *Euro Area Business Cycle Dating Committee*. CEPR.

Chadha, J., Lennard, J., & Thomas, R. (2019). *Dating Business Cycles in the United Kingdom, 1700–2010*. Mimeo.

Chow, G., & Lin, A. (1971). Best Linear Unbiased Interpolation, Distribution, and Extrapolation of Time Series by Related Series. *The Review of Economics and Statistics, 53*(4), 372–375.

Christiano, L., & Fitzgerald, T. (1999). *The Band Pass Filter* (NBER Working Paper 7257).

Crafts, N., & Mills, T. (2017). Six Centuries of British Economic Growth: A Time-Series Perspective. *European Review of Economic History, 21*(2), 141–158.

Davis, J. (2006). An Improved Annual Chronology of U.S. Business Cycles since the 1790s. *American Economic Review, 66*(1), 103–121.

Gayer, A., Rostow, W., & Schwartz, A. (1953). *The Growth and Fluctuation of the British Economy, 1790–1850*. Oxford: Clarendon Press.

Grant, A., & Chan, J. (2017). Reconciling Output Gaps: Unobserved Components Model and Hodrick-Prescott Filter. *Journal of Economic Dynamics and Control, 75*, 114–121.

Hamilton, J. (1989). A New Approach to the Economic Analysis of Nonstationary Time Series and the Business Cycle. *Econometrica, 57*(2), 357–384.

Harding, D., & Pagan, A. (2002). Dissecting the Cycle: A Methodological Investigation. *Journal of Monetary Economics, 49*(2), 365–381.
Harding, D., & Pagan, A. (2005). A Suggested Framework for Classifying the Modes of Cycle Research. *Journal of Applied Econometrics, 20*(2), 151–159.
Harvey, A. (1989). *Forecasting, Structural Time Series Models and the Kalman Filter*. Cambridge: Cambridge University Press.
Harvey, A., & Jaeger, A. (1993). Detrending, Stylized Facts and the Business Cycle. *Journal of Applied Econometrics, 8*(3), 231–247.
Hodrick, R., & Prescott, E. (1980). *Postwar U.S. Business Cycles: An Empirical Investigation* (Carnegie-Mellon University Discussion Paper 451).
Hodrick, R., & Prescott, E. (1997). Postwar U.S. Business Cycles: An Empirical Investigation. *Journal of Money, Credit and Banking, 29*(1): 1–16.
Jordà, Ò., Schularick, M., & Taylor, A. (2013). When Credit Bites Back. *Journal of Money, Credit and Banking, 45*(s2), 3–28.
Morley, J., Nelson, C., & Zivot, E. (2003). Why Are the Beveridge-Nelson and Unobserved-Components Decompositions of GDP so Different? *The Review of Economics and Statistics, 85*(2), 235–243.
National Bureau of Economic Research. (2019). *US Business Cycle Expansions and Contractions*. Cambridge, MA: NBER.
Neftci, S. (1982). Optimal Prediction of Cyclical Downturns. *Journal of Economic Dynamics and Control, 4*, 225–241.
Perron, P., & Wada, T. (2009). Let's Take a Break: Trends and Cycles in US Real GDP. *Journal of Monetary Economics, 56*(6), 749–765.
Romer, C. (1994). Remeasuring Business Cycles. *The Journal of Economic History, 54*(3), 573–609.
Rostow, W. (1972). Cycles in the British Economy: 1790–1914. In D. Aldcroft & P. Fearon (Eds.), *British Economic Fluctuations, 1790–1939*. Basingstoke: Macmillan.
Sefton, J., & Weale, M. (1995). *Reconciliation of National Income and Expenditure: Balanced Estimates of National Income for the United Kingdom, 1920–1990*. Cambridge: Cambridge University Press.
OECD. (2019). *OECD Composite Leading Indicators: Reference Turning Points and Component Series*. Paris: OECD.
Whittaker, E. (1923). On a New Method of Graduation. *Proceedings of the Edinburgh Mathematical Association, 41*, 63–75.
Zarnowitz, V. (1985). Recent Work on Business Cycles in Historical Perspective: A Review of Theories and Evidence. *Journal of Economic Literature, 23*(2), 523–580.

4

GDP Data for Analysing Business Cycles

4.1 Background and Method

Our approach in this volume will be to take the univariate approach and use GDP as a summary measure of activity for dating the business cycle and deriving key metrics under the different approaches. Other data will be brought into the picture in Chapter 6 when we undertake the narrative history of cycles over the past three and a half centuries.

As is well known, GDP can be measured using expenditure, income and output-based approaches. Estimates using each of the three approaches can be averaged to create "compromise" measures that implicitly place equal weight on all three estimates. Alternatively the measures can be balanced where judgement is placed on the reliability of each series, and the relative degree of reliability is then used to weight the series together. Balanced estimates can also be produced for particular benchmark years using input-output analysis where the researcher attempts to make the three estimates consistent using knowledge about the industrial structure and spending

The original version of this chapter was revised: Typographical and grammatical corrections were incorporated. The correction to this chapter is available at https://doi.org/10.1007/978-3-030-26346-1_8

N. Dimsdale and R. Thomas,
UK Business and Financial Cycles Since 1660,
https://doi.org/10.1007/978-3-030-26346-1_4

patterns in the economy for that year. Typically for the C19th such analysis is only feasible for years when a population census was carried out.

Various historical estimates for the UK exist using each of the three approaches. The main work on the UK in the C19th and first half of the C20th was carried out by Charles Feinstein in his 1972 volume *National Income, Expenditure and Output of the United Kingdom 1855–1965*. This monumental work, which is still the bedrock of UK estimates over this period, built on the earlier contributions of many scholars such as Bowley, Stamp, Clark, Deane, Stone, Jeffreys, Walters, Prest, Chapman, Hoffman, and Lewis among others. Work improving the estimates of industrial production and output during the industrial revolution was subsequently carried out by Crafts and Harley in the 1980s and restated in Crafts and Harley (1992). Martin Weale in a series of collaborations (Horrell et al. 1994; Sefton and Weale 1995; Solomou and Weale 1991) pioneered the work on balanced estimates in the UK and constructed an input-output table for the UK in the census year of 1841. Ongoing work by Mark Thomas, building on earlier collaboration with Charles Feinstein, is aiming for a similar input-output table for 1851. More recently the path-breaking work of Broadberry et al. (2015), who took on the task of reconstructing the growth of output and population in England and Great Britain between 1270 and 1870, now allows comparisons of GDP per capita to be made over seven centuries.

For many years little was known about the exact pattern of growth in Ireland especially during the C19th when Ireland experienced the Great Famine and the large overseas emigration that followed. That situation has now changed and major contributions have recently been made by Geary and Stark (2004, 2015, 2018) in a series of papers on regional growth in the UK, and Andersson and Lennard (2019) who have constructed annual estimates for Ireland for the 1842–1913 period.

The various historical estimates of GDP for the UK and Ireland that exist often cover different geographical areas and different time periods. The challenge is to try and construct continuous times series for the three geographically-consistent areas discussed above using the best available compromise and balanced estimates incorporating the information from each of the three approaches to measuring GDP. The Bank of England's Millennium dataset (Thomas and Dimsdale 2017) attempts to construct GDP measures for various different geographical areas on a consistent basis. The challenge for this volume is to derive a measure that provides sufficient continuity that business cycles comparisons can be made over time but that also encapsulates a wide variety of information. Our approach is discussed below.

4.2 Sources and Construction—Annual Data 1660–2018

To evaluate real GDP involves deflating disaggregated expenditure or industry output and input components at current prices using suitable price indices and then weighting the resulting volume components together to create aggregate real indices of output or expenditure. A real measure from the income side can also be constructed by deflating nominal domestic incomes with the GDP deflator from the expenditure side of the account.

Typically for quantity indices a Laspeyres index is used, where current price shares in a base period form the weights and these are used to produce an index calculated over a set number of years. The base period and weights are then shifted periodically to capture any changes in the structure of the economy. The resulting chains of data are then linked together at an appropriate point as an index number to form a "chained volume measure" or CVM. This volume measure can be left in index number form. But it is also sometimes referenced to a particular year's GDP in current prices so that the current price volume measure takes the same value in that year. This is then a chained volume measure expressed in terms of that particular reference year's prices. In older versions of the official accounts the weights were updated around every 5 years. In historical analysis with limited current price data, volume indices are often based on linking fewer and longer chains of historical data where the periods used for weights can be many years apart. Current best practice is to chain-link annually using weights based on the previous year.

4.2.1 1948 Onwards

All UK estimates for the last seventy years are on the basis of post-1922 UK borders (Great Britain + Northern Ireland) and are derived from official Office for National Statistics (ONS) estimates of GDP. The volume estimates in the National Accounts are generally annually chain-weighted estimates where the volume index is built up from the components of GDP weighted appropriately by nominal shares of each component in overall GDP.

The preferred measure of output is gross valued added or GDP valued at basic prices rather than market prices. Basic prices exclude taxes and subsidies on products like VAT and duties. This is to ensure that the weights used to construct volume estimates of GDP are not distorted by indirect taxes. For example, the volume measure of GDP at market prices will, from an output perspective, tend to overstate the weight placed on consumption relative to other expenditure components given the relatively high share of indirect taxes applied to consumer spending. Prior to the introduction of the ESA95 system of accounts GDP volumes were generally measured at factor cost rather than basic prices. Factor cost estimates also exclude taxes on production such as business rates and motor vehicle excise duty paid by companies. But output prices at factor cost are not generally available because such taxes cannot be applied on a per unit basis. This mattered less when estimates of output by industry generally used direct volume indicators of production which were then weighted together by industry estimates of nominal value added at factor cost to generate an aggregate volume measure in factor cost terms. But the move to measuring real industry value added by deflating gross output and inputs in value terms with appropriate price deflators means that basic prices are the most practical basis for constructing GDP volumes.

ONS currently maintain a full set of national accounts based on the ESA2010 system of accounts from 1997. The data are available at a quarterly frequency and annual totals in current price terms are balanced over time through the supply-use framework, with a statistical discrepancy introduced for years which have not been balanced. Volume estimates on the expenditure and output sides of the accounts are annually chain-linked, although prior to 1990 this is only possible for the expenditure side.

Prior to the introduction of ESA95 in 1998 ONS had largely been able to maintain a full set of aggregate and sector income accounts back to 1948 for annual data, 1955 for aggregate quarterly data and 1963 for sector income and financial accounts. These accounts had also been balanced in current price terms using the supply-use framework back to 1986. Following the introduction of ESA95 in 1998 the start date of the full set of accounts was brought forward to 1987 given the cost and difficulty of applying the initial ESA95 changes retrospectively. This has now been brought even further forward to 1997 following successive implementation of subsequent ESA95 and ESA2010 changes. To mitigate the impact of this ONS has tried to maintain a set of core national accounts series back to 1948 and 1955 covering the main expenditure and income aggregates and key sector series. One particular problem after 1998 was that a number of corruptions and errors developed in some of the components of the historic (pre-ESA95) data which ONS continued to make available. These were documented by Martin (2009). This led the ONS to decide that only a set of core series would be maintained back to 1948 (see Everett [2011] and Denley [2016]). When there are methodological revisions to the accounts in the future the ONS remain committed to apply them retrospectively to this set of core series.

Together this means that although a vast amount of official data exist on the national accounts in the post-World War II (WWII) period, a comprehensive set of accounts based on a consistent methodology does not exist and this causes a number of problems for researchers who require a set of aggregate-level data that are also consistent with those across sectors and industries. The most glaring gap is that there is not a set of real industrial output data that are consistent with the core measure of real GDP based on the expenditure and deflated income measures. This means it is not possible to accurately decompose movements in aggregate output and productivity into the contributions of different industries prior to the 1990s.

For the purposes of this volume we use the core chained volume index for GDP at basic prices from 1948 to 2018 but recognising the limitation that we cannot disaggregate this accurately into the contribution from different industries.

4.2.2 1920–1948

The UK data for this period are based on the balanced estimates of GDP at factor cost by Sefton and Weale (1995). They used Feinstein's

(1972) estimates of GDP, which he was able to construct using all three approaches. Instead of constructing a simple average "compromise measure" they used a least-squares approach to weight the three estimates according to their underlying reliability. They showed that the compromise measure would only be the least-squares estimate if each series were considered equally reliable. Chart 4.1 shows the differences between the compromise measure and balanced measure of Sefton and Weale between 1920 and 1948. The differences are not particularly large at the aggregate level with the largest occurring during WWII but at a disaggregated level balancing expenditure and income produced more plausible estimates of the household saving ratio in the early 1920s, so these are to be preferred.

The current price estimates for 1948 by Sefton and Weale are very similar to current ONS estimates for GDP at current prices in the same year, despite Sefton and Weale's estimates being based on the pre-ESA95 system of national accounts. The series are linked using the ratio of the two series in 1948. The constant price estimates at 1938 prices are linked to the ONS chained volume measures in the same way.

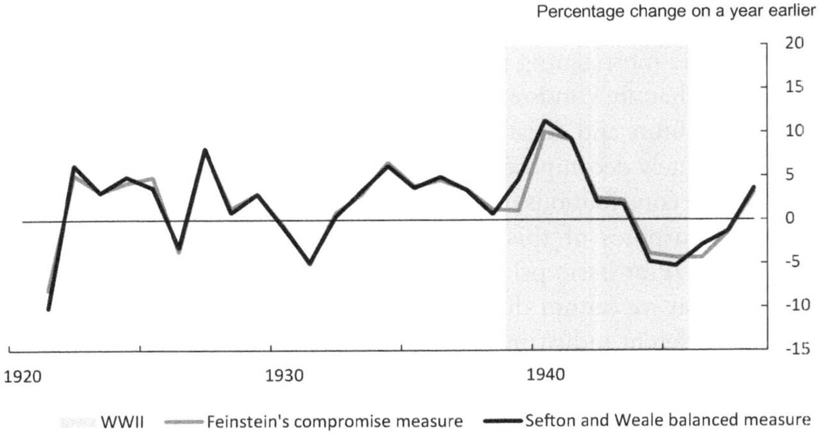

Chart 4.1 Balanced versus compromise measures of real GDP growth 1920–1948 (*Source* Thomas and Dimsdale [2017] based on Feinstein [1972] and Sefton and Weale [1995])

4.2.3 1870–1920

There are a number of estimates for Great Britain, Ireland and UK GDP available over the C19th and early C20th period.

- **Output-based measures**. Feinstein (1972) constructed estimates between 1855 and 1920 for both Great Britain and the UK. Since then Broadberry et al. (2015) have constructed current price and volume measures for Great Britain between 1700 and 1870. Andersson and Lennard (2019) have similarly constructed estimates for Ireland between 1842 and 1913 benchmarked to the decadal estimates of Irish GDP implied by the regional shares of Geary and Stark (2015) based on sectoral wage data.
- **Expenditure-based estimates.** Feinstein constructed expenditure-based estimates of UK GDP from 1870 in his (1972) volume. Subsequently he pushed these back to 1830 using earlier work by Deane (1968), and his own work on investment and trade in Feinstein and Pollard (1988). These improved estimates were published in Mitchell (1988). Estimates are available on a constant and current price basis.
- **Income-based estimates**. Feinstein (1972) constructed current price income estimates back to 1855. However he also subsequently made several improvements to the components on the income side, especially to the estimates of wage earners' incomes (Feinstein 1990). Boyer and Hatton (2002) also improved the estimates of unemployment over the 1870–1913 period. These estimates are in the process of being brought together in an updated income measure by Solomou and Thomas (2019) but these have yet to be peer reviewed and accepted.
- **Compromise and balanced estimates**. Feinstein himself provided compromise estimates based on an average of the three estimates he constructed in his (1972) volume. These were updated to include some revisions on the expenditure side arising from the work on gross capital formation and net trade in Feinstein and Pollard (1988). This "new" compromise estimate appeared in Mitchell (1988). Solomou and Weale (1991) provide balanced estimates

based on Feinstein's updated data for the 1870–1913 period using Feinstein's subjective assessment about the reliability of each of the series. Solomou and Thomas (2019) have provided provisional estimates of a compromise measure based on Feinstein's susbsequent revisions to the income measure.

Our approach in this volume, given the state of current knowledge and until more recent research can be brought together and synthesised, is to use the Solomou and Weale (1991) balanced estimates as the best current estimate for the 1870–1913 period, extended by Feinstein's compromise measure to 1920. We recognise however this estimate is likely to be revised by ongoing work on historical UK accounts discussed above. Chart 4.2 shows how Solomou and Weale's balanced estimates for the 1870 period compare with Feinstein's earlier compromise estimates.

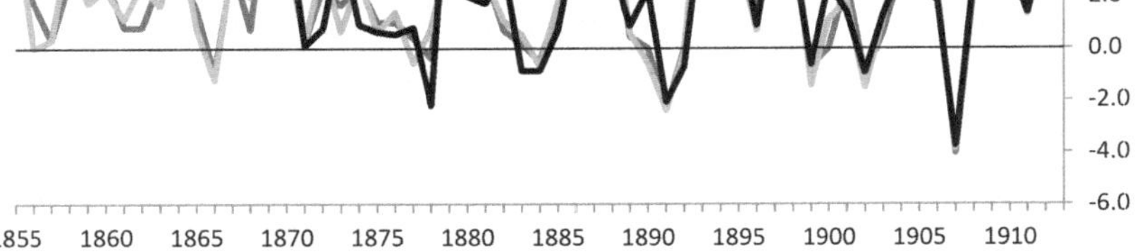

Chart 4.2 Solomou and Weale's (1991) balanced estimates (*Source* Thomas and Dimsdale [2017] based on Feinstein [1972], Mitchell [1988], and Solomou and Weale [1991])

4.2.4 1660–1870

As discussed in the previous section, for the period before 1870 it is now possible to construct measures for the UK as a whole back to 1830 using expenditure data and 1841 based on the income approach and the output-based data for Great Britain and Ireland. The input-output table of Horrell et al. (1994) for 1841 also provides a benchmark estimate that reconciles the measures from the different approaches.

However, there are many issues to resolve before such a UK-wide measure combining the three approaches can be used reliably for business cycle analysis. These are discussed in Solomou and Thomas (2019). We also know the period between 1841 and 1870 covers the period of the Irish famine and subsequent diaspora which reduced the population of Ireland by around a third and is likely to have significant and distinct effects on the pattern of growth in Ireland relative to that in Britain.

So for these reasons we use Broadberry et al.'s (2015) output-based estimates for British GDP from 1870 back to 1700, and extended this further backwards in time to 1660 using their estimates of English GDP. These represent estimates for British growth that from 1700 have been scrutinised by many scholars. In particular, they encapsulate the widely accepted "Crafts-Harley" view[1] of growth during the industrial revolution that suggested only a modest improvement in growth unlike the earlier views of Hoffmann (1955) and Deane and Cole (1962). These estimates have also been used to analyse the shifts in the underlying trend rate of growth of GDP between 1270 and 1870 (Crafts and Mills 2017). So for comparability it is cleaner to use these same estimates for cyclical analysis. UK estimates that incorporate the information from the other measures and include the latest Irish GDP estimates can be found in Thomas and Dimsdale (2017).

When we undertake the narrative analysis in Chapter 6 we will however use some of the components of the expenditure side estimates to help explain what is driving the causes of the cycle. Chart 4.3 shows that movements in the UK expenditure-based measure over the period

[1] See Crafts and Harley (1992).

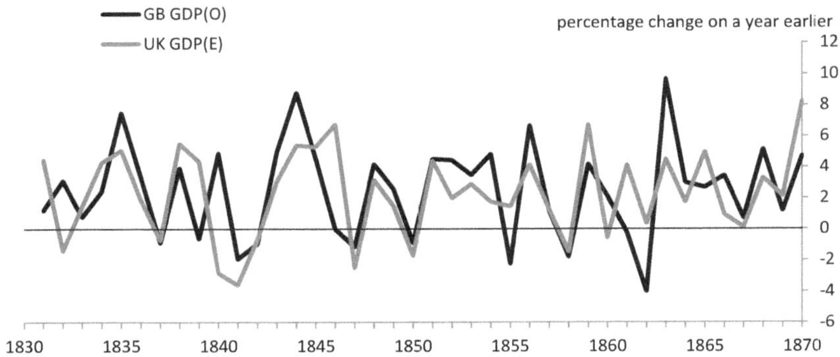

Chart 4.3 Expenditure and output measures compared (*Source* Thomas and Dimsdale [2017] based on Deane [1968] and Broadberry et al. [2015])

1830–1870 do correspond broadly to the fluctuations in British output. The main differences occur in the early 1860s and this needs to be borne in mind when using the expenditure components to explain cycles over this period.

4.3 Quarterly and Monthly GDP Estimates

Official estimates of quarterly GDP begin in 1955. It is possible to construct monthly estimates of GDP by using other partial indicators such as industrial production which can be used to interpolate the quarterly GDP series that go back to 1955 or the annual series stretching back to 1920 and earlier. The National Institute of Economic and Social Research (NIESR) currently constructs a monthly series for GDP which currently goes back to 1985 and they have also produced an earlier series that goes back to 1973.[2]

Mitchell et al. (2012) carried out a similar exercise using quarterly industrial production and a set of monthly indicators from the Economist for the interwar period (1920–1938) benchmarking to Sefton and Weale's (1995) balanced GDP data. This enables both

[2]See https://www.niesr.ac.uk/sites/default/files/files/GDP%20Spreadsheets/dp127.PDF.

monthly and quarterly GDP estimates for the interwar period from 1920 to 1938. In principle, this method could be extended to create a complete monthly series from 1913 to the present based on a comprehensive set of indicators.

The world war periods provide particular issues in providing high frequency estimates. For WWI (1972) Feinstein was able to make estimates on the expenditure and income side although no split between self-employed income and profits was possible. No indices of real output by industry were produced. For WWII estimates of GDP rely on those published in the *Statistical Digest of the War* which was republished with accompanying explanation by Howlett (1995). Again no GDP(O) and industry output estimates are available.

It is possible to interpolate the estimates of GDP with higher frequency information on the output of certain sectors during each war period. For example a quarterly munitions index was produced during WWII and was improved by Harrison (1990). This could be used to interpolate that part of national income and expenditure attributable to wartime procurement of goods and services on the expenditure side of the accounts. Monthly retail sales data also exist over the war period. The accumulation of sufficient indicators would allow the creation of a quarterly and possibly monthly GDP series back to WWI. Preliminary quarterly estimates for 1938–1955 based on a range of indicators are available in Chadha et al. (2019).

For the purposes of this volume we analyse the quarterly data of Mitchell et al. (2012) for 1920–1938 and ONS data for 1955–2018 pending future work on high frequency data for the war periods and their immediate aftermath.

4.4 Summary of GDP Data

For the data in the next chapter we now summarise the GDP data used. The different annual components are combined into an index with a base of 1948. The data represent growth rates of English GDP from 1660 to1700, Great Britain from 1700 to 1870, the UK including all of Ireland, 1870–1920 and the UK including Northern Ireland only from

Table 4.1 Summary of real GDP used for cyclical analysis

Variable	Source	Coverage	Units
Real gross value added at factor cost, output-based	Broadberry et al. (2015, pp. 239–244)	England, 1660–1700	1700 = 100
Real gross value added at factor cost, output-based	Broadberry et al. (2015, pp. 239–244)	Great Britain, 1700–1870	1700 = 100
Balanced estimate of real GDP at factor cost	Solomou and Weale (1991)	United Kingdom, 1870–1913, pre-1922 definition	£ millions in 1900 constant prices
Compromise estimate of real GDP at factor cost	Mitchell (1988, p. 836)	United Kingdom, 1913–1920 pre-1922 definition	1913 = 100
Balanced estimate of real GDP at factor cost	Sefton and Weale (1995, pp. 188–189)	United Kingdom, 1920–1948, post-1922 definition	£ millions in constant prices
Gross value added at basic prices, balanced to 2016	Office for National Statistics. Series ID: ABMM	United Kingdom, 1948–2018, post-1922 definition	Chained volume measure, 2016 reference prices
Quarterly data			
Real GDP at factor cost	Mitchell et al. (2012)	United Kingdom, 1920–1938	£ millions in constant prices
Gross value added at basic prices, balanced to 2016	Office for National Statistics. Series ID: ABMM	United Kingdom, 1955–2018	Chained volume measure, 2016 reference prices

1920. As discussed, the volume series for GDP is on a factor cost or basic price basis. The overall index of real GDP that we use is summarised in Table 4.1.

Taking the data at face value, the volatility of economic growth appears to have changed over time.

During the late C17th and early C18th GDP growth appears to have been particularly volatile (Chart 4.4). As discussed later, this may reflect the use of probate data in measuring agricultural output rather than the more reliable data from farm accounts. Growth became less volatile during the C18th and early C19th. During the mid-to-late C19th, the average growth rate of the economy picked up to around 2% per annum and there was less volatility in output (Table 4.2). But the

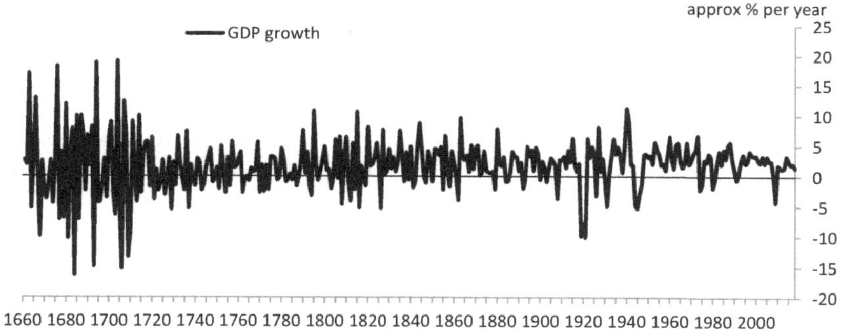

Chart 4.4 Annual GDP growth 1660–2018 (*Source* See Table 4.1)

Table 4.2 Summary statistics on annual GDP growth

	Annual GDP growth	
Period (peak to peak)	Averages	Standard deviation
1663–1720	1.09	8.42
1720–1781	0.71	2.89
1781–1825	1.61	3.79
1825–1878	2.28	3.11
1878–1918	1.99	2.33
1918–1943	1.78	5.49
1943–1973	2.57	2.96
1973–2007	2.35	1.89
2008+	1.16	2.02

volatility returned in the interwar period, during which there were two major recessions. The post-WWII period ushered in a golden age of prolonged periods of positive and relatively stable (annual) GDP growth, such as in the late 1950s/early 1960s, and between the early 1990s and the onset of the recent financial crisis. However growth in the ten years since the start of the financial crisis has been half of that observed in the previous two centuries. These estimates are used in the next section to derive a set of business cycle metrics for the UK since 1660.

References

Andersson, F., & Lennard, J. (2019). Irish GDP Between the Famine and the First World War: Estimates Based on a Dynamic Factor Model. *European Review of Economic History, 23*(1), 50–71.

Boyer, G., & Hatton, T. (2002). New Estimates of British Unemployment, 1870–1913. *The Journal of Economic History, 62*(3), 643–675.

Broadberry, S., Campbell, B., Klein, A., Overton, M., & van Leeuwen, B. (2015). *British Economic Growth 1270–1870*. Cambridge: Cambridge University Press.

Chadha, J., Lennard, J., Tchuente, G., & Thomas, R. (2019). *Quarterly GDP Estimates for the United Kingdom, 1938–55*. Mimeo.

Crafts, N. F. R., & Harley, C. K. (1992). Output Growth and the British Industrial Revolution: A Restatement of the Crafts-Harley View. *The Economic History Review, 45*(4), 703–730.

Crafts, N., & Mills, T. (2017). Six Centuries of British Economic Growth: A Time-Series Perspective. *European Review of Economic History, 21*(2), 141–158.

Deane, P. (1968). New Estimates of Gross National Product for the United Kingdom, 1830–1914. *Review of Income and Wealth, 14*(2), 95–112.

Deane, P., & Cole, W. (1962). *British Economic Growth, 1688–1959: Trends and Structure*. Cambridge: Cambridge University Press.

Denley, H. (2016). *National Accounts Historic Dataset Developments Since Blue Book 2011*. Office for National Statistics Article.

Everett, G. (2011). *Historic National Accounts*. Office for National Statistics Article.

Feinstein, C. (1972). *National Income Expenditure and Output of the United Kingdom 1855–1965*. Cambridge: Cambridge University Press.

Feinstein, C. (1990). What Really Happened to Real Wages? Trends in Wages, Prices, and Productivity in the United Kingdom, 1880–1913. *The Economic History Review, 43*(3), 329–355.

Feinstein, C., & Pollard, S. (1988). *Studies in Capital Formation in the United Kingdom 1750–1920*. Oxford: Oxford University Press.

Geary, F., & Stark, T. (2004). Trends in Real Wages During the Industrial Revolution: A View from Across the Irish Sea. *The Economic History Review, 57*(2), 362–395.

Geary, F., & Stark, T. (2015). Regional GDP in the UK, 1861–1911: New Estimates. *The Economic History Review, 68*(1), 123–144.

Geary, F., & Stark, T. (2018). 150 Years of Regional GDP: United Kingdom and Ireland. In J. Rosés & N. Wolf (Eds.), *The Economic Development of Europe's Regions: A Quantitative History Since 1900*. London: Routledge.

Harrison, M. (1990). A Volume Index of the Total Munitions Output of the United Kingdom, 1939–1944. *Economic History Review, 43*(2), 659–668.

Hoffmann, W. (1955). *British Industry 1700–1950*. Oxford: Basil Blackwell.

Horrell, S., Humphries, J., & Weale, M. (1994). An Input-Output Table for 1841. *The Economic History Review, 47*(3), 545–566.

Howlett, P. (1995). *Fighting with Figures: A Statistical Digest of the Second World War*. London: Central Statistical Office.

Martin, B. (2009). Resurrecting the UK Historic Sector National Accounts. *Review of Income and Wealth, 55*(3), 737–751.

Mitchell, B. (1988). *British Historical Statistics*. Cambridge: Cambridge University Press.

Mitchell, J., Solomou, S., & Weale, M. (2012). Monthly GDP Estimates for Inter-War Britain. *Explorations in Economic History, 49*(4), 543–556.

Sefton, J., & Weale, M. (1995). *Reconciliation of National Income and Expenditure: Balanced Estimates of National Income for the United Kingdom, 1920–1990*. Cambridge: Cambridge University Press.

Solomou, S., & Thomas, R. (2019). *Feinstein Fulfilled: GDP from the Income Side 1841–1920* (ESCoE Technical Report 04).

Solomou, S., & Weale, M. (1991). Balanced Estimates of UK GDP 1870–1913. *Explorations in Economic History, 28*(1), 54–63.

Thomas, R., & Dimsdale, N. (2017). *A Millennium of UK Macroeconomic Data: Bank of England OBRA Dataset*. London, UK: Bank of England. https://www.bankofengland.co.uk/-/media/boe/files/statistics/research-datasets/a-millennium-of-macroeconomic-data-for-the-uk.xlsx.

5

Metrics and Turning Points of Cycles 1660–2018

In this chapter we apply some of the methods discussed in Chapter 3 to the composite GDP data series discussed in Chapter 4. This is to draw out some basic metrics on business and credit cycles based on the existing data. We first consider some of the key metrics using classical business cycle analysis, drawing heavily on Chadha et al. (2019), before going on to look at growth cycles under various methods of de-trending discussed in Chapter 3. We look at annual data from 1660 and quarterly data from 1920 with the break-in World War 2 that was discussed in Chapter 4.

5.1 Classical Cycle Metrics

We first consider classical business cycle dating on annual data from 1660, adopting the simple algorithm from Chapter 3 where we identify expansions and contractions in GDP and GDP per capita. Table 5.1 summarises the annual turning points in chronological order. Chart 5.1 shows this graphically. It charts log levels of GDP over the period with contraction periods marked in grey.

N. Dimsdale and R. Thomas,
UK Business and Financial Cycles Since 1660,
https://doi.org/10.1007/978-3-030-26346-1_5

Table 5.1 Classical cycle peaks and troughs

GDP		Per capita		GDP		Per capita	
Peak	Trough	Peak	Trough	Peak	Trough	Peak	Trough
1663	1664	1663	1664	1796	1797	1796	1798
1667	1668	1667	1668	1802	1804	1802	1804
1669	1672	1669	1672	1805	1806	1805	1806
1673	1674	1673	1674	1807	1808	1807	1808
1676	1677	1676	1677	1810	1812	1810	1812
1678	1679	1678	1679	1813	1814	1813	1814
1680	1681	1680	1681	1815	1816	1815	1816
1683	1684	1683	1684	1817	1819	1817	1819
1685	1686	1685	1686	1825	1826	1825	1826
1688	1689	1688	1689			1827	1829
1692	1693	1692	1693			1831	1832
1694	1697	1694	1697	1836	1837	1836	1837
1698	1699	1698	1699	1838	1839		
1701	1703	1701	1703			1839	1842
1704	1706	1704	1706	1840	1842		
1708	1710	1708	1710	1845	1847		
1711	1713	1712	1713			1846	1847
1714	1715	1714	1715	1849	1850	1849	1850
1718	1719	1718	1719	1854	1855	1854	1855
1720	1721	1720	1721			1856	1858
1722	1724	1722	1724	1857	1858		
1725	1727	1725	1727	1860	1862		
1728	1729	1728	1729			1861	1862
1730	1731	1730	1731			1866	1867
1733	1735	1733	1735			1871	1873
1736	1737	1736	1737			1874	1879
1738	1740	1738	1740	1878	1879		
1742	1744	1742	1744	1883	1885	1883	1886
1747	1749	1747	1749			1889	1890
1750	1751	1750	1751	1891	1893	1891	1893
1753	1754	1753	1754	1899	1900	1899	1900
1755	1756	1755	1756	1902	1903	1902	1903
1761	1765	1761	1765	1907	1908	1907	1908
1769	1770	1769	1770			1916	1917
1771	1772	1771	1772	1918	1921	1918	1921
1773	1774	1773	1774	1925	1926	1925	1926
1777	1779	1777	1779	1929	1931	1929	1932
1781	1783	1781	1785	1943	1947	1943	1947
1784	1785			1973	1975	1973	1975
1786	1788	1786	1788	1979	1981	1979	1981
		1790	1791	1990	1991	1990	1991
1792	1794	1792	1794	2007	2009	2007	2009

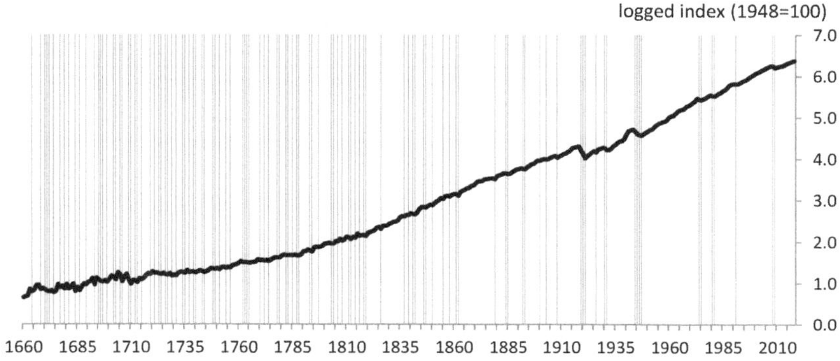

Chart 5.1 Expansions and contractions in GDP

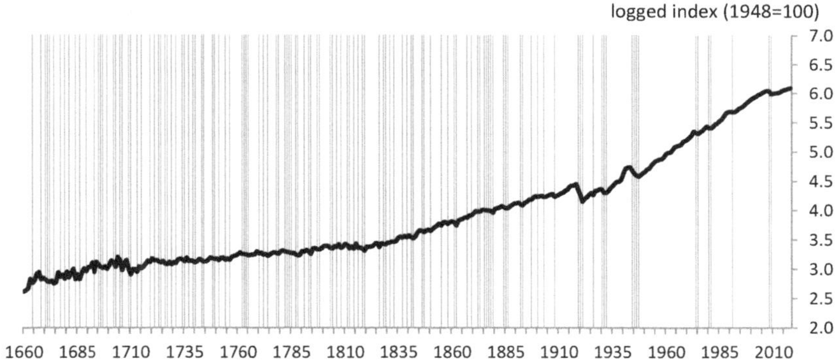

Chart 5.2 Expansions and contractions in GDP per capita

The chart suggests that for GDP there have been 72 cycles between the peak of 1663 and the trough of 2009 using a simple rule based on annual turning points. For GDP per capita there have been 78 cycles. A comparison of Charts 5.1 and 5.2 shows that many of the differences occur during the mid-late C19th when population growth rates were relatively large and positive implying many more contractions in GDP per capita.

Tables 5.2 and 5.3 ranks these cycles in terms of the size of the contraction in GDP from peak to trough and looks at the frequency and amplitude of cycles over time. Prior to 1825 the economy was in

Table 5.2 Ranking of individual annual contractions

Rank	Peak	Trough	Duration	Output loss (% of GDP)
1	1918	1921	3	−25.4
2	1708	1710	2	−21.2
3	1704	1706	2	−19.6
4	1683	1684	1	−16.4
5	1692	1693	1	−14.9
6	1943	1947	4	−13.7
7	1680	1681	1	−10.3
8	1667	1668	1	−9.9
9	1694	1697	3	−9.0
10	1701	1703	2	−8.8
11	1669	1672	3	−7.6
12	1676	1677	1	−7.2
13	1685	1686	1	−7.2
14	1678	1679	1	−6.9
15	1929	1931	2	−5.8
16	1728	1729	1	−5.6
17	1825	1826	1	−5.4
18	1736	1737	1	−5.4
19	1663	1664	1	−5.3
20	1815	1816	1	−5.3
21	1810	1812	2	−5.1
22	1792	1794	2	−4.8
23	1807	1808	1	−4.7
24	1673	1674	1	−4.5
25	2007	2009	2	−4.5
26	1711	1713	2	−4.4
27	1860	1862	2	−4.2
28	1761	1765	4	−3.9
29	1720	1721	1	−3.9
30	1907	1908	1	−3.8
31	1742	1744	2	−3.7
32	1725	1727	2	−3.7
33	1973	1975	2	−3.7
34	1698	1699	1	−3.6
35	1722	1724	2	−3.4
36	1925	1926	1	−3.3
37	1840	1842	2	−2.9
38	1714	1715	1	−2.8
39	1753	1754	1	−2.8
40	1891	1893	2	−2.8
41	1769	1770	1	−2.7
42	1733	1735	2	−2.7
43	1771	1772	1	−2.6

(continued)

Table 5.2 (continued)

Rank	Peak	Trough	Duration	Output loss (% of GDP)
44	1979	1981	2	−2.5
45	1688	1689	1	−2.4
46	1738	1740	2	−2.3
47	1854	1855	1	−2.3
48	1773	1774	1	−2.2
49	1813	1814	1	−2.2
50	1802	1804	2	−2.2
51	1878	1879	1	−2.2
52	1750	1751	1	−2.2
53	1786	1788	2	−1.9
54	1857	1858	1	−1.8
55	1718	1719	1	−1.8
56	1817	1819	2	−1.8
57	1883	1885	2	−1.7
58	1755	1756	1	−1.7
59	1747	1749	2	−1.7
60	1730	1731	1	−1.6
61	1781	1783	2	−1.5
62	1845	1847	2	−1.2
63	1777	1779	2	−1.0
64	1902	1903	1	−0.9
65	1849	1850	1	−0.9
66	1836	1837	1	−0.9
67	1796	1797	1	−0.7
68	1784	1785	1	−0.7
69	1990	1991	1	−0.7
70	1838	1839	1	−0.6
71	1899	1900	1	−0.6
72	1805	1806	1	−0.4

contraction for just under half of the time. After 1825 this drops to around a quarter of time for the next century or so before falling to around 10%. This can be seen visually in Charts 5.1 and 5.2. So it is the infrequency of large contractions that underpins the underlying shift in the growth rate of per capita incomes noted in Chapter 4. Contractions however have lengthened over time, with C20th recessions lasting longer than those in earlier centuries. Expansions have generally lengthened and increased in size during the C20th. The length of the classical cycle as a whole, measured as the sum of expansion and contraction periods, has increased fivefold since the late C17th.

Table 5.3 Summary statistics on cycles

	1659–1721	1721–1826	1826–1908	1908–1947	1947–2009	**1659–2009**
Contractions (Peak to trough)						
Number	20	30	14	4	4	**72**
Average length (years)	1.4	1.5	1.4	2.5	1.8	**1.5**
Average frequency (%)	45.2	43.8	23.2	25.6	11.3	**31.4**
Average amplitude (%)	−8.4	−2.9	−2.5	−12.0	−2.8	**−4.7**
Expansions (Trough to peak)						
Number	20	30	14	4	4	**72**
Average length (years)	1.7	2.0	4.5	7.3	13.8	**3.3**
Average frequency (%)	54.8	56.2	76.8	74.4	88.7	**68.6**
Average amplitude (%)	13.4	6.8	10.0	32.0	61.8	**14.9**
Total cycle (Peak to peak)						
Number	20	30	14	4	4	**72**
Average length (years)	3.3	3.5	5.9	9.0	16.0	**4.9**

Note The bold signifies results for the whole period 1659–2009

Table 5.2 ranks individual annual contractions in terms of output loss. The worst historical contractions largely occurred in the late C17th and early C18th. However the worst fall in output occurred after the end of World War 1 from a peak in 1918 to the trough in 1921, when GDP fell by a quarter over three years. Another large fall occurs at the end of World War 2 when output falls by 14%. By contrast the Great Depression and the Great Recession rank 15th and 25th on the all-time list of contractions. The recession after the South Sea Bubble in 1720 ranks 29th on the list while that in the early years of Mrs. Thatcher's government is 44th.

Table 5.4 provides a summary of recovery periods following recessions documenting how long it takes for output to recover to its previous peak. The length of recovery is measured from peak to peak rather

Table 5.4 Contractions ordered by length of time taken to recover to previous peak

Peak	Length of recovery	Cumulative loss (% of GDP)
1704	16	−204.4
1918	16	−187.7
1720	16	−77.3
1736	11	−34.7
1943	9	−67.5
1761	8	−18.9
1781	8	−9.3
1694	7	−43.7
1769	7	−13.8
2007	6	−8.8
1683	5	−48.4
1815	5	−18.5
1747	5	−5.4
1973	4	−7.1
1979	4	−4.8
1883	4	−3.6
1680	3	−17.6
1701	3	−11.8
1792	3	−6.6
1807	3	−6.5
1810	3	−6.3
1907	3	−5.0
1891	3	−4.9
1840	3	−4.9

(continued)

Table 5.4 (continued)

Peak	Length of recovery	Cumulative loss (% of GDP)
1860	3	−4.6
1802	3	−4.4
1777	3	−1.7
1845	3	−1.2
1990	3	−0.9
1692	2	−16.2
1920	2	−5.5
1753	2	−2.8
1688	2	−2.4
1854	2	−2.3
1813	2	−2.2
1878	2	−2.2
1857	2	−1.8
1755	2	−1.7
1902	2	−0.9
1849	2	−0.9
1836	2	−0.9
1796	2	−0.7
1838	2	−0.6
1899	2	−0.6
1805	2	−0.4

than trough to peak given that many recoveries were interrupted by ups and downs in output. So it is defined as the length of time it takes output to recover from the start of the recession in that year. The table also documents the cumulative loss in output (relative to its previous peak) in percentage terms.

The recovery from the 1704–1705 recession represents the longest and most costly length of time that output took to return to its previous peak. So on this metric it outscores the fall in output at the end of WW1 in terms of cumulative loss, even though it took 16 years in both cases for output to recover. The third row of the table shows that no sooner had output returned to its 1704 peak in 1720 then another recession occurred around the same time as the South Sea Bubble and again it took another 16 years for the level of output to recover. Note that in all these 16 year periods, the recovery was interrupted by several contractions in output most notably by the Great Depression in the case of the recovery following the contraction in output at the end of

World War 1. Output in 1929 was still 3% below its 1918 level when the Wall Street Crash hit.

Charts 5.3 and 5.4 together with Table 5.5 show quarterly turning points over the 1920–1938 and 1955–2018 periods based on the rule that a technical recession should involve at least two consecutive quarters of negative growth. It reveals subtleties about certain recessions that are masked by the annual data. In particular it reveals the double-dip recessions in the Great Depression and in the mid-1970s which we will

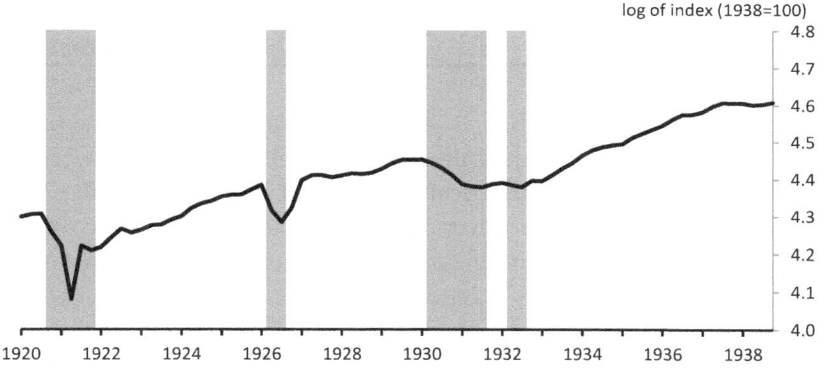

Chart 5.3 Quarterly expansions and contractions (2 quarter rule) 1920–1938 (*Notes* Recession periods are shaded)

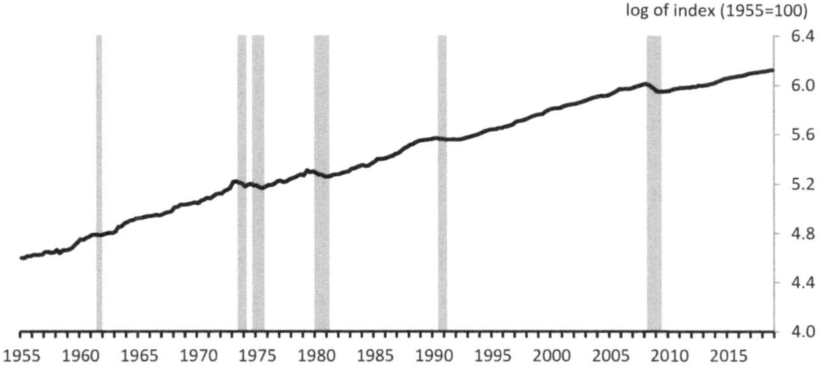

Chart 5.4 Quarterly expansions and contractions (2 quarter rule) 1955–2018 (*Notes* Recession periods are shaded)

Table 5.5 Quarterly turning points in the United Kingdom, 1920–1938/1955–2018

Peak	Trough
1920Q3	1921Q2/Q4
1926Q1	1926Q3
1930Q1	1931Q3
1932Q1	1932Q3
1961Q2	1961Q4
1973Q2	1974Q1
1974Q3	1975Q3
1979Q2	1981Q1
1990Q2	1991Q1
2008Q1	2009Q2

return to in the narrative chapter. There is also an issue about the timing of the trough in 1921 which is affected by the miner's strike between 3rd of April and 28th June of that year as discussed in Mitchell et al. (2012) and can be seen clearly in Chart 5.3 with a large dip and recovery in 1921Q2 and Q3. This also affects the assessment about the size of the contraction in 1921 which is based on total output produced over the year. Note that in this case, where we have no quarterly data for 1918 and 1919, the 1930s recovery would be separate from that after 1920Q3 where output had returned to its previous "peak" by mid-1924. So the treatment of World War 1 matters quite a bit for this type of metric.

To complete our analysis of classical economic cycles we also estimate a simple two-regime Markov Switching model in order to determine contraction periods, using Hamilton's (1989) method that was discussed in Chapter 3. The results on annual and quarterly data are shown in Tables 5.6 and 5.7. The annual model suggests an expansion growth regime of just under 2% a year and a contraction regime of a 9% fall in output. As Chart 5.5 shows the model is able to detect turning points in large recessions but some contractions, such as the Great Depression of 1931, shows a probability of under 0.5 of being such a regime reflecting the relative mildness of that recession in output terms (although as we will see not in unemployment terms). The quarterly model shown in Chart 5.6 is able to pick out the key C20th recessions very well with all the major contractions showing a conditional probability of >0.5 of being in a contractionary state with the exception of the early 1990s recession.

Table 5.6 Markov-Switching model results—annual data 1660–2018

Variable	Coefficient	Std. error
Contraction regime		
μ_1	−0.091298	0.012901
Expansion regime		
μ_2	0.019634	0.001807
Autoregressive coefficients		
ϕ_1	−0.296041	0.062804
ϕ_2	−0.094423	0.062223
ϕ_3	0.114245	0.062140
ϕ_4	0.113993	0.065220

Table 5.7 Markov-Switching model results—quarterly data 1955–2018

Variable	Coefficient	Std. error
Contraction regime		
μ_1	−0.011831	0.002468
Expansion regime		
μ_2	0.007409	0.000727
Autoregressive coefficients		
ϕ_1	−0.038421	0.073830
ϕ_2	0.144159	0.076249
ϕ_3	0.109879	0.070418
ϕ_4	0.016628	0.068886

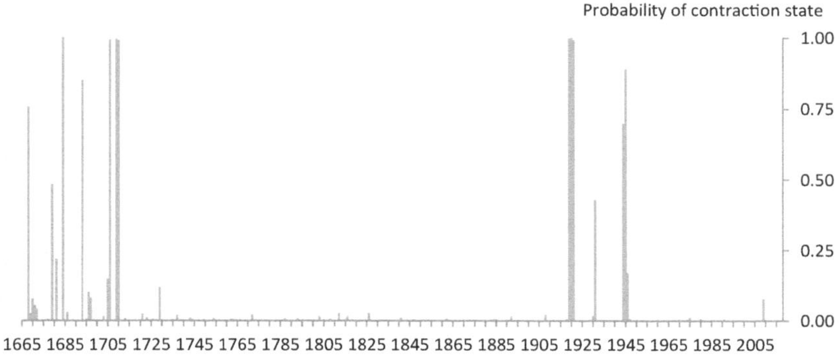

Chart 5.5 Annual turning points 1660–2018: Markov-Switching model

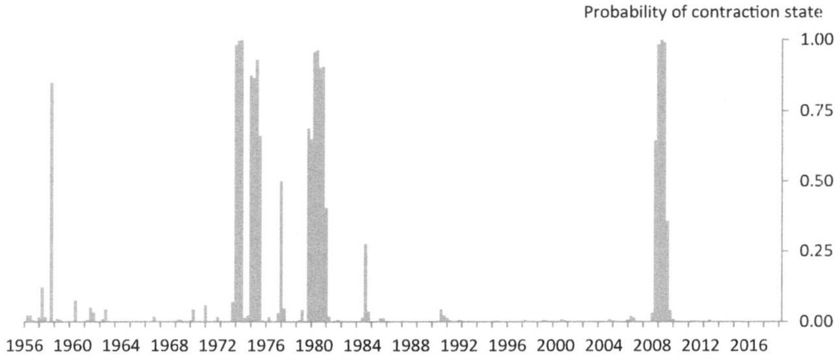

Chart 5.6 Quarterly turning points 1955Q1 to 2018Q4: Markov-Switching model

5.2 Growth Cycle Metrics

For growth cycle metrics we derive de-trended measures using the various methods discussed in Chapter 3. We estimate the following models on annual data:

- Hodrick Prescott filtered (HP) estimates using the "standard" lambda parameter of 100.
- A Band-pass filter (BP) based on the Christiano-Fitzgerald asymmetric approach where the lower and upper bands are set at 2 and 8 years.
- An Unobserved Components (UC) model based on the local-linear trends model of Chapter 3. The cycle is modelled as an AR(2) process so that the data can determine whether the roots are complex or not, rather than impose the complex roots via specifying an explicit trigonometric cycle.
- A segmented-trend model (ST) where the cycle is backed out by removing a series of split-deterministic time trends. We use GDP per capita for the data here so implicitly the trends relate to labour productivity and the employment ratio. The time trends are linear.
- A Beveridge-Nelson (BN) decomposition derived from an ARIMA(2,1) model.

For each model we chart the implied cycles in Charts 5.7, 5.8, 5.9, and 5.10. In each case the Hodrick Prescott filter is used as a benchmark for comparisons. We then derive peak and trough points under each approach based on the deviation of each cycle from trend. As discussed in Chapter 3, we apply censoring rules to ensure that troughs represent negative deviations from trend and peaks are positive, in order to avoid mini-peaks and troughs. We also ensure that peaks and troughs alternate making judgements about where the peak or trough lies depending

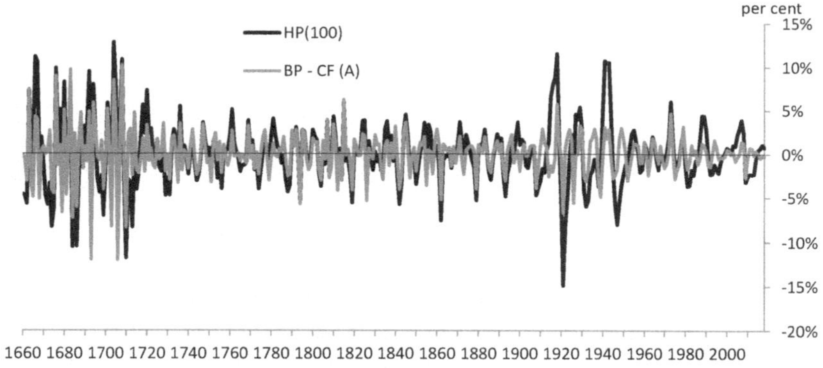

Chart 5.7 Cycles based on Hodrick Prescott filter and band-pass filter

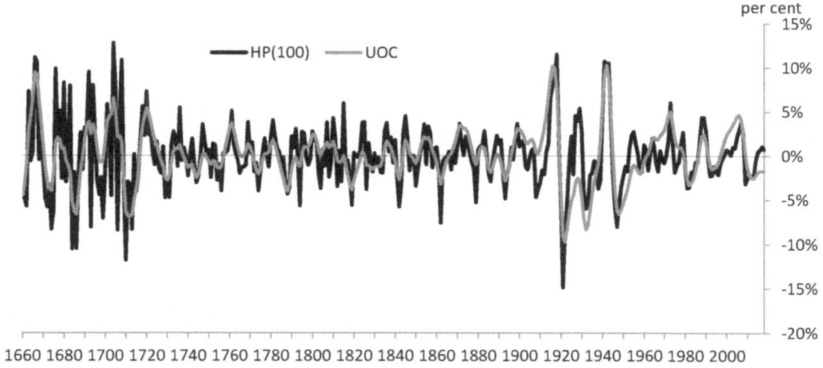

Chart 5.8 Cycles based on Hodrick Prescott filter and unobserved component model

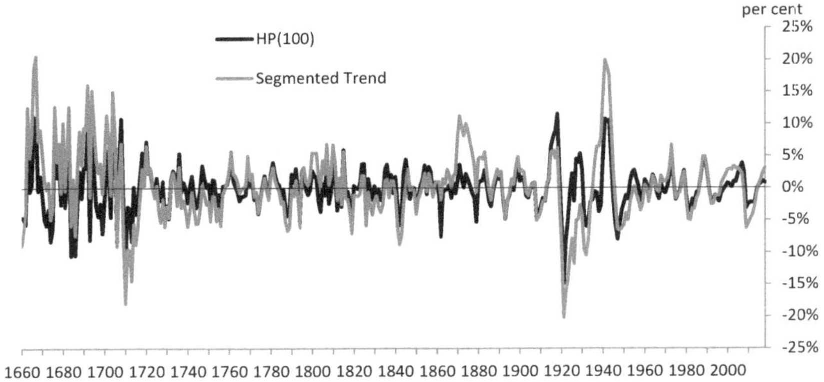

Chart 5.9 Cycles based on Hodrick Prescott filter and segmented trend model

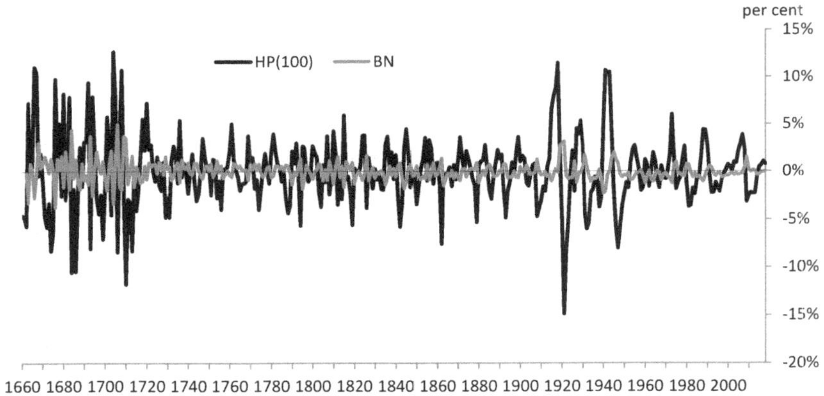

Chart 5.10 Cycles based on Hodrick Prescott filter and Beveridge Nelson decomposition

on the pattern of observations. This allows us to derive the metrics about the timing, length and amplitude of cycles which are shown in Tables 5.8, 5.9, 5.10, 5.11, 5.12, and 5.13.

The results of applying the different de-trending methods are largely what would be expected from our discussion in Chapter 3. Upturns and downturns are more symmetric than classical cycles. The Band-pass filter delivers cycles that are slightly less volatile than the HP filter and slightly shorter, though peaks and troughs are fairly coincident.

Table 5.8 Classical versus growth cycle dating

Classical		HP		UC	
Peak	Trough	Peak	Trough	Peak	Trough
1663	1664	1663	1664		
1667	1668	1666	1668	1666	1674
1669	1672	1669	1674		
1673	1674				
1676	1677	1676	1679	1677	1686
1678	1679				
1680	1681	1680	1681		
1683	1684	1683	1684		
1685	1686				
1688	1689	1688	1689		
1692	1693	1692	1693	1692	1698
1694	1697	1694	1699		
1698	1699				
1701	1703	1701	1703		
1704	1706	1704	1706	1704	1711
1708	1710	1708	1710		
1711	1713				
1714	1715	1714	1715		
1718	1719				
1720	1721	1720	1724	1720	1730
1722	1724				
1725	1727	1725	1727		
1728	1729	1728	1729		
1730	1731				
1733	1735	1733	1735		
1736	1737	1736	1737	1736	1744
1738	1740	1738	1740		
1742	1744	1742	1744		
1747	1749	1747	1751	1748	1755
1750	1751				
1753	1754	1752	1756		
1755	1756	1761	1765		
1761	1765	1769	1774	1761	1766
1769	1770			1769	1774
1771	1772				
1773	1774				
1777	1779	1777	1779		
1781	1783	1781	1788	1781	1788
1784	1785				
1786	1788				
1792	1794	1792	1794		
1796	1797	1795	1798		

(continued)

Table 5.8 (continued)

Classical		HP		UC	
Peak	Trough	Peak	Trough	Peak	Trough
1802	1804	1800	1804	1801	1804
1805	1806	1805	1806		
1807	1808	1807	1808		
1810	1812	1810	1812	1810	1813
1813	1814	1813	1814		
1815	1816	1815	1819	1815	1819
1817	1819				
		1820	1822		
1825	1826	1825	1826	1824	1829
		1827	1829		
		1830	1834		
1836	1837	1836	1839	1836	1842
1838	1839				
1840	1842	1840	1842		
1845	1847	1845	1850	1845	1850
1849	1850				
1854	1855	1854	1855	1854	1862
1857	1858	1856	1858		
1860	1862	1860	1862		
		1866	1867		
		1868	1869		
1878	1879	1871	1879	1871	1879
1883	1885	1883	1886	1882	1886
1891	1893	1889	1893	1889	1893
		1896	1897		
1899	1900	1899	1904		
1902	1903				
1907	1908	1907	1908	1906	1909
1918	1921	1918	1921	1916	1922
1925	1926	1925	1926		
1929	1931	1929	1932	1929	1932
1943	1947	1943	1947	1942	1948
		1955	1958		
		1960	1962		
		1964	1967		
		1968	1970		
1973	1975	1973	1975	1973	1982
1979	1981	1979	1981		
1990	1991	1988	1992	1989	1993
2007	2009	2007	2009	2006	2013

Table 5.9 Growth cycles—HP filter (λ = 100)

Period	Number	Average length of cycle (years)			Amplitude (%)	
	Std Dev	Downturn	Upturn	Total	Downturn	Upturn
1663–1720	13	2.08	2.31	4.38	−5.45	7.37
1720–1781	12	2.75	2.33	5.08	−2.38	2.77
1781–1825	10	2.70	1.70	4.40	−3.04	2.79
1825–1874	11	2.18	2.00	4.18	−2.72	2.22
1874–1918	6	3.67	4.17	7.83	−3.28	3.68
1918–1943	3	2.33	6.00	8.33	−7.64	6.04
1943–1973	5	2.80	3.20	6.00	−2.84	2.53
1973–2007	3	2.67	7.25	9.92	−2.59	4.25
2008+	1	2.00			−3.17	

Table 5.10 Growth cycles—band-pass filter

Period	Number	Average length of cycle (years)			Amplitude (%)	
		Downturn	Upturn	Total	Downturn	Upturn
1663–1720	14	1.86	2.21	4.07	−5.66	5.93
1720–1781	14	2.21	2.14	4.36	−1.80	2.19
1781–1825	11	2.18	1.82	4.00	−2.59	2.50
1825–1874	11	2.45	1.73	4.18	−2.59	1.93
1874–1918	8	2.88	3.00	5.88	−2.03	2.17
1918–1943	4	2.50	3.75	6.25	−5.07	2.74
1943–1973	5	2.80	3.20	6.00	−1.90	2.09
1973–2007	4	2.75	5.20	7.95	−1.80	2.42
2008+	1	2.00			−2.65	

Table 5.11 Growth cycles—unobserved components model

Period	Number	Average length of cycle (years)			Amplitude (%)	
		Downturn	Upturn	Total	Downturn	Upturn
1663–1720	4	7.50	5.40	12.90	−4.54	5.44
1720–1781	5	7.00	5.20	12.20	−1.79	1.63
1781–1825	4	4.25	6.50	10.75	−2.15	1.13
1825–1874	4	6.00	5.75	11.75	−2.07	2.24
1874–1918	4	4.75	6.50	11.25	−1.35	3.34
1918–1943	2	4.50	8.50	13.00	−9.05	3.72
1943–1973	1	6.00	25.00	31.00	−6.63	5.03
1973–2007	2	6.50	15.00	21.50	−2.38	4.04
2008+	1	7.00			−2.57	

Table 5.12 Growth cycles—segmented trend

Period	Number	Average length of cycle (years)			Amplitude (%)	
		Downturn	Upturn	Total	Downturn	Upturn
1663–1720	11	2.18	2.75	4.93	−4.53	10.82
1720–1781	8	4.25	3.38	7.63	−3.60	2.78
1781–1825	5	3.80	4.80	8.60	−4.88	3.47
1825–1874	7	2.29	4.43	6.71	−3.46	3.19
1874–1918	5	4.20	5.20	9.40	−2.75	4.10
1918–1943	2	3.00	8.50	11.50	−15.38	8.60
1943–1973	4	3.75	4.25	8.00	−3.27	2.29
1973–2007	3	2.67	7.00	9.67	−3.12	4.38
2008+	1	6.00			−6.33	

Table 5.13 Growth cycles—Beveridge Nelson decomposition

Period	Number	Average length of cycle (years)			Amplitude (%)	
		Downturn	Upturn	Total	Downturn	Upturn
1664–1719	15	2.13	1.50	3.63	−1.76	2.23
1719–1779	13	2.38	2.23	4.62	−0.59	0.84
1779–1826	11	1.91	2.36	4.27	−1.13	0.92
1826–1873	12	1.50	2.42	3.92	−0.92	0.61
1873–1917	9	2.56	2.33	4.89	−0.55	0.59
1917–1945	5	2.20	3.40	5.60	−1.04	1.65
1945–1975	4	4.75	2.75	7.50	−1.14	0.31
1975–2009	3	6.00	5.33	11.33	−0.75	0.96
2009+	2	2.00	1.00	3.00	−0.24	0.13

The UC model filters out more of the fluctuations in output as noise and delivers fewer and longer, more persistent cycles. However the roots of the estimated AR(2) component are real rather than complex so there is no periodic cycle underlying the generated cycle. Charts 5.11, 5.12, and 5.13 summarise the AR(2) trend, cyclical and noise components.

The segmented trend model has the least volatile trend and unsurprisingly leads to cycles that are generally larger in amplitude, although again the turning points in the growth cycle are very similar. The Beveridge Nelson has the most volatile trends and leads to very noisy cycles with little amplitude. The predicted turning points are also very different.

After applying the censoring rules most of the approaches suggest a narrowed-down set of turning points (Table 5.8) and, overall, they suggest that the length of growth cycles increases after 1870

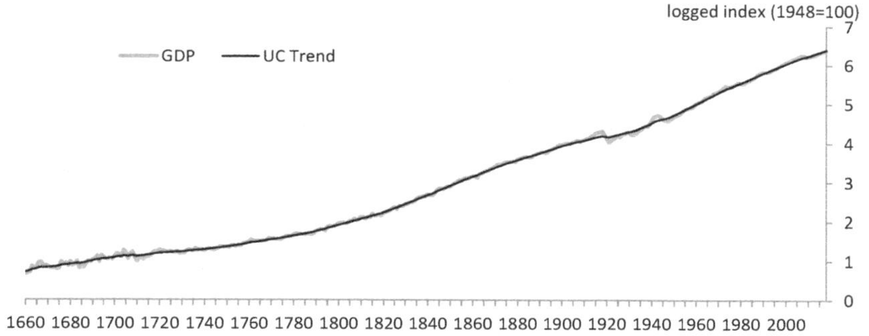

Chart 5.11 Unobserved components model—trend

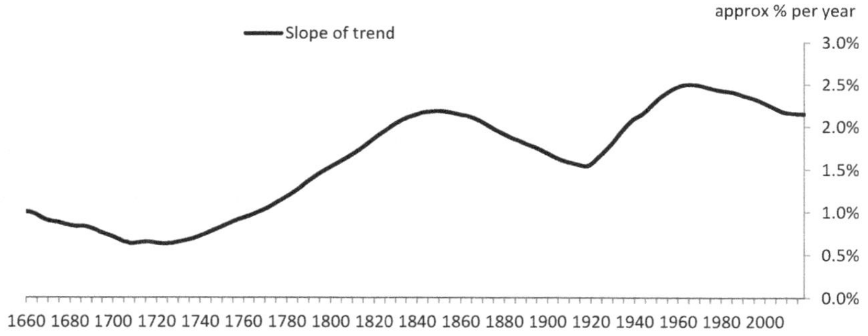

Chart 5.12 Unobserved components model—slope of trend

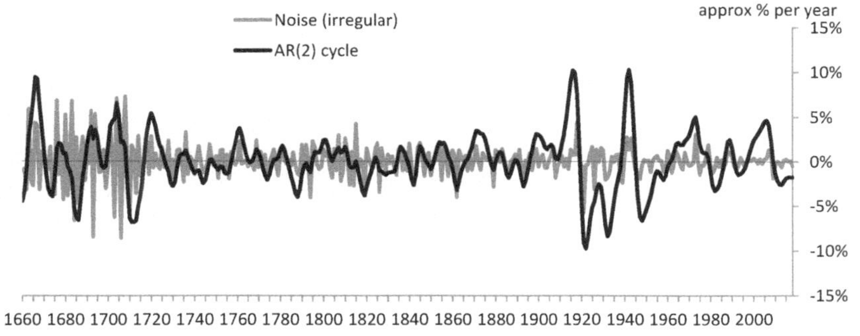

Chart 5.13 Unobserved components model—noise and AR(2) cycle

(Tables 5.9, 5.10, 5.11, 5.12, and 5.13). The HP and BP models suggest that the business cycle lengthens from around 4–5 years to between 6 and 9 years. The UC model however appears to show that cycles mostly increase in length after World War 2, with a total cycle duration of 11–13 years between 1663 and 1943. The interwar periods and the 1660–1720 period show the greatest amplitude which is unsurprising given these contain the deepest recessions.

Overall the tables show quite a range in business cycle metrics, suggesting deriving stylised facts on the business cycle is difficult and very dependent on the method used. The BN decompositions in particular suggest that most of the fluctuations in GDP can be attributed to the trend component and that the cyclical component is noisy with low duration and amplitude. That would imply that many shocks lead to permanent shifts in output either because they reflect supply shocks as in the real business cycle model or demand shocks that have hysteretic effects on potential supply as discussed earlier in Chapter 2. The HP and BP models tend to reflect the "conventional wisdom" of a lengthening cycle over time but one that lies within traditional business cycle territory of between 2 and 10 years. The UC model results are particularly interesting in that they suggest that the duration of cycles are, on average, very much in the range of what modern consensus would deem to be credit cycle territory—a duration of between 8 and 20 years. As we show in Chapter 6 many of the peaks and troughs in the UC model bookend financial crises. On post-WW2 data the annual UC model suggests a long upswing of almost 25 years between 1948 and 1973, once censoring is applied.

We also apply some of the de-trending methods to the quarterly GDP data available from 1920–1938 and from 1955. Charts 5.14, 5.15, 5.16, and 5.17 consider the peaks and troughs for both the interwar and post-WW2 periods and a comparison is made between the HP filter (HP), Band-pass filter (BP(CF)) and an AR(2) cycle from an unobserved components model applied to quarterly data. Once again the BP and HP filters show similar patterns although the BP filter is smoother as it excludes high frequency movements that the HP filter lets through. The UC model exhibits more significant differences particularly in the post-WW2 period. The UC model suggests a more

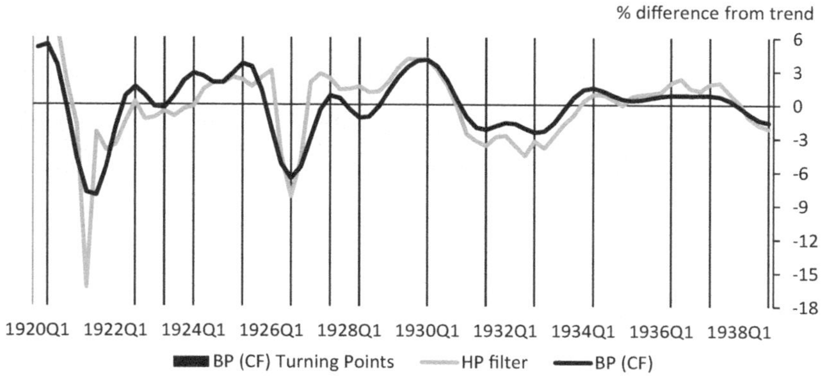

Chart 5.14 Interwar growth cycles using quarterly data—HP and BP models compared

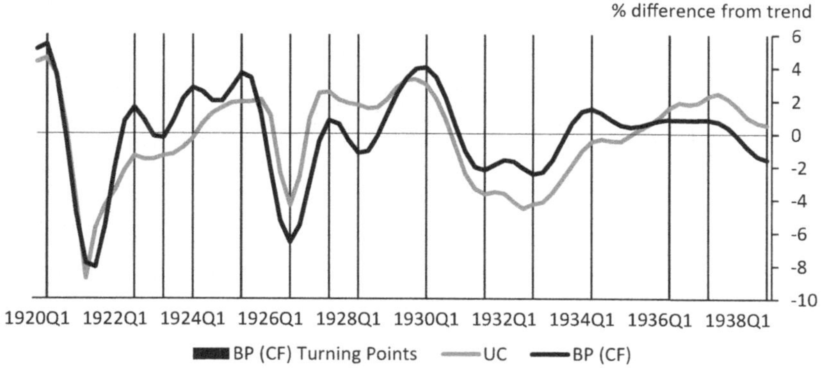

Chart 5.15 Interwar growth cycles using quarterly data—UC and BP models compared

persistent boom in the build-up to the Great Financial Crisis in 2008 and a more persistent contraction relative to trend thereafter. Also note that applied to quarterly data from 1955, the UC model shows more peaks and troughs over the post-WW2 period than the annual UC model (with censoring rules applied). Clearly the development of quarterly GDP data over the 1938–1955 period would be beneficial so a longer quarterly assessment of growth cycles can be made.

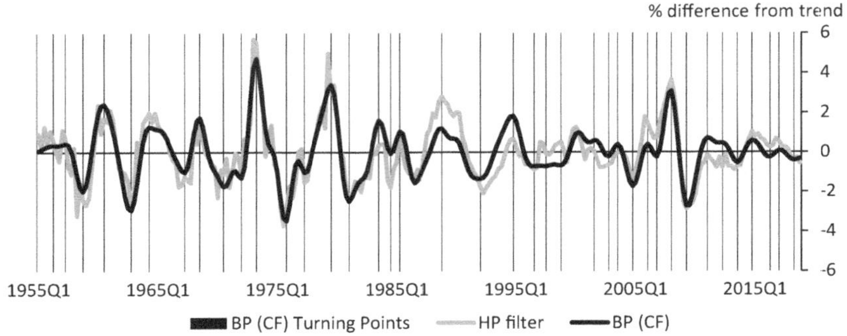

Chart 5.16 Post-war growth cycles using quarterly data—HP and BP models compared

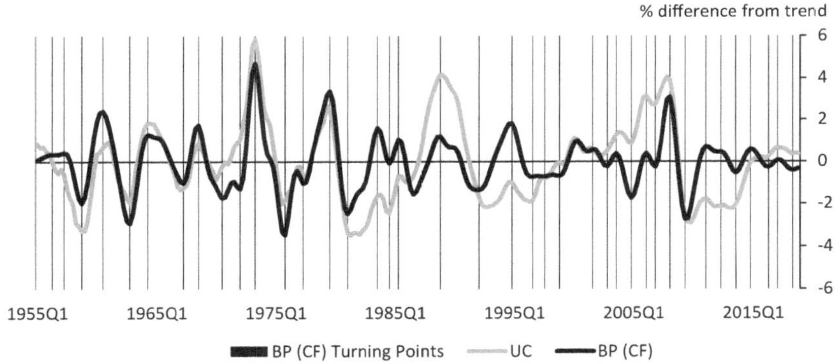

Chart 5.17 Post-war growth cycles using quarterly data—UC and BP models compared

Overall the results reaffirm the conclusion that, although many of the peaks and troughs derived from the various statistical methods show similar patterns, the business cycle metrics can vary quite a lot. None of this is surprising given the discussion of Chapter 3 and it is clear statistical methods alone are not sufficient to uncover the nature of business cycles. A key test is whether these metrics when combined with the historical narrative from contemporary and secondary sources can tell a consistent story over time. This is the focus of Chapter 6.

References

Chadha, J., Lennard, J., & Thomas, R. (2019). *Dating Business Cycles in the United Kingdom, 1700–2010*. Mimeo.

Hamilton, J. (1989). A New Approach to the Economic Analysis of Nonstationary Time Series and the Business Cycle. *Econometrica, 57*(2), 357–384.

Mitchell, J., Solomou, S., & Weale, M. (2012). Monthly GDP Estimates for Inter-War Britain. *Explorations in Economic History, 49*(4), 543–556.

6

A Narrative History of UK Business Cycles

This chapter draws on the existing economic history literature to examine the key drivers of past economic cycles, linking them to developments in the world economy, domestic fiscal and monetary policy, and past financial crises. The main discussion covers the period 1720–2007 and we break the analysis into the periods 1720–1830, 1830–1913, 1919–1939, 1945–1971 and 1971–2007. These dates are in part chosen due to the availability of data, but they also correspond approximately to distinct economic phases in the United Kingdom's economic history. However, we "bookend" the 1720–2008 period with a scene-setting "prologue" covering 1660–1720, and an "epilogue" covering the period since 2008. Each chapter starts with an overview of institutional factors and key drivers. This is aimed at readers who want a general overview of the cycles in this period, the institutional background to them and the key factors driving fluctuations in output. This is then followed by a chronological narrative that sketches out the nature of each cycle informed by the business cycle metrics in Chapter 5. This is aimed at readers who want a more detailed assessment of each

The original version of this chapter was revised: Typographical and grammatical corrections were incorporated. The correction to this chapter is available at https://doi.org/10.1007/978-3-030-26346-1_8

N. Dimsdale and R. Thomas,
UK Business and Financial Cycles Since 1660,
https://doi.org/10.1007/978-3-030-26346-1_6

particular cycle. For each section we summarise the results of Chapter 5 by showing charts of annual growth cycles over the relevant period with turning points in classical cycles highlighted in the background.

6.1 Prologue—The Emerging Market Economy 1660–1720

6.1.1 Overview—Institutional Factors and Key Drivers

Our overview of British economic cycles begins with a prologue covering the period 1660–1720. There are several motivations for this.

First, as Crafts and Mills (2017) show in their analysis of the Broadberry et al. (2015) GDP data, this is the period when we begin to see a positive trend in the growth of per capita incomes (as shown earlier in Chart 1.1) which is the hallmark of modern industrial and commercial economies. In part, the scene had been set earlier. As Broadberry et al. (2015) show the British economy was already highly industrialised and commercialised in 1600 and those trends continued throughout the C17th so that by the end of the C17th agriculture had fallen from around 40% of GDP to around a quarter with the rest accounted for by increased shares of both industry and services (Chart 6.1).

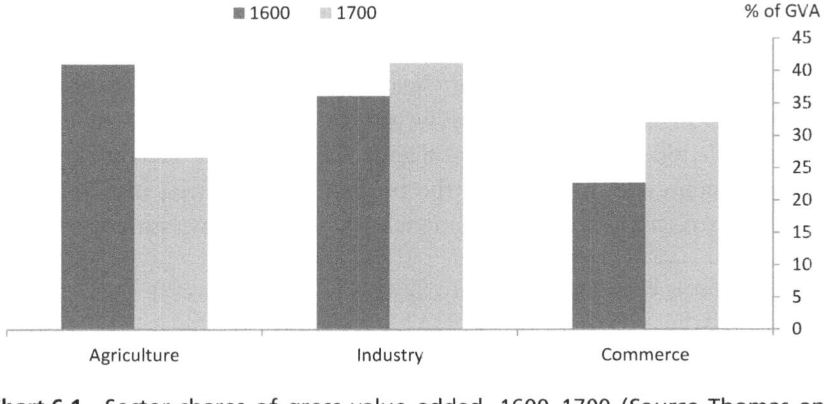

Chart 6.1 Sector shares of gross value added, 1600–1700 (*Source* Thomas and Dimsdale [2017] derived from Broadberry et al. [2015])

Second, this period witnesses the birth of corporate Britain and the start of a commercial revolution. Mirowski (1985) suggests the emergence of joint-stock companies and banking firms over this period marks this period as the "birth of the business cycle" with increasing trade in financial instruments and an associated growth in money and credit. These developments facilitated the cyclical swings typically observed in capitalist economies and which begin to emerge over this period.

Third, this is a period when there is a major re-orientation of British trade away from a narrow specialisation, based on the export of woollen cloth to Europe, towards a more diversified pattern both in terms of commodities and geography, based on Britain's growing commercial empire (Davis 1954, 62).

A final and related development is the development of the mercantilist fiscal-military state (O'Brien 1988) that was required to support this new commercial trade policy. The Navigation Acts (1651 and 1660) first introduced by Cromwell, and re-affirmed by the restored Stuart monarchy, required trade between Britain and its colonies to be carried in domestic or colonial vessels. This prompted a hostile reaction from the Dutch who had developed a highly profitable entrepôt trade between East and West. The Dutch had built by far the largest mercantile fleet in Europe and had control over the extremely lucrative trade in spices after conquering most of Portugal's overseas trading posts. The Dutch had also infiltrated England's trade with her developing North American colonies. The Commonwealth and Restoration period were to see the initiation of the Royal Navy and a series of mercantilist wars—first with the Dutch and then, when William of Orange secured the throne in 1688, the start of many wars with the French during C18th. The development of a mercantilist fiscal-naval state engendered a revolution in finance both in terms of taxation and government borrowing (Dickson 1967).

Each of these factors had implications for the course of economic fluctuations over this period. These do show evidence of recurrent cycles (see Chart 6.2). The Unobserved Components (UC) model suggests a cycle length of 10 years over this period while the HP filter shows a more erratic set of peaks and troughs reflecting a high degree of variability in output during the late C17th and early part of the C18th discussed earlier. As shown in Table 5.4 the recovery from the recession

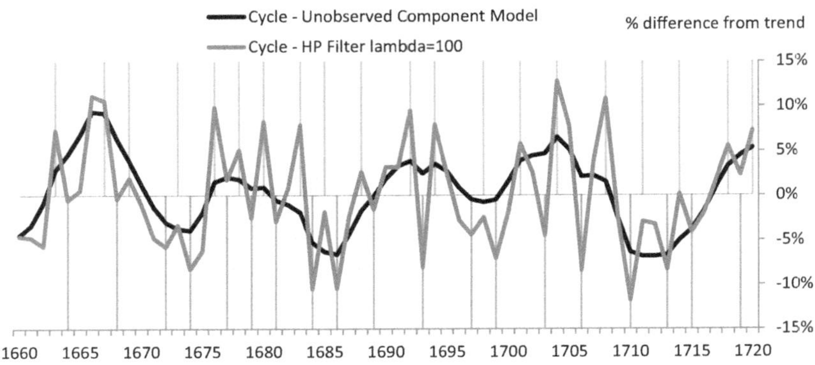

Chart 6.2 Cycles 1660–1720 (*Notes* Lines above the axis represent classical cycle peaks, lines below represent classical cycle troughs. *Source* Chapter 5)

between 1704 and 1705 was the longest and costliest in terms of cumulative loss over the past three and a half centuries. Output only recovered to its 1704 peak in 1720 after which there was a further recession and equally long-lived recovery period.

Much of the large degree of variability in GDP reflects agriculture (Chart 6.3). That could result from the need to rely upon probate records as the basis for estimating crop yields before 1720. After 1720 estimates of agricultural output are derived from the more reliable farm accounts (see Broadberry et al. [2015] for a discussion). The availability of farm accounts enables estimates of agricultural output to be improved as shown by Turner et al. (2001). The only alternative indicator here is to follow earlier scholars who had to rely mainly on the price of wheat in assessing the bounty of harvests such as Tooke and Newmarch (1838), Ashton (1959), Hoskins (1968), and Hoppit (1987) but here the inference can only be indirect at best.

The other major financial development over this period was the foundation of the Bank of England in 1694, chiefly an act to raise money for the government. In return for the loan to the government the private owners of the Bank were given certain privileges. After 1708 it was the only joint-stock bank permitted in England (other banks were limited to partnerships of 6 or less) and the Bank was allowed to issue notes and discount bills. That meant the number of banks increased only slowly over this period (see Chart 6.4) at least up until the early 1710s.

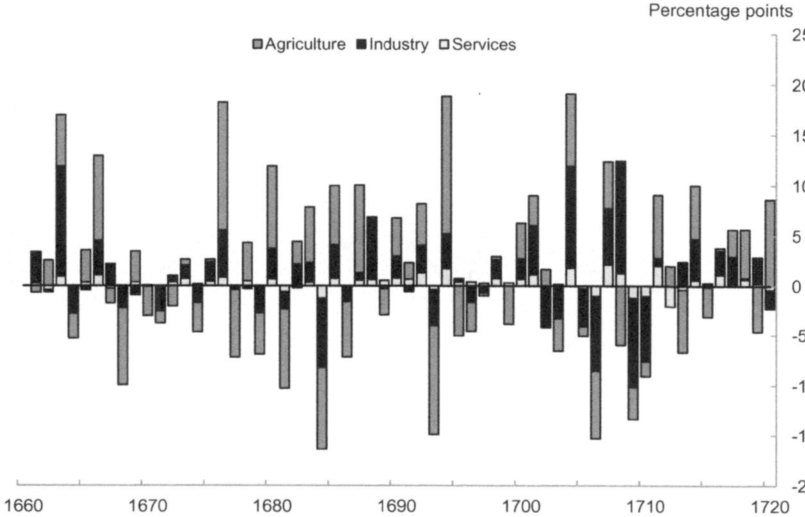

Chart 6.3 Contributions to output growth 1660–1720 (*Source* Thomas and Dimsdale [2017] derived from Broadberry et al. [2015])

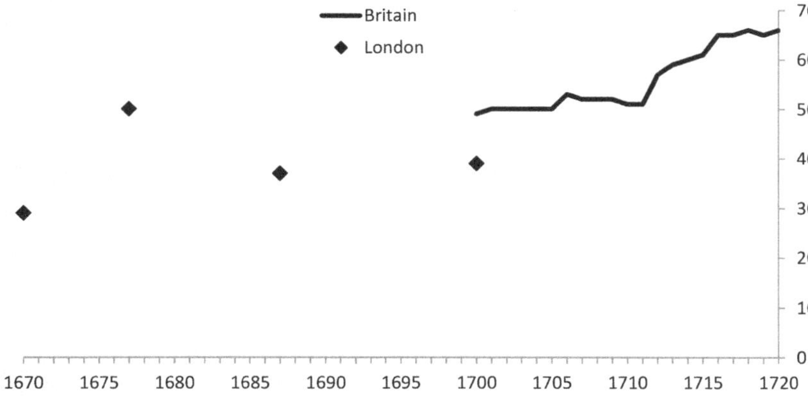

Chart 6.4 Number of banks in London and Britain 1670–1720 (*Source* Melton [2002] and Michie [2016])

Price (1992) notes that the Bank was keen to increase its private discounting business over this period in order to get more notes into circulation and increase profitability. Chart 6.5 shows the Bank increased its private sector lending to the order of 3.5% of GDP by 1715. There

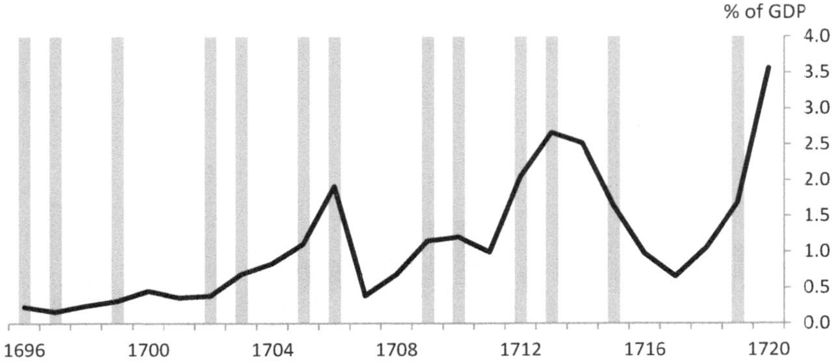

Chart 6.5 Bank of England discounts and other security holdings (*Notes* Annual recession periods shaded. *Source* Thomas and Dimsdale 2017)

were sharp movements in discounts to the tune of 1% of English GDP in certain years. One hypothesis raised by Lovell (1957) is whether the Bank in its first hundred years or so of its existence stepped in to act as a lender of last resort during panics and crises. However, before 1720 the Bank had not fully established itself and the sharp contractions in discounts appear largely due to runs on the newly formed Bank, largely due to political events and sentiment (French invasions and Jacobite uprisings) that threatened the state's viability. Nevertheless, the Bank does appear to have increased its discounts during several recessions (Chart 6.5). This may have alleviated the number of bankruptcies that occurred. Hoppit's (1986) data suggest that in those periods where the Bank increased its discounts private bankruptcies increased by less, although changes in the bankruptcy law in 1706 make quantitative comparisons before and after that date difficult (Chart 6.6).

Wars could lead to upturns in the early stages of a conflict if there was a pick up in government spending and activity directed towards supporting soldiers and horses. If wars were anticipated they could also trigger cyclical recoveries before the start of hostilities as trade picked up in anticipation that an impending conflict would lead to future disruption (Chart 6.7). But wars could ultimately cause downturns as growing export industries coped with weaker demand and disruption and indeed poor trade performance was one reason parties were keen to see

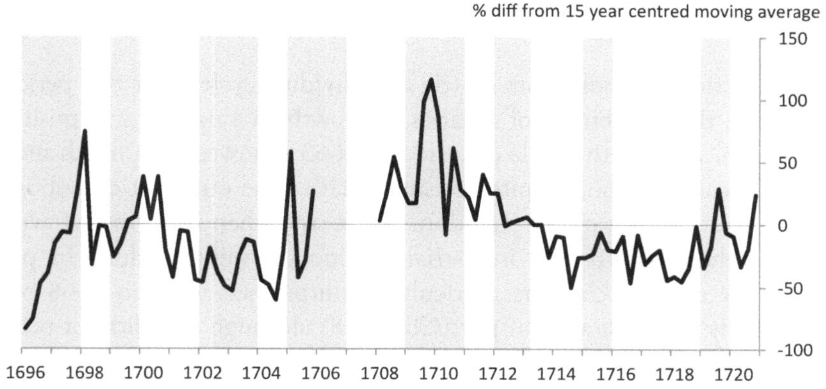

Chart 6.6 Bankruptcies and recessions (*Notes* Annual recession periods shaded. *Source* Hoppit 1987)

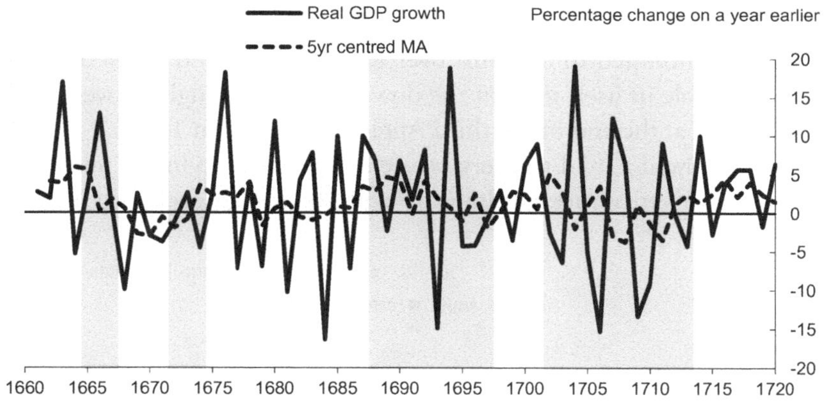

Chart 6.7 GDP growth and wars 1660–1720 (*Notes* War periods shaded. *Source* Thomas and Dimsdale 2017)

conflict end. There is some evidence of this pattern for the late C17th wars and the War of Spanish Succession. Jones (1988) discusses in detail the impact of the War of the League of Augsburg and the Spanish Succession on the economy. He shows that the disruptions of war could work both ways. For example, in the early 1700s war ruined a number of industries on the continent to the benefit of England which saw record sales of grain and woollen textiles.

6.1.2 The Birth of Modern Business Cycles 1660–1720

In this section we look more closely at individual cycles over this period. Following the restoration of Charles II growth in England was positive and a mini-peak in the cycle occurred in 1663 followed by a much more defined peak in 1666, despite disasters such as the outbreak of bubonic plague and the Great Fire London. There was then a period of weak growth when exports and industrial production were subdued in part due to the two Dutch Wars. Agricultural output was weak in 1668 predominantly due to arable output (Chart 6.8) although this did not occur alongside an increase in wheat prices used by Hoskins (1968) to assess the quality of wheat harvests. So this may represent sampling issues with the probate data in this period. Taxation increased markedly with a doubling of revenue in 1672–1674 from around 2.5% of GDP to around 5% (O'Brien and Hunt 1999). Expenditure directed towards the rebuilding of London following the Great Fire peaked in 1672 (see Coffman et al. 2019) but amounted to only just over £100,000 (around 0.2% of GDP) and was unable in itself to stem the downturn. The trough in overall output occurred at the end of the third Anglo-Dutch war in 1674.

There followed a mild recovery before a further slump in the mid-1680s affecting both agriculture and industry with the trough occurring in 1684.

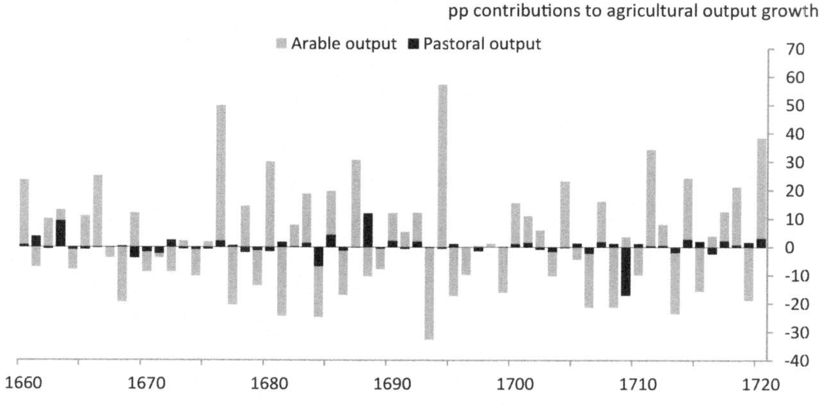

Chart 6.8 Contributions of arable and pastoral output (*Source* Thomas and Dimsdale [2017] derived from Broadberry et al. [2015])

Recovery then ensured following the Glorious Revolution in 1688 with a further peak in output in 1693 in the early part of the war of the League of Augsburg. There was then a downturn with a mini-trough in 1697 which may have been due to the disruption caused by the recoinage of that year which caused a shortage of coin and a fall in the money supply (Chart 6.9).

Growth varied widely during the War of the Spanish Succession 1701–1713. Exports were hampered in the early part of the war but soon recovered reflecting the record sales of grain and woollen textiles noted by Jones (1988) and discussed above. By implication fluctuations in industrial production seem to have been more influenced by domestic demand (Chart 6.10). The slow recovery from the trough of 1704 has already been noted.

The disturbances over the period may have arisen from fluctuations in harvests as well as from the war itself. The harvest was poor in 1708–1709 and there was a financial crisis in 1710, as discussed in Ashton (1959), which represented a significant trough in the cycle. Bankrutpcies picked up sharply (Chart 6.6) and as discussed in Hoppit (1987). This financial crisis was exceptional for the early C18th as it coincided with a major setback to the real economy. Alongside the poor harvests of 1708 and 1709 there were sharp falls in both industrial production and GDP. The crisis had arisen from a burst of speculative

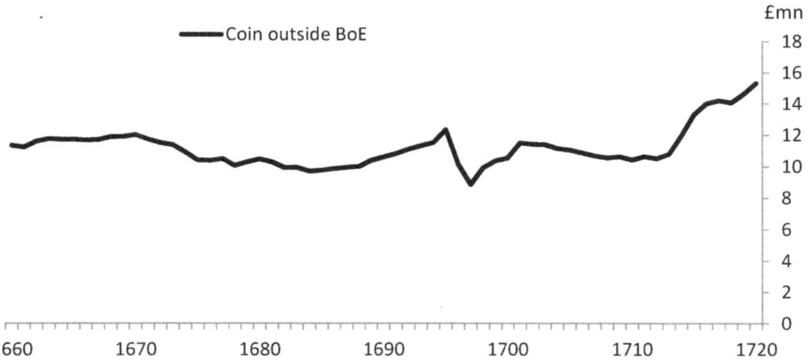

Chart 6.9 Coin in circulation outside the Bank of England (*Source* Thomas and Dimsdale [2017] derived from Palma [2018])

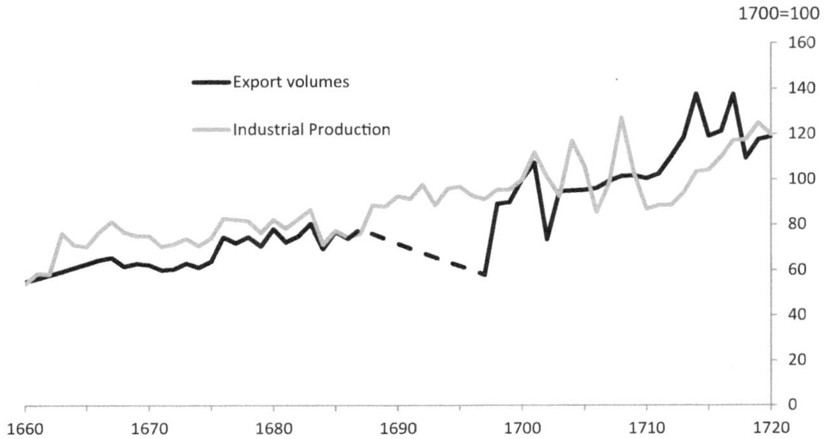

Chart 6.10 Export volumes and industrial production (*Source* Thomas and Dimsdale [2017] and Broadberry et al. [2015])

activity in the promotion of insurance companies in the City of London and some political uncertainties.

After 1710 the pattern of separation between financial crises and fluctuations in the economy asserted itself. The threatened ejection of the Hanoverian regime by the first Jacobite rebellion in 1715 caused a run on the Bank of England, but this did not have a noticeable effect on GDP. There was then a sustained recovery to 1720, a year in which agriculture was highly productive but where industry and services had already started to turn and overall output had only just recovered to the peak of 1704.

6.2 The Long C18th 1720–1830

6.2.1 Overview—Institutional Factors and Key Drivers

The data for this period suggest the pattern of GDP growth after 1720 showed lower variability than before, although fluctuations were still volatile from year-to-year. However, looking through the year-to-year volatility an apparent cyclical pattern of around 11 years emerges when looking at the filters that exclude noisy high-frequency movements in output such as the UC model. So in this regard it is similar to the 1660–1720 period (Charts 6.11, 6.12).

There are a number of underlying factors affecting the business cycle over the long C18th. For the first half of this period they were similar to those in the 1660–1720 period.

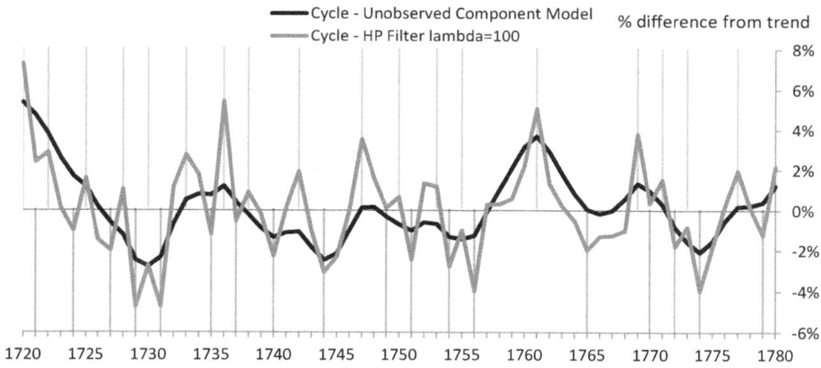

Chart 6.11 Cycles 1720–1780 (*Notes* Lines above the axis represent classical cycle peaks, lines below represent classical cycle troughs. *Source* Chapter 5)

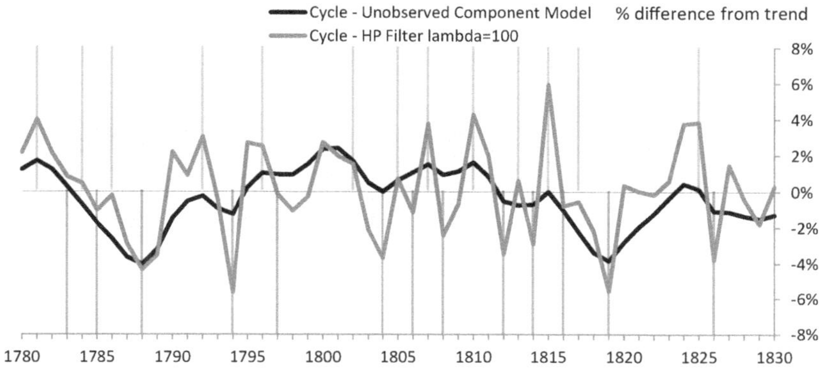

Chart 6.12 Cycles 1780–1830 (*Notes* Lines above the axis represent classical cycle peaks, lines below represent classical cycle troughs. *Source* Chapter 5)

First, Britain in this period was still heavily dependent on agriculture and the impact of poor harvests continued to have a direct impact on the business cycle and an indirect role in financial crises. Agricultural output was a large contributor to the swings in output (Chart 6.13), especially in the early C18th, and may have also had an impact on industry to the extent agricultural produce was used as an input. It could also affect the balance of payments and gold flows which would affect the Bank of England's willingness to lend and would have far-reaching consequences for the rest of the country given the Bank's links with the London private banks. These in turn were connected to the "country banks" outside London which emerged as the century wore on Ashton (1959). Data for the C18th are still inevitably uncertain but as noted after 1720 estimates of agricultural output are derived from the more reliable farm accounts (Chart 6.14).

The second feature of this period was that Britain was at war for almost half of it. As noted, wars frequently led to downturns as growing export industries coped with weaker demand. But they could also trigger cyclical recoveries if military spending was directed towards

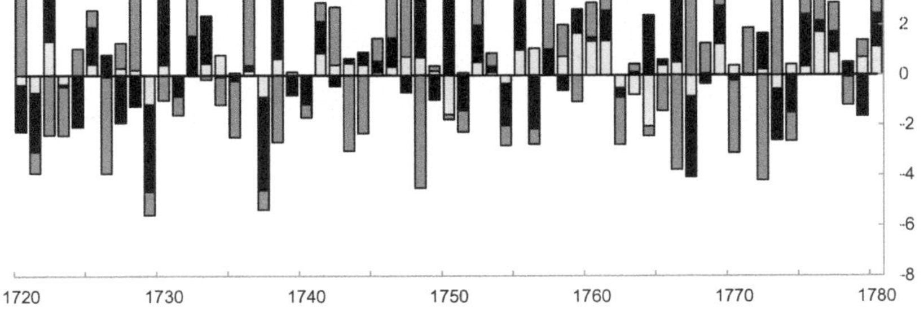

Chart 6.13 Contributions to GDP growth by industry, 1720–1780 (*Source* Thomas and Dimsdale [2017] derived from Broadberry et al. [2015])

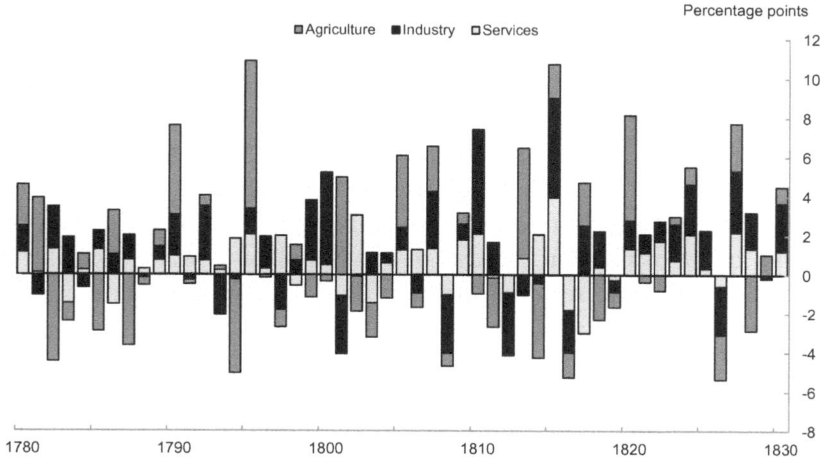

Chart 6.14 Contributions to GDP growth by industry, 1780–1830 (*Source* Thomas and Dimsdale [2017] derived from Broadberry et al. [2015])

domestic production. While the impact of war on growth is apparent before 1714 and from 1790 to 1815, it is less obvious in the intervening period. The War of the Austrian Succession (1739–1748), the Seven Years War (1756–1763) and even the American War of Independence (1776–1783) do not appear to have had much direct effect on the rate of growth of GDP in the middle part of the century. The impact of wars and international trade may have been overstated in earlier accounts based on a narrower range of indicators than GDP such as Ashton (1959). It is however clear that the Napoleonic war had a major impact on activity.

A third, and equally important reason, for the volatility of growth in this period was the emergence of a domestic investment cycle. Investment projects of the time—such as road (turnpike) and canal building—fluctuated in the mid-to-late C18th, particularly in the mid-1790s, as the industrialising economy of Britain developed (Ginarlis and Pollard 1988).

Both government and private investment may have indirect effects on the economy through financial markets which imparted their own influence on the cycle. During this period downturns were also often associated with financial crises (Ashton 1959; Hoppit 1986). In part, these were crises of public finance especially in the early to mid-part of the C18th. For instance, the South Sea Bubble of 1720 was largely a crisis in public finance given the relatively small number of bankruptcies that followed it. And these crises mainly reflected fluctuations in the fortunes of war. Public debt rose throughout the C18th, reaching around 200% of GDP at the end of the Napoleonic Wars. Increases in the public debt ratio resulting from military spending were often associated with increased government bond yields and public finance crises such as in 1745 and 1761 (Chart 6.15) (Barro 1987).

However towards the end of this period financial crises in the private sector became more prominent as the number of banks in Great Britain increased from around 60 in 1720 to around 300 in 1780, peaking at over 1100 in the financial crisis of 1810 (see Michie (2016) and Chart 6.16). Hoppit (1986) shows that bankruptcies increased during crises (Chart 6.17). The Bank of England itself is also argued to have stepped in as a lender of last resort during the C18th crises (see Lovell 1957) perhaps helping to ameliorate some of their impact on the real economy (Chart 6.18). During the second half of the period, financial crises increasingly began to involve the private sector more widely and

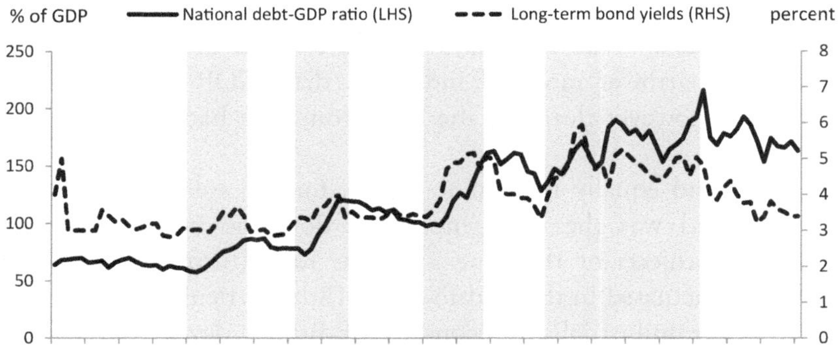

Chart 6.15 Debt and long-term interest rates during wars of the C18th (*Source* Thomas and Dimsdale 2017)

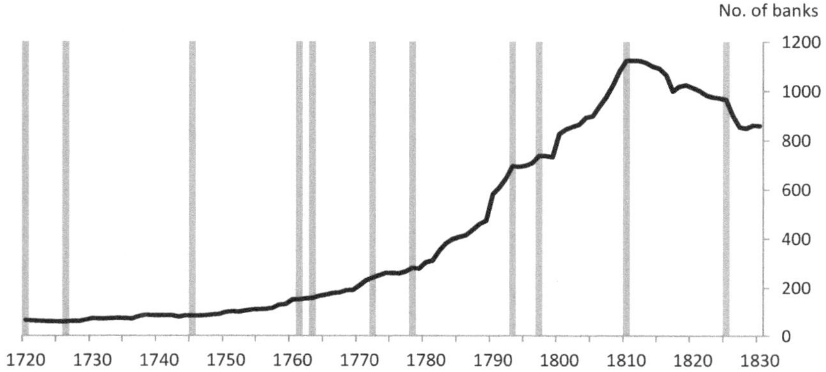

Chart 6.16 Number of British banks 1720–1830 and financial crises (*Source* Michie 2016)

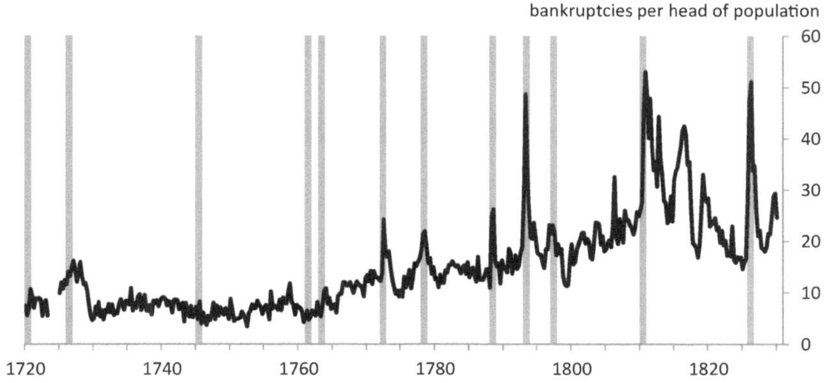

Chart 6.17 Bankruptcies and financial crises (*Source* Hoppit [1986] and Gayer et al. [1953]. Financial crises shaded)

often occurred at the peak of the economic cycle. This was arguably the natural outcome of the growing pains of an industrial economy, with growth occurring in spurts at a stage when the United Kingdom's financial system was still relatively underdeveloped (Hoppit 1986). The worst crises involved both the public and private sectors. For example, in 1793, there was a sharp rise in government bond yields linked to the

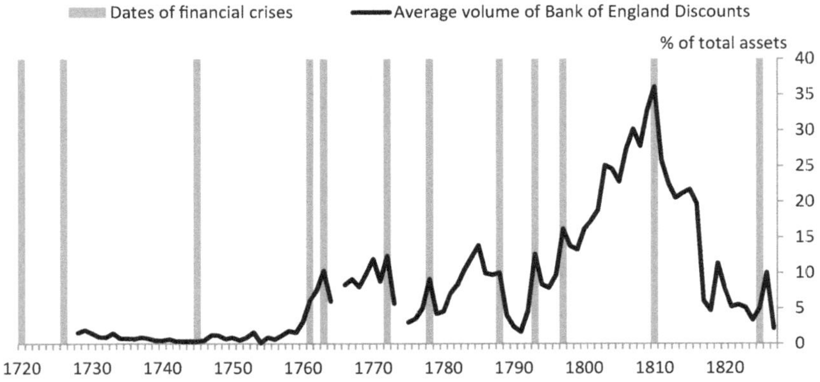

Chart 6.18 Bank of England discount activity and financial crises (*Source* Lovell 1957)

opening of hostilities with France and a widespread collapse in trade credit, leading to a large increase in bankruptcies.

6.2.2 The Expansion of Empire 1720–1780

In this section we consider each cycle over the long C18th in more detail. 1720 was a year in which both agricultural production and GDP attained a peak level of output. It occurred at the same time as the South Sea Bubble which caused a major disturbance to government finance. The events leading up to the peak in share prices and their sharp reversal have been discussed in an extensive literature. In summary, the aim of the South Sea scheme was to reduce the cost of financing the national debt which had swollen as a result of both the Nine Years War and the War of the Spanish Succession. The transfer of government bonds to the South Sea Company offered a convenient way of reducing the cost of servicing the debt. This objective could be achieved since the interest payable to the South Sea Company would be lower than the interest due to the holders of annuities of which the debt was mainly composed. The over-exploitation of issues by the South Sea Company combined with a wave of speculation on the part of the public led to an unsustainable rise in the price of South Sea stock. Purchases of part-paid stock at greatly enhanced prices implied that speculators were assuming liabilities which were well in excess of their resources. The bursting of the bubble led to a collapse in the price of South Sea stock and other securities (Chart 6.19).

What is less clear is the impact which the boom and bust had on the real economy (Dickson 1967; Temin and Voth 2013). The direct impact on the real economy appears to have been slight apart from a small rise in bankruptcies among financial firms in the City of London.

1720 was followed by a period of slowing growth for the rest of the decade. The slowdown was largely attributable to a decline in agricultural output. The years from 1725–1729 were notable for poor crops and there is evidence of a rise in mortality at this time, see Stratton (1978) and Wrigley and Schofield (1989). There was also a slowdown in industry in the later 1720s. As a result, the level of output remained below its 1720 peak for almost 15 years. Chart 6.20 compares this with slow recovery from the 2008 crisis which had a similar initial impact on GDP but took only around 5 years for output to recover to its previous level (Chart 6.21).

After poor harvests during the later 1720s, there was an improvement in the 1730s and a spike in the growth rate in 1738. The 1730s were a period of predominately favourable harvests and low prices of wheat.

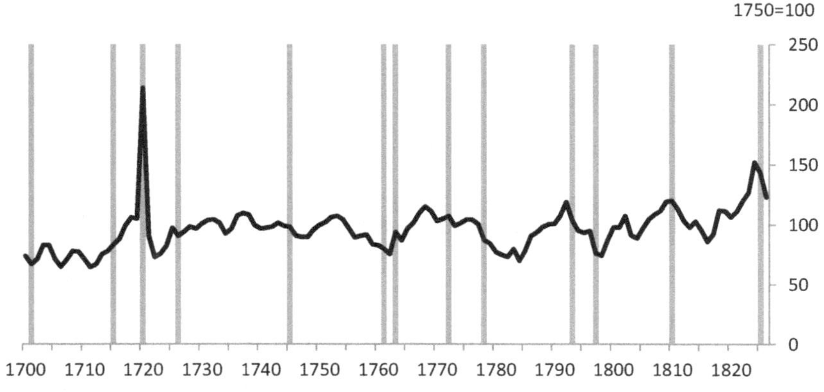

Chart 6.19 Share prices 1700–1780 (*Source* Mirowski 1981)

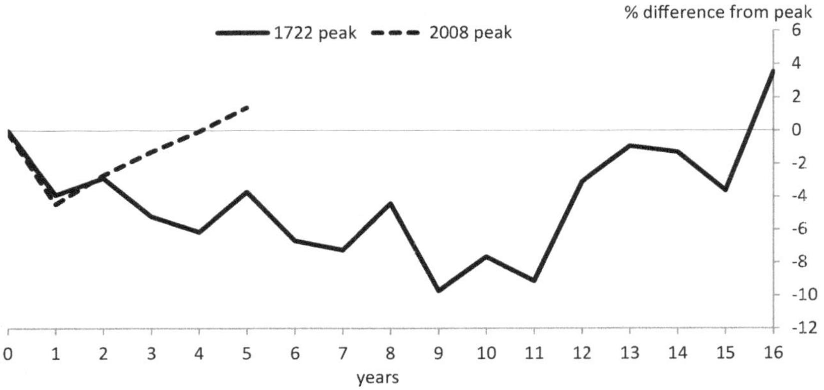

Chart 6.20 The slow post-1720 recovery compared with 2008 (*Source* Thomas and Dimsdale 2017)

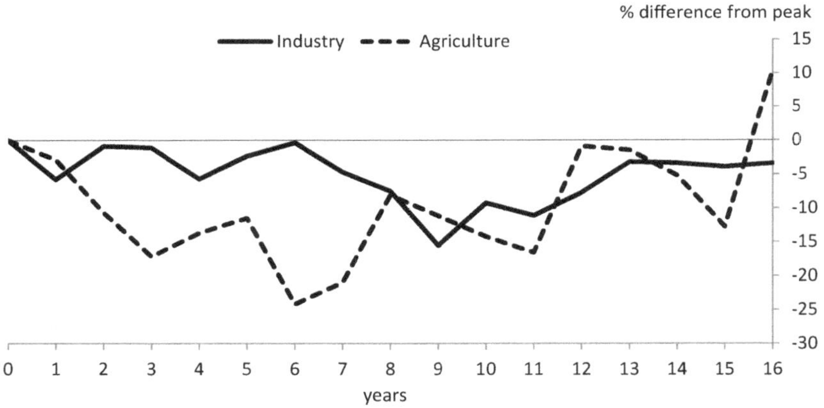

Chart 6.21 The slow post-1720 recovery: industry versus agriculture (*Source* Thomas and Dimsdale [2017] derived from Broadberry et al. [2015])

Both agriculture and GDP reached peaks in 1733 and 1736. The run of good harvests was broken towards the end of the decade. There were crop failures in 1739 and 1740, when there was a slight fall in agricultural output and a check to GDP.

The major political disturbance of the 1740s was the invasion of England by the Young Pretender in 1745. When the Jacobites reached as far south as Derby, there were signs of concerns in the City, as the prices of securities fell sharply. Markets rallied sharply with the news of the defeat of the Jacobites at the battle of Culloden. There was no sign of a reduction in economic activity in 1745. But there was a boost to confidence as GDP increased between 1745 and 1750. The Jacobite Rebellion of 1745 did not have a noticeable effect on GDP as the growth rate was not checked until 1749.

Growth in the early 1750s was marked by a recovery in 1751–1752 followed by a downturn in 1753–1754. This pattern of two years of expansion followed by two years of contraction was typical of cycles in the C18th. A strong recovery did not take place until 1757, a year in which there was also a sharp rise in the price of wheat, which had doubled since 1755 (Stratton 1978). The growth rate appears to have been stronger following the outbreak of the Seven Years War, in particular from 1757 to 1761. The strong growth of GDP in the later 1750s may be explained by the high level of agricultural output during the Seven Years War.

There was however a setback to growth in the early 1760s. The economy may have been affected by the financial crisis of 1763, which was centred on Amsterdam. The bullion of the Bank was reduced as Dutch investors ran down their holdings of British securities. It was a commercial crisis, but it was not located in Britain although it had some impact on British financial markets. The crisis arose from the finance of an indemnity to be paid to victorious Prussia at the end of the Seven Years War (1756–1763). The payment of the indemnity was financed by bankers in Amsterdam who extended credit liberally. The bankers were hit by a sudden collapse in commodity prices, which undermined their solvency. In particular, the leading house of De Neuvilles of Amsterdam found itself in difficulties and defaulted. There were substantial holdings of British securities in the portfolios of Dutch financial institutions, which sought to increase liquidity by selling the stock. This put pressure on the Bank and led to a fall in its holdings of bullion. There was a marked decline in the ratio of bullion to deposits at the Bank. The effects on the British economy appear negligible if the output nad bankruptcy figures are reliable over this period.

During the later 1760s there was a slowdown in the rate of growth of exports (Ashton 1949), which resulted from the ongoing dispute over trade with the American colonies (Chart 6.22). Interruption of trade with America may have contributed to the failure of the Ayr Bank in 1772, which led to the first home-grown financial crisis, Hoppit (1986) and Kosmetatos (2018). It arose from a high level of investment activity in 1771–1772, which was particularly vigorous in Scotland. Full advantage of opportunities was taken by the Ayr Bank, which led the way in the issue of small notes in Scotland and using commercial bills to borrow in London. The trouble started as a result of speculation in East India Company Stock by Alexander Fordyce, a partner in the London bank of Neale, James, Fordyce and Down, which had close connections with the Ayr Bank. When his speculations failed, he fled to France.

News of these events spread rapidly to Edinburgh. As a result, there was a collapse of confidence in both banks which failed. The Ayr Bank was a note-issuing joint-stock bank, which was permissible in Scotland but not in England, given the Bank of England's monopoly. The directors of the bank were men of high social standing but little understanding of banking. Adam Smith who had an intimate knowledge of the affairs of the bank attributed its failure to abuses of bill finance. Following the Scottish crisis, there were failures among a number of London banks (Checkland 1975).

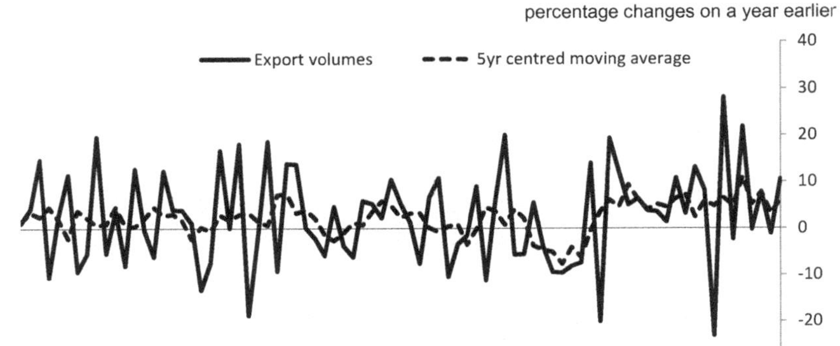

Chart 6.22 Growth rate of exports 1720–1800 (*Source* Thomas and Dimsdale 2017)

In the early 1770s annual changes in GDP were choppy with a year of growth being followed by a year of contraction. However, growth was stronger when hostilities started in 1775 and the upturn continued until 1778. Harvests were favourable at this time and there was a boom in building as measured by imports of timber, Ashton (1959). When France entered the war in 1778, the level of activity declined. Construction was checked by the threatened interruption of supplies of timber from Scandinavia as well as a loss of confidence and a rise in interest rates (Ashton 1949).

6.2.3 The French Wars and the Restriction Period 1780–1830

The slowdown of 1778–1779 was only temporary as output reached a peak in 1780, largely on account of a major increase in agricultural output. However, this burst of production was not sustained.

As the American War drew to a close in the early 1780s there was an upsurge in arable output in 1780–1781. This major peak was followed by a sustained reduction in agricultural output. However, the disappointing performance of agriculture was offset by the vigorous growth of industrial production and improved prospects for exports following the end of the war with the United States (Chart 6.23).

Industry was by then sufficiently important to usurp the dominance of agriculture in economic fluctuations, which had been a characteristic of the economy in the C18th. The growth of industry in the 1780s and 1790s was made possible by the rapid expansion of British exports, which took place after the end of the American War of Independence in 1783. The recovery of exports owed much to the strong demand of the American market for British manufactures. The revival of exports improved the trade balance and strengthened the Bank's reserves. This was much needed because of the low level of bullion held by the Bank at the end of the war (Clapham 1944). The rise in the reserves was accompanied by a reduction in interest rates and a relaxation of credit. The growth of credit was financed by the country banks, which expanded their numbers and, according to recent estimates from Gent (2016), the volume of credit (Charts 6.24, 6.25).

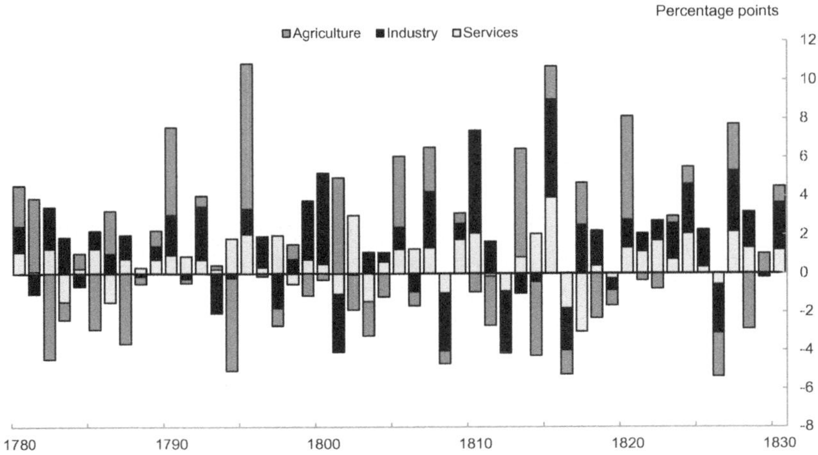

Chart 6.23 Contributions to GDP growth by major sectors (*Source* Thomas and Dimsdale [2017] derived from Broadberry et al. [2015])

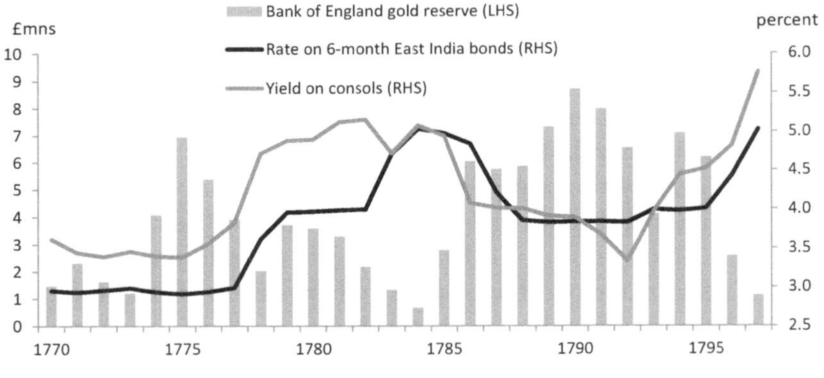

Chart 6.24 Bank of England gold reserves and market interest rates (*Source* Thomas and Dimsdale 2017)

The outcome was slow overall growth of GDP in the 1780s given the sharply different contributions from the two major sectors of the economy. Gayer et al. (1953) relying on the growth of exports and the Hoffman index of industrial production as indicators, conclude

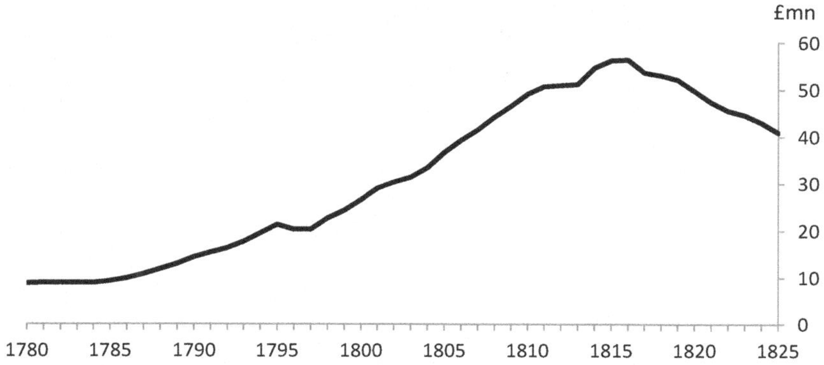

Chart 6.25 Country bank assets 1780–1825 (*Source* Gent 2016)

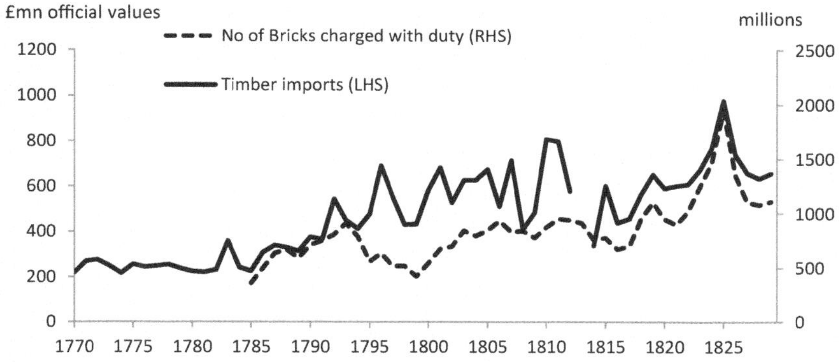

Chart 6.26 Investment indicators 1770–1830 (*Source* Mitchell 1988)

that economic growth was rapid in the 1780s. The recent data from Broadberry et al. (2015) on GDP indicates that this interpretation needs qualification for overall activity in the economy (Chart 6.26).

The result of the relaxation of credit in 1780s was a major boom in building canals and turnpikes as well as the enclosure of agricultural land. However, signs of financial stress began to emerge. The late 1780s saw a check to activity resulting from a financial crisis which mainly affected the Lancashire cotton industry, see Pressnell (1956). The recovery which followed this setback however was vigorous. Output grew

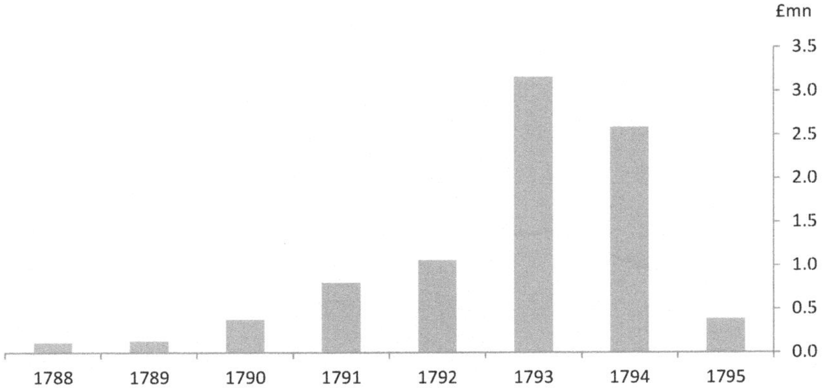

Chart 6.27 Canal building authorised by parliament 1788–1795

strongly reaching a peak in 1792. The boom was associated with high activity in building and the rapid growth of exports, in particular trade with the former American colonies flourished. Canal building also increased rapidly peaking in 1793 leading to the term "Canal mania" being applied to this period (see Chart 6.27).

The boom reached a peak in 1792–1793 and was then follwed by a downturn with a severe financial crisis in 1793. The underlying cause of the crisis can be attributed to the excessive expansion of credit by the new country banks, whose numbers and assets had greatly expanded as shown above. But its timing may have been determined by the outbreak of war with France in 1793. Contemporaries argued on this issue, but Tooke made a strong case for the excessive growth of credit as the underlying cause of the financial turmoil. The Bank was severely criticised over its handling of the crisis for its refusal to provide assistance to banks outside London.[1] Relief came through an issue of Exchequer bills, which provided the money market with a source of reliable liquidity. A small issue of Exchequer bills was sufficient to check the panic. These provided City traders with a much-needed source of liquidity and rapidly restored confidence in markets. However, the lack of direct

[1] Especially since the Bank was able to bail out a former governor of the Bank to whom it made a loan of £60,000.

assistance to the rest of the country meant that failures among the country banks were high (Hayek in Thornton 1962).

The recession which followed the crisis was short but sharp. GDP declined by 4.8% from 1792 to 1794. The fall was more severe in industry where output fell by 6.7%. In 1795 there was an upsurge in the wheat price on account of the severe winter of 1794/1795. Bread was scarce and there were riots over the price of food. The government responded by introducing the Speenhamland System, which was in essence a form of wage subsidy, see Stratton (1978). Harvest failure caused hardship, but did not check economic recovery in 1795. GDP then rose fairly steadily to a peak in 1802 having increased by 12.1%. The recovery was interrupted by a brief contraction in 1797 when output fell by 0.73%. This minor setback to GDP was of considerable financial significance. The heavy burden of war finance pushed the budget into a major deficit and sterling was weakened as a result much of the war expenditure being overseas. A poor harvest meant that imports of wheat were abnormally high. In addition, the pound came under pressure as there was a rise in price of gold in Paris on account of the French government's decision to abandon assignats and to adopt a metallic currency. The market price of gold exceeded the price at the mint and so gold coins were being hoarded or exported. The Bank's reserves fell sharply and the government ordered the Bank to suspend cash payments (Hawtrey 1919; Silberling 1924). This decision meant that sterling became a paper currency and Britain would remain with a paper pound until the restoration of the Gold Standard in 1821 (Gayer et al. 1953).

During what has become known as the "Restriction Period" the Bank was authorised to issue small notes to meet the demand for currency and the country banks were permitted to issue small notes which had previously been prohibited. The public readily accepted the new paper currency and the transition was remarkably smooth. It seems likely that the long tradition of sound finance by the Bank in the C18th had created public confidence in the belief that the Bank would not abuse its powers of issuing paper currency despite the demands of war finance (O'Brien and Palma 2017). However these were also supplemented with a concerted effort by key players in the City of London to ensure the new paper system on money worked and by the efforts of the government to try and finance the war as possible through increased taxation and long-term borrowing (see Chadha and Newby 2013).

The macroeconomic impact of the 1797 currency crisis was slight. The economy continued to grow strongly under the influence of a high level of war-related spending, the continuing growth of exports and investment. Industrial production was buoyant and reached a peak in 1800 before declining. While British industry and trade flourished during the French Revolutionary war, it did not fare so well in the Napoleonic war which started in 1803 after the brief Peace of Avignon. French policies were directed against British trade under the Continental System. British exporters lost access to major European markets. Trade became more restricted as the area of Europe controlled by the Napoleonic regime increased. As a result, there was a marked decline if not stagnation on the growth of exports and industrial production. GDP slowed from 1803–1806. Relief came with the Spanish revolt against Napoleon in 1807 which opened up Spanish markets to British traders, in particular markets in South America. Gayer et al. (1953) provide a detailed account of the effects of French policies directed against British trade and the consequences of obtaining access to Spanish markets following the start of the Peninsular War. From 1806 to 1807 GDP rose by 6.5% and Industrial production by 8.7%. Further expansion came with a boom in both exports and domestic demand which reached a peak in 1810. Domestic investment recovered and there was renewed speculation in the capital market. Credit expanded with a rapid increase in the number of country banks and their assets. From 1808 to 1810 GDP and industrial production rose by 9.8 and 19.4% respectively. Michie (2016) estimates the number of British banks peaked in 1810 and that there was a financial crisis in this year (Chart 6.16). As a result, the boom proved to be short-lived as GDP and industrial production fell back from 1810 to 1812 by 5.1 and 4.1%, respectively.

The boom of 1810 is of interest because of the close relationship between overseas markets and domestic activity. It was also important for the role of financial policy. The Bank not only financed government spending through its discounts, it also increased its discounts for the private sector heavily over the first decade over the C19th (Chart 6.28) the reasons

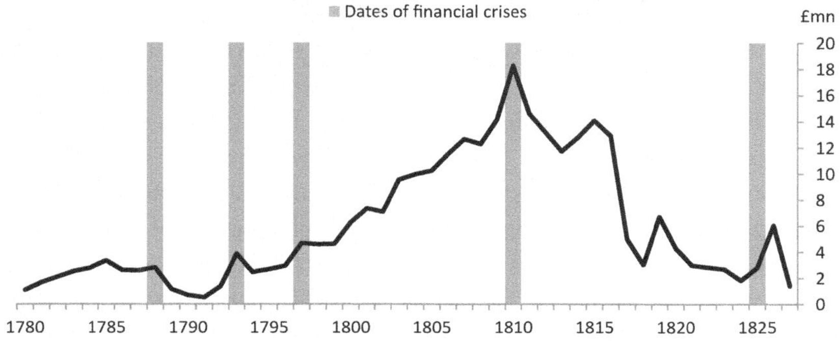

Chart 6.28 Bank of England discounts (*Source* Anson et al. 2017)

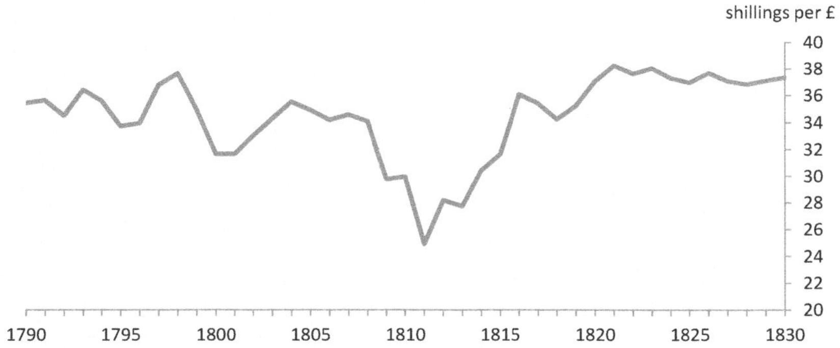

Chart 6.29 Price of Hamburg Bills on London (*Source* Gayer et al. 1953)

for which are discussed in Duffy (1982). The expansion of the Bank's issues was, as noted already, accompanied by a renewed growth in the number of country banks which contributed to the rapid growth of credit. A major controversy developed over the weakness of the sterling exchange rate, the benchmark rate at the time was the price of Hamburg bills. This fell by 27% between 1808 and 1811 shown in Chart 6.29. This led to the appointment of the Bullion Committee to examine the causes of this.

The Committee attributed the fall in sterling to the expansionary policy of the Bank. It recommended linking the Bank's lending to the level of its reserves, which would have implied a restoration of the gold standard. The Government rejected this advice because it assigned priority to being able to borrow from the Bank to finance expenditure on the war. While the Bullionists argued that excessive issues and lending by the Bank were responsible for the sharp fall in the exchange rate, they were opposed by the Anti-Bullionists who related the problems of sterling to high level of overseas expenditure needed to finance the Napoleonic War combined with unusually high imports of wheat which were necessary on account of poor domestic harvests.

The boom was ended as a result of overoptimistic assessments of the capacity of South American markets to absorb British exports. In addition, there was a tightening of the Continental System and the effects of an embargo on trade imposed by the United States. These factors account for the decline in exports from 1810 to 1812 and the fall in GDP of 5.1%. The defeat of Napoleon's expedition to Russia undermined the Continental System and opened up European markets to British exports. There was, therefore, an upsurge in the volume of exports from 1812 to 1815 and GDP increased by 14.1% and industrial production by 10.4%. The boom in exports went sharply into reverse in 1816 when it became clear that export markets had become seriously overstocked in both Europe and South America. The Bank did not participate in the boom by expanding its discounts but there was a renewed increase in the number of country banks. The recession was sharp as GDP declined by 5.25% from 1815 to 1816. There was a temporary check to the decline in activity in 1817 and 1818 followed by a renewed decline in 1819, which brought GDP to the same level as in 1816. This was the low point of the contraction which started in 1815 with the ending of the Napoleonic War. Exports and industrial production also declined during the long post-war recession. Exports were adversely affected by a downturn in activity in the United States in 1819 and depressed conditions in Europe and the rest of the world Chart 6.30.

The period from 1815 to 1820 was of considerable difficulty for the British economy. The growth of GDP was interrupted and expectations were depressed by the downward trend in prices. The GDP deflator fell by from 1815 to the low point in 1819. There has been an ongoing debate over the causes of the decline in prices which followed the end of the Napoleonic War. It could be argued that the contraction in the Bank's

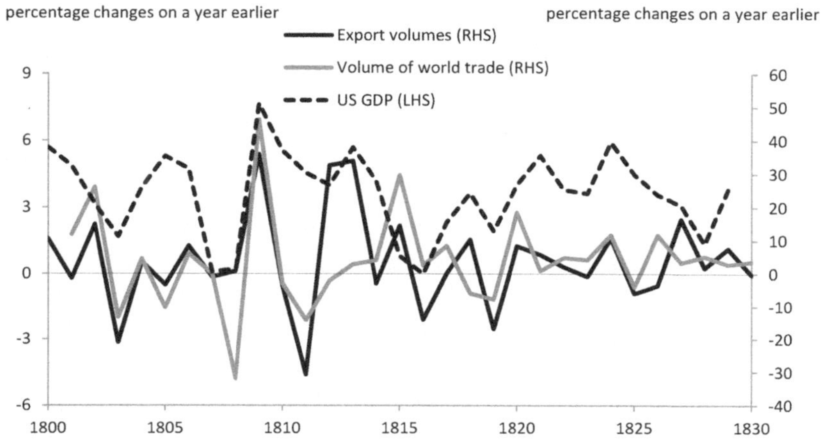

Chart 6.30 Exports, US GDP and world trade 1800–1830 (*Source* Thomas and Dimsdale 2017)

lending to both private sector (see Chart 6.28) and public sector borrowing was the driving force behind the deflation, combined with the expectation that specie payments would be restored at the 1797 exchange rate soon after the end of the war. This could have required a severe decline in the price level. Gayer et al. (1953) question this monetary explanation and argue that the post-war decline in prices and continuing depressed state of the economy was caused by the weakness of agricultural prices, the reduction of military spending at the end of the war and the stagnation of exports on account of depressed markets in both Europe and the United States. Domestic investment was also weak as a result of a lack of interest in canal building and other investments in infrastructure (Chart 6.26). Lack of enthusiasm for domestic investment and low-interest rates prompted a rise in loans to foreign governments in 1819.

From the depths of depression in 1819 the economy then staged a sustained recovery, reaching a peak in 1825 before relapsing into a sharp recession in 1826. The upturn was longer than found in the typically short cycles of the C18th. GDP rose by 18% from 1819 to 1826 and industrial production by 26%. The initial impetus came from a recovery of exports of British goods which rose by around 30% from 1819 to 1824. There was also vigorous expansion of investment indicated by the output of bricks which rose by 76.9% from 1819 to 1825. A major factor behind the recovery was a revival of confidence and willingness to bear risks as compared with the depressed confidence of the preceding deflation of 1815–1820. There was a greater willingness to invest in new ventures at home and abroad.

During 1817 and 1818 four European governments had raised loans on the London capital market at a time when domestic investment was depressed. From 1820 interest shifted to investing in mining ventures, particularly in Latin America and also loans to newly liberated Latin American republics. In addition, there was enthusiasm for investing in infrastructure projects at home, such as railways, docks water and gas works. The burst of investment activity was partly the result of the buoyancy of expectations. It was also a response to the policies of the Treasury and the Bank.

The economic revival was assisted by the relaxed stance of the Bank of England but this may have contributed to the financial crisis of 1825 and the subsequent downturn. The Bank of England had made provision to replace the small notes which it had issued following the suspension of payments in 1797 with gold coins in 1816. In the event the public, which had become used to using paper notes, was not interested in exchanging notes for coins contrary to the Bank's expectations. As a result, the Bank ended up with holding more reserves than it required. It reduced Bank Rate from 5 to 4% in June 1822 and assisted the Treasury in its conversion of part of the national debt to a lower interest rate. The yield on consols declined from 4.4% in 1820 to 3.2% in 1824. The reduction in the yield of British securities below the levels to which investors had become accustomed during the Napoleonic War encouraged a switch of investment in the direction of overseas issues. The returns on overseas securities were higher than on British government securities as also were the risks, which investors were willing to accept (Neal 1998).

The vigour of the boom gave rise to an increase in prices. The Gayer, Rostow Schwartz index of the price of domestic goods rose from a low point in 1822 to a peak in 1825, rising by 39% (Chart 6.31). The increase in economic activity was associated with the rapid growth of imports and a marked deterioration of the trade balance in the later

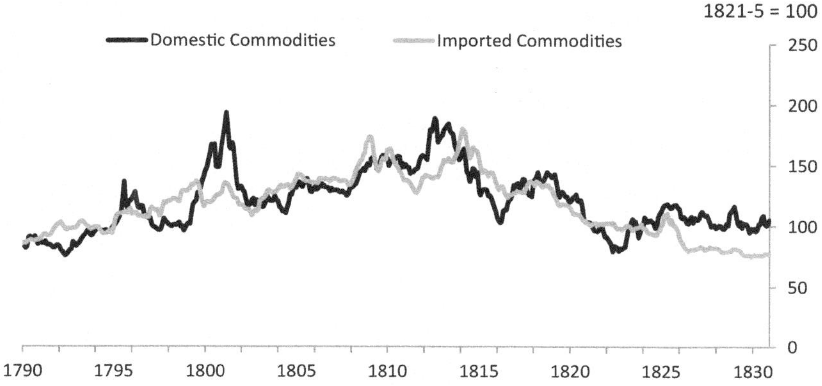

Chart 6.31 Wholesale prices (*Source* Thomas and Dimsdale 2017)

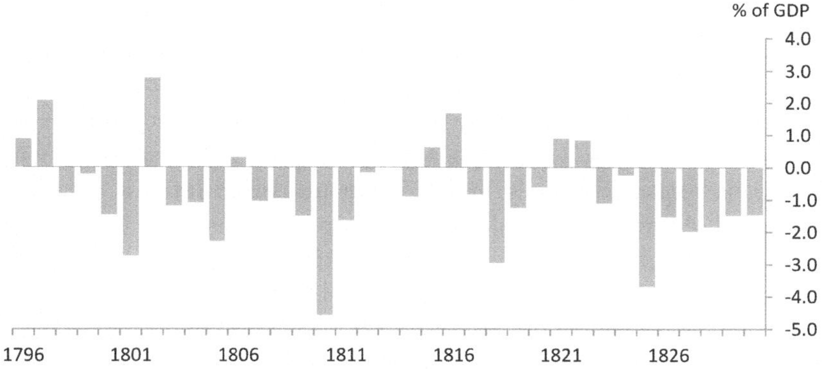

Chart 6.32 Balance of trade in goods (*Notes* Imports of goods are on a balance of payments "free on board" basis in this calculation. *Source* Thomas and Dimsdale 2017)

stages of the boom. The deficit on merchandise trade deteriorated as the boom progressed, rising from 1.1% of GDP in 1823 to 3.7% in GDP in 1825. This exceeded even the deficit reported in 1818 which was a peak year for imports (see Chart 6.32). There was a severe crisis in the banking system, which was attributed to the over issue of notes by the

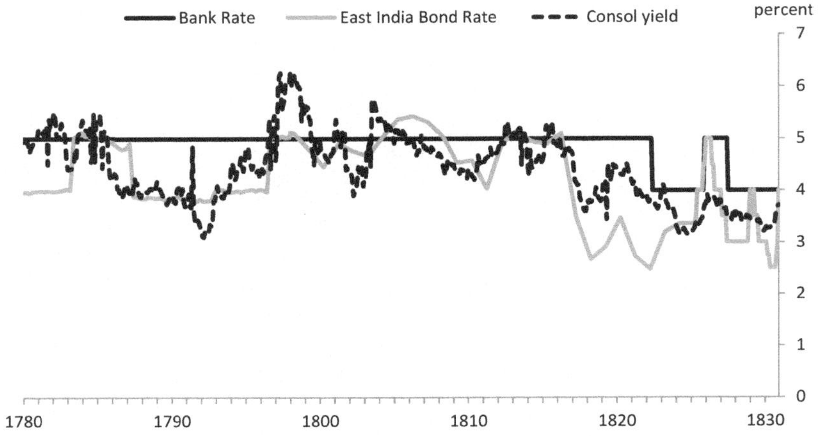

Chart 6.33 Interest rates (*Source* Thomas and Dimsdale 2017)

country banks. Whether the country banks were responsible for the crisis remains an unsettled issue (Turner 2014).

The Bank has been criticised for its expansionary policy stance during the early 1820s. There was a tightening in the form of a major sale of Exchequer bills early in 1825, but no rise in interest rates until December. At this time Bank rate went up from 4% to the maximum of 5% allowed by the usury laws, when the financial crisis was at its height (Chart 6.33). The Bank's reserves fell steeply from £14 million at the start of 1824 to only around £2 million in December 1825. The reserves benefited from a timely loan from France at a critical juncture. The Bank restricted its discounts as pressures in the money market mounted during 1825, but it did discount freely in the later stages of the crisis. At this late stage, it lent generously on a wide range of assets in order to check the panic in the money market. The Bank was starting to learn about its responsibility towards the money market in a time of crisis. But it had much further to go before it accepted its duties as lender of last resort. This function was not fully recognised until the financial crisis of 1866 (Bagehot 1873; King 1936; Anson et al., 2017).

6.3 The Victorian and Edwardian Economy 1830–1913

6.3.1 Overview—Institutional Factors and Key Drivers

The economic cycle in GDP that emerged during the Victorian age can be seen in Chart 6.34. The average rate of growth rose to around 1¾–2¼%—double that in the 1720–1830 period—reflecting the growing pace of industrialisation and technological progress. There were few downturns that were severe and actual recessions were less frequent than in the C18th. The UC model suggests there were four major cycles from 1830 to 1870 and four major cycles in the period 1870–1913. A major cycle had duration of about 11 years and was accompanied by a number of mini cycles as shown by the HP filter estimates. The shorter cycles were characteristic of the C18th, but a longer cycle had also been apparent in the early C19th as typified by the cycle which gave rise to the crisis of 1825.

The improved availability of disaggregated data for this period allows the analysis of movements in individual GDP expenditure components so that we can meaningfully explore the effect of demand shocks on the cycle

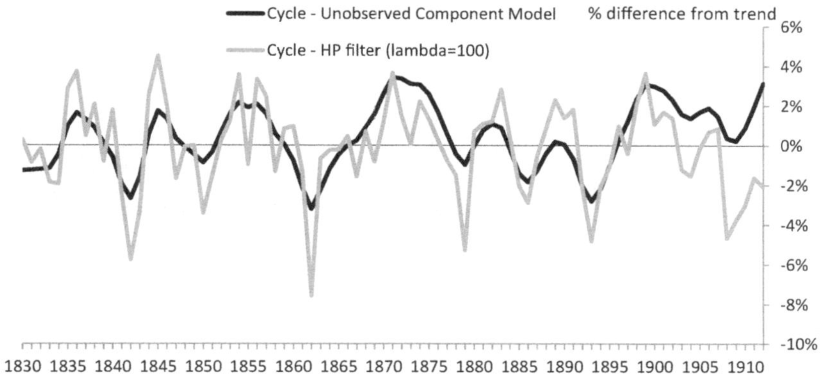

Chart 6.34 Growth cycles—the Victorian economy (*Source* Chapter 5)

rather than infer them from other indicators (this is in large part thanks to Deane 1968). A Keynesian analysis would typically split these into "exogenous" components that drive movements in GDP and "endogenous" components that would be expected largely to respond to movements in GDP. Referring back to Table 2.1 exogenous drivers include: fluctuations in investment spending (including consumer durables) that are the result of shifts in expectations and "animal spirits"; the impact of government purchases resulting from changes in fiscal policy; and movements in exports dependent on the world economy. In contrast, "endogenous" components, typically include non-durable consumption, stockbuilding and imports. Since "exogenous" components have a second round impact on the endogenous components, they are likely to have a larger impact on growth than measured by their direct contributions to GDP.

Investment was an important driver of demand growth in the Victorian age especially in the early part (Chart 6.35). The pattern of industrialisation during the C19th was far from smooth and investment cycles were important. There were waves of railway building throughout the century, similar to those associated with canals and road building in the C18th. In particular, domestic investment made a major contribution to growth in the 1830 and 1840s, which largely reflected such railway building. Dwellings investment also contributed to the domestic boom from 1893 to 1899 (Chart 6.36).

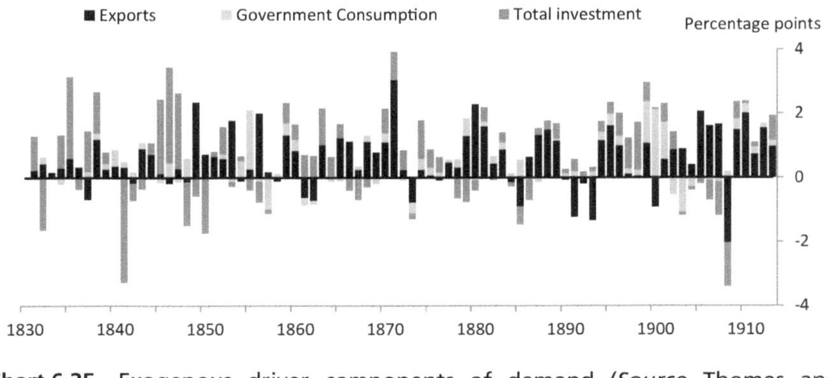

Chart 6.35 Exogenous driver components of demand (*Source* Thomas and Dimsdale 2017)

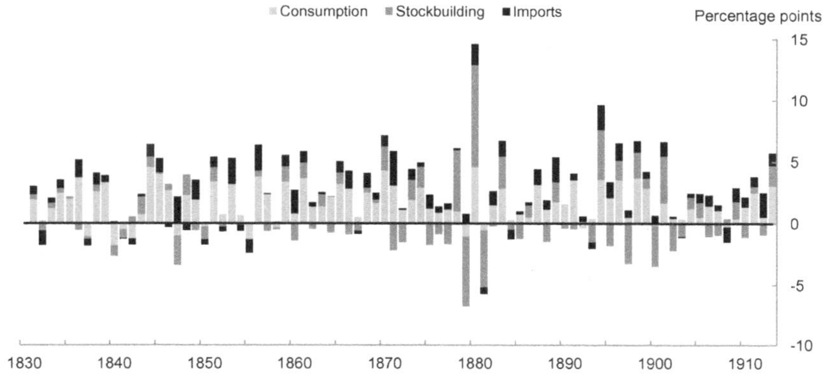

Chart 6.36 Endogenous components of demand (*Source* Thomas and Dimsdale 2017)

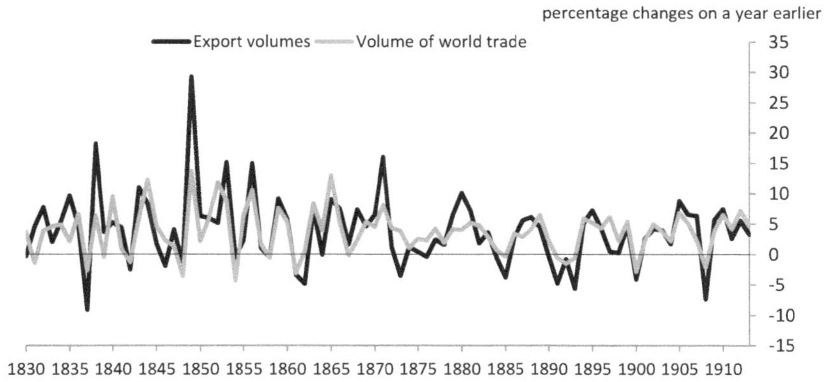

Chart 6.37 Exports and world trade (*Source* Thomas and Dimsdale 2017)

Exports also played an important cyclical role during the second half of the C19th. Between 1850 and 1875, Britain participated in a boom associated with gold discoveries and a move towards free trade. UK exports and world trade were closely correlated over this period (Chart 6.37). And the relative competitiveness of the UK economy had an increasingly important influence on the export cycle from 1870, as

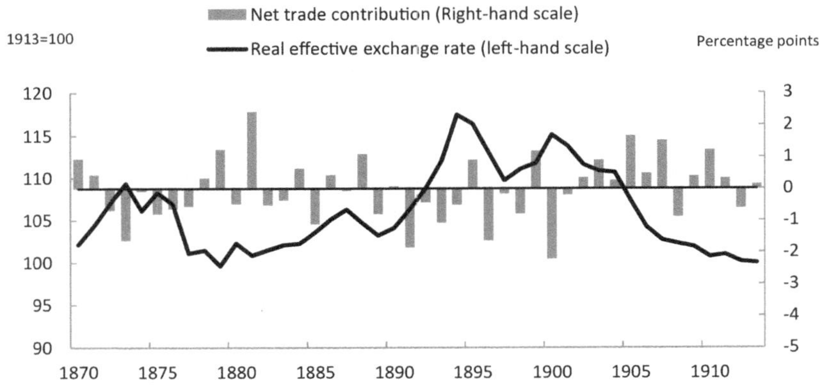

Chart 6.38 Net exports and the real exchange rate (*Source* Thomas and Dimsdale 2017)

shown by the negative relationship between the real exchange rate and net trade (Chart 6.38).

Over and above the business cycle an additional feature was the alternating pattern of revivals in home and foreign investment that accompanied movements in population and migration which have been discussed by Cairncross (1953), Brinley Thomas(1954), and Edelstein (1981, 1982). Foreign investment was high in the 1880s and after 1900, while there was a major upsurge in home investment in the boom of the late 1890s in which housebuilding played a leading role. Over a longer period than the standard business cycle, home and foreign investment moved in opposite directions and in line with Kuznets cycle discussed in Chapter 2 with a period of around 15–20 years.

Shifts in consumption behaviour do not appear to have played a major role in economic cycles during this period (Matthews et al. 1982). On average, consumption generally tracked incomes growing at a pace equal to, or a little below, GDP growth. Consumption was also generally less volatile than GDP growth. Declining fertility and the associated fall in the number of young people in the population did, however, contribute to a structural fall in the consumption-income ratio in the latter part of the period (Dimsdale 2013a). This rise in the saving ratio implied large capital exports between 1870 and 1914.

Up to 1878, domestic financial crises continued to be a significant factor in downturns (Hicks 1982; Dimsdale 1990). And again there were links with agricultural output as poor harvests and high agricultural prices would lead to a decline in the trade balance and pressure on the Bank's gold reserves prompting a rise in interest rates and a tightening of the Banks' credit policy. So even though by this stage agricultural production represented less than a quarter of GDP (Broadberry et al. 2015) it could still have a significant indirect effect on output through this channel. In 1837–1839, 1848 and 1857, for example, output fell following a financial crisis. And the failure of the City of Glasgow Bank in 1878 was an important factor in aggravating the downturn in that year (Collins 1989). However, the recessions that followed each financial crisis appear to get smaller over time. After 1878 domestic financial crises appear to have played a less significant role, reflecting the increasing stability of the United Kingdom's monetary system underpinned by the Bank of England as lender of last resort. Anson et al. (2017) discuss in more detail how the Bank of England evolved into an effective Lender of Last Resort over the course of the major crises in the mid C19th and in accordance with the rules advocated by Bagehot in *Lombard Street* (1873). Capie (2007) however also ascribes this stability down to the prudent behaviour of banks over this period. As an example, he cites the influence of George Rae, a banker in Liverpool, who was the author of a textbook for bankers *The Country Banker* highlighting the need for a bias towards prudence. But the role of mergers and the move to limited liability, particularly after the City of Glasgow bank failure, were also key developments in the structure of banking over this period (Turner 2014). By the end of the century the banking system had become concentrated with the five largest banks accounting for around 70% of deposits (Capie 2007).

After 1870 the British economy became increasingly sensitive to real and monetary disturbances elsewhere in the world at a time when its own financial system was better able to cope with both internal and external shocks. The UK business cycle became more closely aligned with external factors as international linkages became more important following the widespread adoption of the Gold Standard system of exchange rates. Under the system, there were close linkages through trade flows and capital movements between the major financial centres. The impact of trade flows on the cycle has been emphasised by Ford (1969). He argues that fluctuations in exports were the main cause of cyclical movements in national income, while exports were responding to variations in the pace of foreign investment. The connections between economies through financial channels have been emphasised by Bordo (1985). Interest differentials between market rates in the major financial centres were narrowed by improvements in communications, following the introduction of the electric telegraph. This increased the speed of communication and so acted to promote the international mobility of capital. That meant the UK was vulnerable to global spillovers from international financial crises, such as the 1907 crisis, which began in the United States.

This period also ushered in the gradual loss of the UK's pre-eminence in manufacturing. In the middle of the C19th the UK reached its industrial apotheosis, accounting for almost half of world trade in manufacturing. By 1913 this share was already down to a quarter and would continue to fall thereafter (Chart 6.39). In international trade Britain was encountering growing competition from other industrial countries as the predominant position which it had enjoyed in world trade in manufactures before 1870 was progressively undermined. This process did not prevent the balance of payments showing a massive surplus on current account, which was matched by the accumulation of foreign securities by British investors. Thus a variety of influences were at work which might be expected to alter cyclical fluctuations after 1870, quite

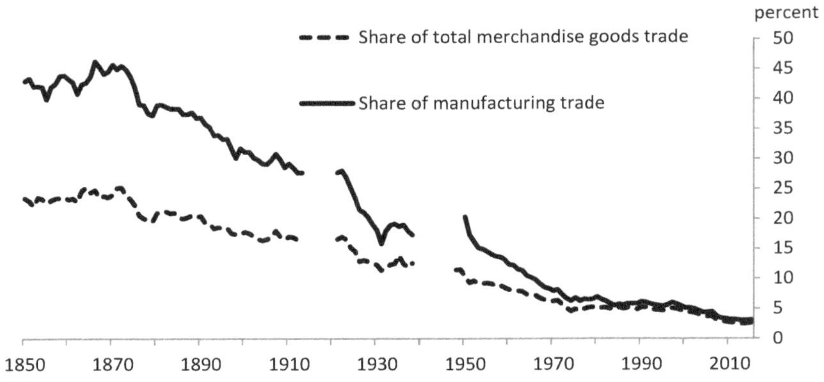

Chart 6.39 UK share of world trade (*Source* Thomas and Dimsdale 2017)

apart from the improvement in the quantity and quality of available data, which could modify the statistical measures of cycles.

From the 1830s onwards it also becomes increasingly relevant to talk of monetary policy. Up until 1833 the usury laws had prevented active use of the Bank's discount rate (henceforth Bank Rate) by setting a ceiling on rates of 5%. After 1833 the laws were repealed and Bank Rate was used more actively to pursue various private and public policy goals. What amounted to monetary policy in this period was largely the maintenance of the international Gold Standard, at the heart of which was London and the Bank of England. After the Bank Charter Act of 1844, the Bank was given the exclusive right to issue notes, but these had to be backed at the margin by gold. Bank Rate would typically therefore rise in response to external deficits and flows of gold overseas. This would both attract gold back to the United Kingdom and encourage fewer notes to be held. As noted above this implied that even though agriculture was increasingly a small part of the overall economy poor harvests could still have a big impact on the economy through the balance of payments given the UK was a net importer of food. For example, Bank Rate rose in the late 1830s and 1840s in order to protect reserves as poor harvests and higher overseas corn prices led to a deterioration in the balance of payments (Chart 6.40). But this further exacerbated the downturns during these periods.

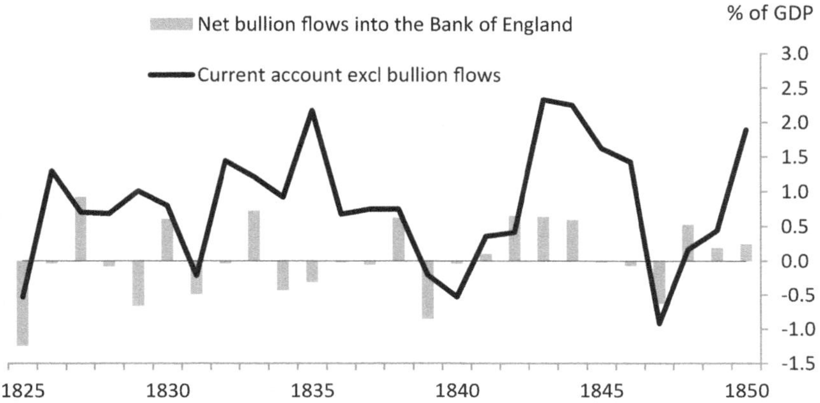

Chart 6.40 Current account of the balance of payments and bullion flows (*Source* Thomas and Dimsdale 2017)

From 1870 until 1913 we have much improved monetary data as a result of the work of Capie and Webber (1985). It is therefore possible to get a better idea of the role of money in trade cycles. The rate of growth of broad money 1870–1913 was generally similar to the rate of growth of nominal GDP, resulting in little variation in the velocity of circulation (see later in Chart 6.73). The stability of velocity combined with pro-cyclical variation in short-term interest rates readily explains the stability of the money demand function found by Capie and Wood (1996) and Dimsdale (2015). However, inferring causality is much more difficult. The stability could result from a causal relationship running from the money supply to nominal income as argued by Hawtrey (1928). An alternative and more modern approach is to emphasise the endogeneity of the money supply with a fixed exchange rate and capital mobility under the Gold Standard. For example, during an upswing in activity the demand for money would rise, raising short market interest rates. This would induce a capital inflow, increasing the Bank's reserves and increase either notes or bankers' deposits at the Bank. As noted above, much would then depend on what the Bank of England would do in terms of Bank Rate (which commercial bank loan and deposit rates were linked to) and how commercial banks themselves responded to a changed reserve position. The view that the money supply was endogenous accords with the argument of Ford (1962, 1981) that cycles under the Gold Standard were driven by fluctuations in home and foreign investment. It is also consistent with the view of Hicks (1982) that under the international gold standard real factors generated cycles which were relatively weak. While this interpretation holds for much of the period it does not apply to the strong recovery of the mid to late 1890s. At this time there was a massive inflow of gold arising from new discoveries of gold, chiefly in South Africa. The rise in the Bank's reserves led to a fall in interest rates and set off a major boom in housebuilding and in investment in infrastructure. The empirical analysis of Capie and Mills (1991) suggests a weak overall cyclical relationship between money and activity over this period but if anything there is a lead of output over broad money. This will be reviewed in the second volume of this study.

However, the Bank Charter Act gave some discretion to the Bank. Part of the overall note stock was held inreserve by the Banking Department and deposits held at the Bank by the banking system (bankers' balances) were not subject to any limit. This allowed the Bank some discretion and enabled it to use lending to the private sector (discounts of bills and secured lending or "advances") or purchases and sales of securities to sterilise movements in the money supply arising from gold flows. Whether the Bank used that discretion over this period as a stabilisation tool and take into account domestic output and unemployment is more contentious (see Goodhart 1972; Dutton 1984; Pippenger 1984; Dimsdale 2013b). The Bank certainly used that discretion in the immediate aftermath of the 1844 Act when it actively competed for commercial lending business with a discount rate that was sometimes below market rates. This contributed to the boom that would lead to the 1847 financial crisis.

What is true is the Bank Rate was used much more actively in the late C19th than the equivalent lending rates of other central banks as the Bank strove to make its rate influential in the market (Chart 6.41). It complemented this with other tools in order to make Bank Rate effective (Sayers 1976; Ugolini 2016). Lennard (2018) and Green (2018) both use archival evidence to uncover the reaction function of the Bank and both look at the impact of unanticipated changes on the UK economy and also the US economy.

Given the absence of major wars over this period, fiscal policy was largely concerned with managing the public debt that had built up in the C18th and early C19th (Chart 6.42). Throughout the mid-C19th,

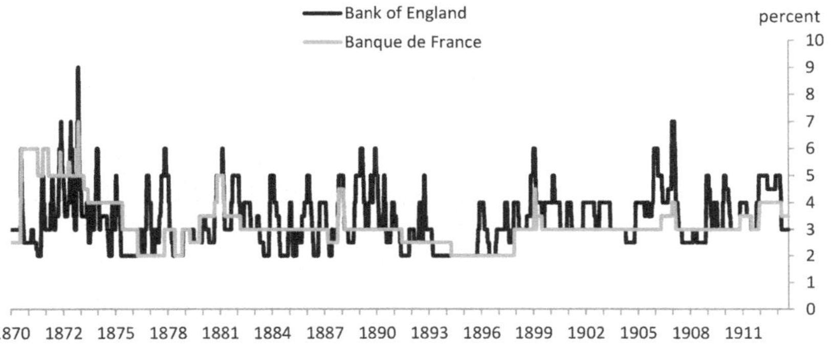

Chart 6.41 Central bank policy interest rates (*Source* Neal and Weidenmeier 2002, http://ebutts05.tripod.com/nealweidenmiergsd/)

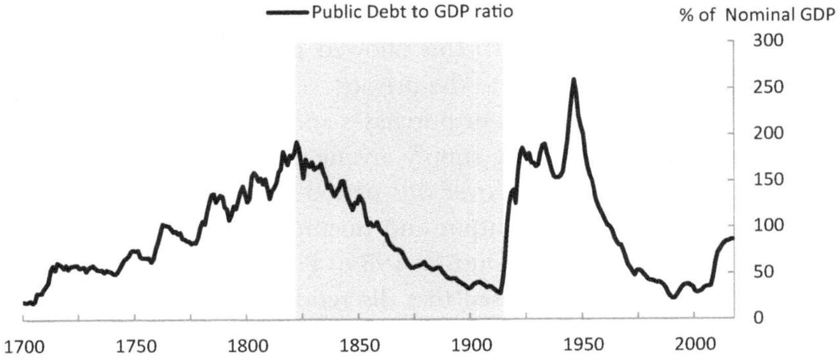

Chart 6.42 Public debt to GDP ratio (*Source* Thomas and Dimsdale [2017]. The gold standard period from 1821–1913 is shaded)

the United Kingdom ran a substantial primary surplus (Chart 6.43), thereby allowing it to service the considerable national debt commitments and maintain a balanced budget overall. Given the growth of nominal national income, the positive primary surplus ensured the national debt-income ratio fell substantially in periods of peacetime up to 1914.

6.3.2 From Crisis to Crisis 1832–1867

The first major cycle of the 1830s started from a trough in 1832 which followed a decline from the major cyclical peak of 1825. The expansion culminated in a peak in 1836 before lapsing into a trough with a low point in 1842 according to the UC model. However the HP filter estimates brings out the choppiness of fluctuations in the late 1830s and which inevitably contributed to financial instability over this period (Chart 6.44).

The recovery to 1836 was marked by the growth of both exports and fixed investment. The increase in exports was associated with a vigorous burst of expansion in the United States and the rise in investment implied by the first domestic boom in railway building. In 1836–1837 the upswing was interrupted by a fall in exports to the

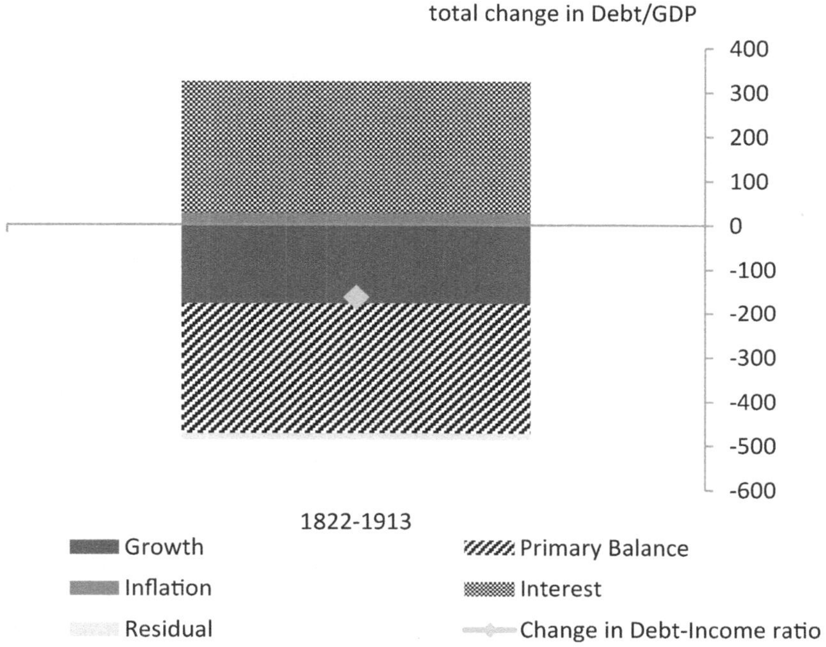

Chart 6.43 Accounting for the change in the public debt-income ratio (*Source* Thomas and Dimsdale 2017)

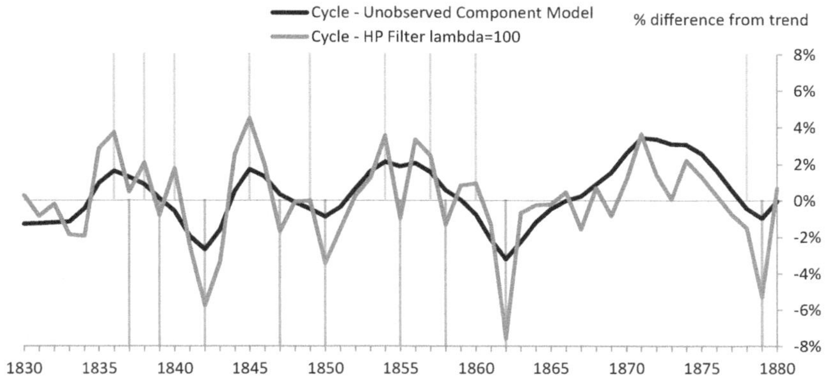

Chart 6.44 Cycles—1830–1880 (*Notes* Lines above the axis represent classical cycle peaks, lines below represent classical cycle troughs. *Source* Chapter 5)

United States. Matthews (1954) argues that the crisis in the United States arose from internal factors. This was supported by Lévy-Leboyer (1982) in later work. But American writers have emphasised causation running from Britain to the United States, as in Huffman and Lothian (1984), Rockoff (1971), and Temin (1974). The rise in short-term interest rates and other restrictive measures taken by the Bank were intended to strengthen the reserves by checking the outflow of capital to the United States. According to this view the tightening of credit in Britain was sufficient to precipitate a financial crisis and real downturn in the United States, which resulted in a reduction in demand for British exports. However domestic investment under the impetus of a growing boom in railway building sustained domestic demand in 1836–1837, reducing the impact of the decline in exports. The offset was not complete as the share of exports in GDP was higher than that of domestic investment.

Growth was resumed in 1837–1839 with the renewed growth of exports to Europe and the United States, combined with a continuing rise in fixed investment. The financial crisis which occurred in 1839 was precipitated by a rise in imports of corn, following the failure of the harvest and a rise in import prices. There was an increase in the merchandise trade deficit from £20.8 million (2.4% of GDP) in 1838 to £28.4 million (3.4% of GDP) in 1839. Bullion at the Bank declined from an average level of around £10 million in 1838 to around £4 million in 1839. Bank Rate was raised from 4 to 6% during 1839 and was held at 5% in 1840–1841. The trade deficit remained stubbornly high because of a succession of poor harvests from 1839 to 1841, which necessitated large imports of corn. The recession which followed the financial crisis was severe and was marked by a substantial fall in fixed investment because of a reduction of investment in railway building. Investment had been well maintained during the early stages of the recession because of railway projects which had been started during the later stages of the boom. But investment fell steeply as these projects reached completion. The high price of corn depressed real incomes and so curbed consumer spending, which fell by 4% between 1839 and 1842. Harvest failure was a critical factor in precipitating the downturn and the continuing high price of corn aggravated the recession.

Recovery started in 1842 following a reduction in imports of corn on account of a more favourable harvest, which contributed to reducing the trade deficit which recovered to its 1838 level. The Bank's reserves were under less pressure as bullion rose between 1841 and 1842, enabling Bank rate to be reduced from 5 to 4%. Lower market rates of interest helped to promote recovery, particularly of fixed investment in the form of renewed railway building and there was also a recovery of exports. Further reductions in interest rates were made as the Bank's bullion rose from around £8 million to £15 million between 1842 and 1844, while Bank rate was reduced to 2.5%.

A major institutional change during the recovery was the passing of the Bank Charter Act in 1844. This divided the Bank into separate Issue and Banking Departments in accordance with the doctrines of the Currency School. The Bank accepted the view of the Currency School that the Banking Department should be free to compete with other banks, while the quasi automatic operations of Issue Department ensured the convertibility of the note issue. The willingness of the Bank to enter into competition with other lenders prompted it to hold Bank rate below market rates of interest, so helping to promote the domestic boom (King 1936). This was an unforeseen consequence of the Bank Charter Act and was presumably not what the currency school had in mind when advocating this aspect of the arrangements.

Expansion was checked in 1845 due to a shortage of raw cotton which reduced the growth of industrial production and exports of cotton goods (Ward-Perkins 1962). However, the growth of GDP was maintained by an upsurge of fixed investment which jumped by more than 70% between 1845 and 1847 in the final stages of the boom in railway building. What interrupted the boom and caused the recession was the growth in imports of corn and the financial pressures which resulted from it. Difficulties started with the Irish Potato Famine of 1846 and continued with crop failures and high corn prices in 1847 (Turner 2014; Campbell 2014). The merchandise trade deficit doubled from £20 million in 1846 to more than £42 million in 1847, almost 5% of GDP.

The financial crisis of 1847 came in two waves. There was an external drain of gold in April 1847 caused by heavy imports of corn. It was followed by a sudden collapse of prices of corn and cotton in the summer leading to a wave of bankruptcies among those who had speculated on a repeat of the bad harvest of the previous year and prices remaining high. There were fears that the Bank would not continue to discount bills because of the threatened exhaustion of the reserve of the Banking Department, which aggravated the situation. Pressure on its reserve arising from an internal drain forced the effective suspension of the Bank Charter Act in October—strictly speaking this was a letter from the Government indemnifying the Bank from breaching the provisions of the Act rather than a formal suspension—and prompted a rise in Bank rate to an unprecedented 8% (Campbell 2014).

The financial crisis swept away the confidence of the upswing and the economy slid into recession with a steep decline in fixed investment because of the end of the boom in railway building. Prices fell sharply in the recession and there was a significant decline in narrow and broad money. The downturn proved not to be severe as rising exports offset declining investment from 1847 to 1850 (Ward-Perkins 1962).

Overall in the cycles of the 1830s and 1840s growth was checked by a financial crisis, which was initiated by a reduction in the reserves of the central bank on account of abnormally high imports of corn following a harvest failure. Losses of reserves forced the Bank to take remedial action in order to remain on the gold standard. Uncertainty about the behaviour of the Bank under a new monetary regime aggravated the crisis of 1847, but otherwise the two trade cycles seem to have much in common, in particular the buoyancy of fixed investment on account of railway building.

The main component of demand which expanded in the recovery of the 1850s was exports which surged by more than 50% between 1850 and the cyclical peak of 1857, while GDP rose by 23% in the same period. The initial stage of the recovery from 1850 to 1852 was marked by a massive inflow of gold following new discoveries in Australia and California (Hughes 1960; Clapham 1944). The Bank's bullion rose from £13.9 million in 1851 to £20.1 million in 1852, which led to a reduction in Bank rate to 2% in 1852 and an even lower level for bill rates. During the period up to 1857 the monetary base grew by around a third and broad money doubled between 1848 and 1857. Monetary expansion gave rise to an increase in prices as the GDP deflator rose by around 13.5% between 1850 and 1857. This was in contrast to the two previous recoveries in which prices rose only moderately. Cycles in nominal GDP were more pronounced than those in real GDP on account of the pro-cyclical movement of prices.

As the recovery of the 1850s proceeded, the Bank raised Bank rate from below 2% in 1852 to 6% in 1856 in line with rising market rates. The increase in Bank rate was not sufficient to prevent a continuing erosion of the reserve of the Banking Department. The merchandise trade deficit rose during the recovery, rising from £18.9 million in 1852 to £41.6 million in 1857. This occurred despite the vigorous growth of exports, because of a deterioration of the terms of trade on account of rising commodity prices. Hughes (1960) has emphasised the unsound expansion of credit which took place in the later stages of the boom. The financial structure became increasingly vulnerable and unable to resist the shock which occurred when Bank Rate was increased to 10% in November 1857 to protect the Bank's diminished reserve. The crisis of 1857 had an external aspect, since the growth of exports was checked because of an acute banking crisis in the United States, which in turn has been attributed to previous increases in British interest rates. The domestic financial crisis arose from failures among Scottish banks and the failure of the Borough Bank of Liverpool (discussed in detail by Turner 2014). These events led to a general scramble for liquidity which forced a repeat of the suspension of the Bank Charter Act. As in 1847 the crisis resulted from a combination of an external drain followed by an internal drain on the Banking Department's note reserve, which made the suspension of the Bank Charter Act unavoidable.

Overall it seems that monetary factors played an important role in both the upturn and the financial crisis. The inflow of gold in the early 1850s created the basis for low-interest rates which promoted recovery. In the later stages of the recovery the weakening reserve of the Bank combined with the rapid growth of bank credit created conditions in which the financial system became increasingly vulnerable to both internal and external shocks. The experience of the 1850s accords well with elements of the monetary and credit theories of the business cycle discussed in Chapter 2.

The recession which followed the crisis of 1857 was not severe because the growth of exports revived quickly in 1858–1860. Recovery was hampered by a rise in Bank Rate to 8% in early 1861, which was intended to check the outflow of gold to the United States before the outbreak of the Civil War. The effect of the war was to depress exports because of the disruption of the cotton industry which arose from a severe shortage of raw cotton—the "cotton famine". This did not prevent the economy from recovering although the pace of the upturn was modest. It was led by a revival in fixed investment in the form of renewed railway building. Despite the modest recovery a financial crisis occurred in 1866 with the failure of Overend and Gurney, the leading firm in the London discount market. There was a severe financial panic with an internal drain on the Bank's reserve of notes (see Sowerbutts et al. 2016). This however was not accompanied by a decline in its holding of bullion, which confirmed that the drain on the Bank's reserve was internal rather than external. Bank Rate was raised by steps to 8% in January followed by a further rise to 10% in May and the Bank discounted freely at this rate (Anson et al. 2017). In the crisis of 1866 the Bank followed the course later recommended by Bagehot (1873) of discounting freely at a high rate of interest. Furthermore, it established its own credibility by not coming to the aid of an insolvent Overend and Gurney.

The crisis of 1866 resulted from the failure of a leading financial institution. The cause of the crisis and downturn was a domestic financial shock. The background to the financial boom and downturn is described in Collins (1988). The situation was more clear cut than in 1857, when a deteriorating external position as well as domestic financial problems contributed to the crisis. Supply-side shocks arising from harvest failure were important features of the cycles of the 1830s and the 1840s and were aggravated by financial factors. In the cycle of the 1850s both real and monetary factors stimulated the upturn and contributed to the crisis. In the 1860s the recovery was impeded by supply-side factors on account of the cotton famine, but the crisis in 1866 appears to have been largely financial.

6.3.3 Industrial Apotheosis, Boom and Slump 1867–1879

The beginning of the cycle of the 1870s lies in the recovery from the downturn of 1866. The rise in Bank Rate during the crisis of 1866 induced a massive increase in the Bank's holding of bullion which rose from £14 million in 1866 to £20 million in 1867. Both Bank Rate and the market rate were reduced, the latter falling from a high of 9.6% in 1866 to under 2% for much of 1867 and 1868. The recovery which started gradually in 1867 was led by a substantial rise in exports, which rose by over a third during the upswing to the peak of the cycle in 1871. The surge in exports was associated with the international boom of the early 1870s, which followed the end of the American Civil War and the Franco Prussian War. British exports responded to the high level of overseas issues on the London capital market, which reached a peak in 1873 and also coincided with a peak in the current account surplus on the balance of payments. Fixed investment which had dominated the previous recovery remained relatively subdued in the late 1860s but rose in the early 1870s as the economy started to experience boom conditions. The rise in exports was the main force behind the long recovery. It resulted from an international boom and a high level of overseas lending (Lewis 1978; Cairncross 1953; Matthews et al. 1982).

Prices, in particular those of exports and capital goods, rose steeply in the early 1870s. The strength of the boom comes out more strongly in the rise of nominal GDP and the low level of unemployment than the course of real output or industrial production. The pressure on capacity in the coal and iron and steel industries was particularly severe. The productive potential of the economy may have been reduced by the general reduction in normal weekly hours worked (Chart 6.45) which occurred

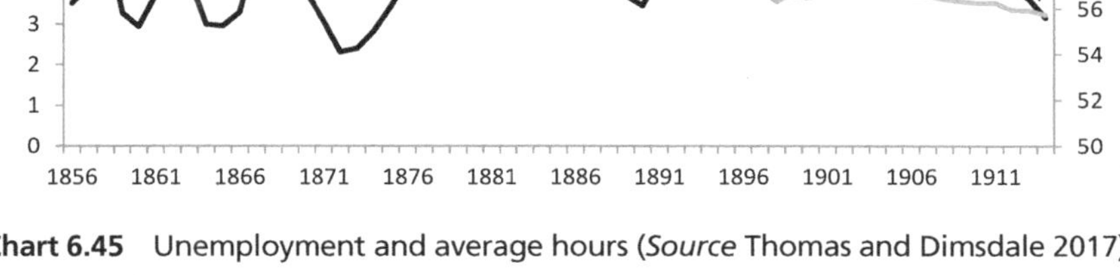

Chart 6.45 Unemployment and average hours (*Source* Thomas and Dimsdale 2017)

in the early 1870s. The reduction in hours of work could have acted as a supply-side shock, checking output and raising prices .The combination of sharply rising prices and relatively modest expansion of output in the boom of 1871–1873 can be explained by the high level of demand combined with a reduction in potential supply as a result of a reduction of weekly hours of about 10%. This outcome contrasts with the assumption by Matthews et al. (1982) that the reduction in hours was fully offset by higher productivity.

The boom was brought to an end by an international financial crisis in 1873, which occurred initially in Germany and later and more seriously in the United States. There was a drain of gold from London to New York following the failure of Jay Cooke & Company and the financial difficulties experienced in US railroads (Clapham 1944; Hawtrey 1962; Friedman & Schwartz 1963). Although Bank Rate was raised to 9% in November 1873, there was no domestic financial crisis. Capital exports, which had been high during the boom, collapsed as British investors turned away from overseas investments. The terms of trade declined as the price of exports, in particular the prices of coal, iron and steel products, fell back from the peak levels reached at the height of the boom. The upward movement of the economy was ended by an external shock which prompted a rise in interest rates and a decline in both exports and overseas capital issues. The international transmission mechanism operated through both trade flows and capital markets.

The decline in foreign investment after 1873 went with the stagnation of exports, but there was offsetting rise in domestic fixed investment, which rose by 26% between 1873 and 1876. Housebuilding made a major contribution to the revival of domestic investment. When the housing boom slackened in 1876, the economy subsided into a severe recession, which reached a low point in 1879 (Cairncross 1953). The recession was aggravated by a rise in Bank Rate because of the erosion of the Bank's reserves as a result of the failure of the City of Glasgow Bank, which is discussed by Turner (2014). The Bank also experienced losses of gold as a result of a series of bad harvests which necessitated a rise in imports of corn. The depression of the late 1870s was aggravated by a tightening of monetary policy arising from a domestic monetary shock combined with loss of reserves following harvest failure.

There was a long decline from the cyclical peak of 1871 to the trough of 1879. This was unlike the typical pattern of C19th cycles, which had short but sharp recessions followed shortly by a recovery. The pattern of the 1870s can be explained by the boom in home investment which maintained activity after the cyclical peak and the contractionary monetary measures introduced by the Bank towards the end of the downturn. The sustained rise in unemployment from about 2% in 1872–1873 to 8% in 1879 may, as noted, have been aggravated by the reduction in hours worked during the boom which increased labour costs (Boyer and Hatton 2002).

6.3.4 The Mature Industrial Economy 1880–1913

The recovery after the trough of 1879 was led by exports and was accompanied by a revival in overseas investment. The boom petered out in 1883 and the economy fell into recession in 1886 with both exports and fixed investment declining in the downturn. Exports led the recovery in 1886 and there was a renewed boom in overseas issues. Home investment also revived in the recovery. In both cycles exports appear to have been the main source of fluctuations in GDP and neither boom was particularly vigorous. The cyclical peak between 1889 and 1891 was chiefly notable for the Bank's intervention to avoid a financial crisis which could have occurred following the failure of Barings as a result of investment prospects in Argentina. The Bank's timely intervention to avoid an incipient crisis in 1890 contrasts with its unwillingness to assist Overend and Gurney in the financial crisis of 1866. However, unlike Overend Gurney, Barings was an important accepting house and a guarantor of many of the bills circulating in London and so its failure would have had more systematic ramifications for the City of London and the wider world economy (Chart 6.46).

Monetary policy may have played some part in the cycles of the 1880s. Hawtrey (1962) argued that the sharp movements of Bank rate in this period discouraged investment. The reluctance of the Bank to reduce Bank Rate in recessions and the tendency to raise it at an early stage in recoveries could be explained by the shortage of reserves which

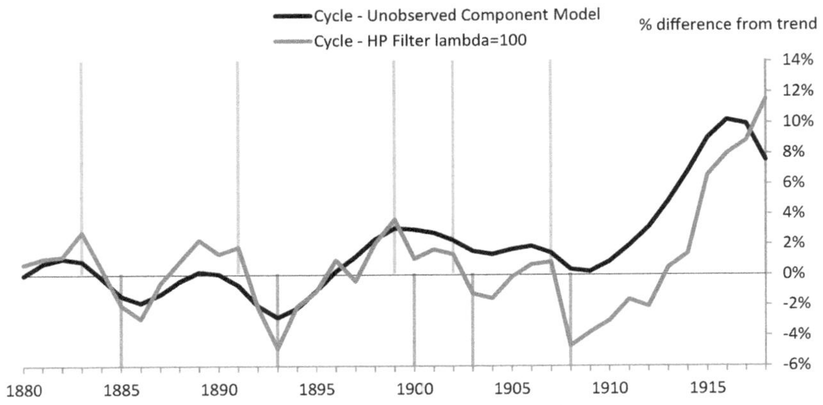

Chart 6.46 Growth cycles 1880–1918 (*Notes* Lines above the axis represent classical cycle peaks, lines below represent classical cycle troughs. *Source* Chapter 5)

the Bank experienced in the 1880s. The international demand for monetary gold was raised by the adoption of the gold standard by Germany and France in the 1870s and the resumption of specie payments by the United States in 1879. This increased demand for gold took place at a time when there was no commensurate increase in the stock of monetary gold. The Bank's reserves were considered to be low in the late 1870s and the 1880s and this may explain the volatile movements of Bank Rate observed by Hawtrey. The shortage of gold in the 1880s implied that there was little growth in the monetary base, but as noted earlier there was considerable flexibility within the monetary system which allowed the money supply to rise. Under the gold standard with much of the money supply consisting of bank deposits, the relationship between the metallic base of the system and the money supply might be weakened, but it would not disappear completely as suggested by Hicks (1977) given the Bank of England's reaction function.

During the 1890s the monetary situation changed markedly, since gold flowed in abundance to London on a scale not seen since the early 1850s, following gold discoveries, principally in South Africa. The note reserve in the Banking Department rose steeply in 1895–1896 together with its associated ratio (known as 'the Proportion'). Short-term rates were reduced from 1890 to 1895, while long-term rates which showed little movement over the whole period up to 1913 moved downwards in the mid-1890s. The reduction in the yield on Consols well below the barrier of 3% postulated by Hicks (1967) was achieved in the 1890s, following Goschen's successful debt conversion operation of 1888. The low point was reached in 1897 when the yield was only 2.25% after which it rose gradually to 3.5% in 1913. Hawtrey (1962) argued that the long-term rate can hardly have had a major impact on fixed investment, since its variation was so slight in the trade cycles from 1860 to 1913. The experience of the 1890s provides a counterexample to this view, since the reduction in both short and long-term interest rates at that time was associated with a rise in share prices, followed by a major boom in fixed investment.

The inflow of gold and also lack of interest among investors in foreign investments, following the Baring crisis created conditions which were highly favourable for home investment. Gross fixed investment rose by 75% in the recovery from 1893 to 1899, while broad money increased by 24% in the same period. The strength of the boom slackened as the backlog of investment opportunities, principally in housing and infrastructure were worked through. While the boom was initiated by a monetary shock, it was ended by a temporary exhaustion of domestic investment opportunities. The recession which started in 1899 was mild, unemployment rose while fixed investment continued to grow at a reduced pace. After the cyclical peak activity was maintained by the rise in government spending arising from the Boer war. The end of the war led to reduced military spending, which pushed the economy into a mild recession with a low point in 1903.

The two subsequent booms which peaked in 1907 and 1913 follow the pattern outlined by Ford (1969, 1981). British overseas capital issues and world economic activity provided a stimulus to exports which rose by 25% from 1903 to 1907 and by 27% between 1908 and 1913 (Chart 6.47). The high level of capital exports and the massive current account surplus from 1900 to 1913 are shown in Chart 6.48. These years can be regarded as a sustained export-led boom which was interrupted by an external shock arising from a major financial crisis in 1907. The crisis led to an outflow of gold to New York and Bank Rate was raised to 7%. The rise in Bank Rate and disturbed international conditions pushed the economy into a sharp

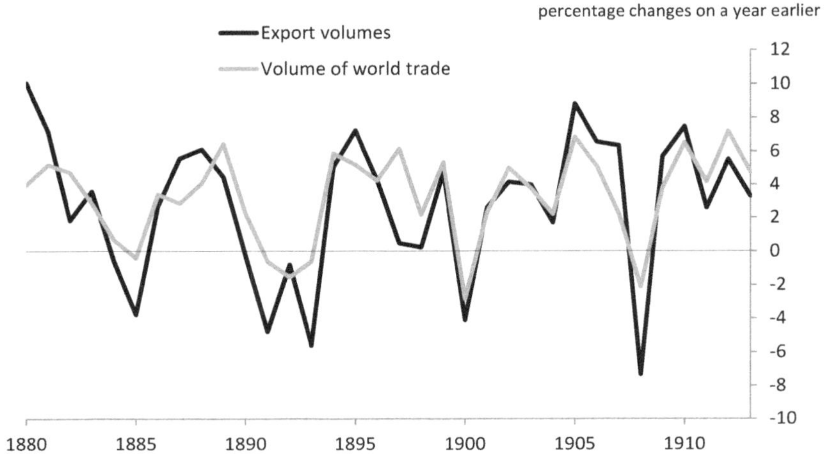

Chart 6.47 Export volumes and world trade (*Source* Thomas and Dimsdale [2017] and Federico and Tena-Junguito [2019])

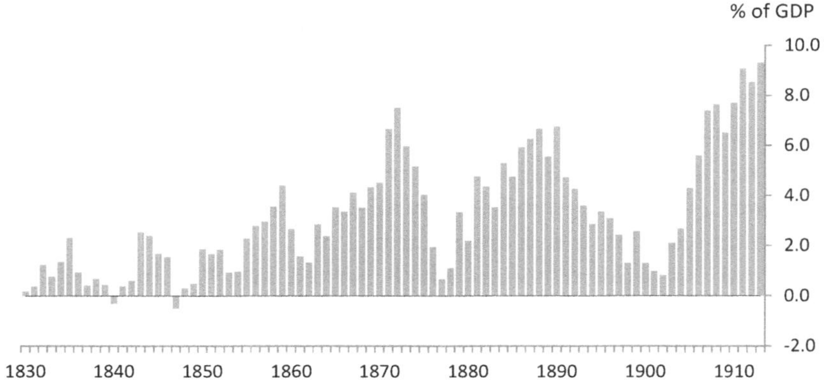

Chart 6.48 Current account of the balance of payments (*Source* Thomas and Dimsdale 2017)

recession with declines in both exports and domestic investment. There was no domestic financial crisis and both overseas lending and exports rebounded from the recession after 1908.

Overall, the main contributions to British fluctuations from 1870 to 1913 came from variation in the level of exports, which were linked to the pace of British overseas lending and to world economic activity. External shocks arising from overseas financial crises were important in ending booms in both 1873 and 1907. The massive gold inflow of the 1890s created a positive monetary shock which initiated a major domestic investment boom in the late 1890s. Supply-side factors were less important than the period before 1870, when harvest failures created acute problems for the balance of payments. However, the reduction in working hours in the early 1870s served to constrain the response of GDP to a strong boom in exports. The role of domestic financial crises in causing downturns was greatly reduced compared with the period before 1870.

6.4 The Interwar Economy 1919–1939

6.4.1 Overview—Institutional Factors and Key Drivers

Output became more volatile during and after WW1 and as identified in Chapter 5 there were several periods of major recession. During the period 1919–1939, three cyclical peaks can be identified from the various filters applied to quarterly data 1920Q2, 1929Q3–1930Q1 and 1937Q2/3, and three cyclical troughs 1921Q2/4, 1932H2 and 1938Q4 as shown in Chart 6.49. As Chapter 5 showed however the growth cycle peak in annual terms occurred in 1916 or 1918 rather than mid-1920 although the latter is often taken as the start point for analysis of peacetime cycles that are not affected by demobilisation and the inevitable contraction of government spending and labour utlisation that occurs at the end of major wars. The General Strike in 1926 also represents a trough in the cycle in 1926Q3. Overall the cyclical pattern over this period in classical terms is characterised by relatively long recoveries in the 1920s and 1930s with rapid downturns in 1920–1921 and 1929–1932.

Much of the interwar literature, particularly in the United States, focuses on the Great Depression of the 1930s. But Dowie (1975) and

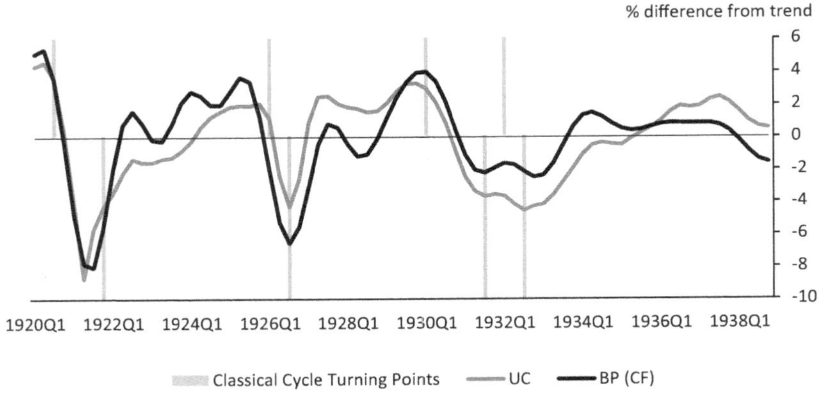

Chart 6.49 Interwar cycles (*Source* Chapter 5)

Broadberry (1990) argue that equal attention needs to be paid to the recession of 1919/20–1921. For the United Kingdom, although the recession of the 1930s was large by historical standards, it was smaller than that of 1919/20–1921 which remains a significant outlier in UK historical recessions given the amplitude and period of that cycle. Indeed, the 1930s recession was milder in GDP terms than the slump experienced in the United States whereas the 1920–1921 recession was materially worse.

One feature that became ingrained in the interwar period as a result of these two recessions was high unemployment. It increased to over 10% in 1921 which in itself was not a surprise given the collapse in output. But it failed to fall significantly in the early 1920s years despite the recovery in output. As a result, it increased to over 15% when the Great Depression hit and was still around 8% at the outbreak of World War 2 (Chart 6.50).

Hatton and Thomas (2010) argue there was a rise in the natural rate of unemployment in the early 1920s reflecting increased union power and the spread of collective bargaining and the introduction of wide-spread national unemployment insurance which they argue increased bargaining power. Benjamin and Kochin (1979) also emphasise the impact of unemployment benefits arguing it reduced effective labour supply and job search intensity. Hatton and Thomas (2010) also argue that weaker productivity (output per head), in part driven by a large

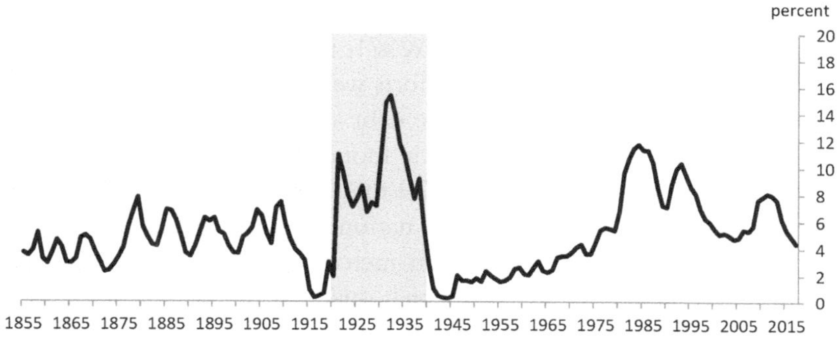

Chart 6.50 Interwar unemployment (*Source* Thomas and Dimsdale [2017]. Interwar period shaded)

fall in average hours worked at the end of World War I, had a persistent effect on unemployment as real product wages adjusted only gradually.

In a similar vein Dimsdale and Horsewood (1995) estimate a small macroeconomic model which provides estimates of the equilibrium rate of unemployment in the 1920s and 1930s. This provides a breakdown between unemployment which is induced by the supply side and unemployment which is caused by deficiency of demand. The natural rate of unemployment in their framework is influenced by the benefit replacement ratio and the real price of imports. They estimated the natural rate was higher in the 1930s than in the 1920s and the actual rate of unemployment was higher than the natural rate in both decades. So that there was unemployment resulting from deficient demand as well as unemployment attributable to the supply side. At the peak of 1937, they estimate the level of unemployment was approximately at the natural rate of unemployment. Unemployment was 7.8% and Keynes himself commented at the time that any further increase in demand would be likely to raise the rate of inflation.

Monetary policy in the 1920s was initially dominated by the large recession of 1920–1921 and then by the subequent return to the Gold Standard in 1925. Eichengreen et al. (1985) show that Bank Rate under the interwar gold standard was used less actively than before WW1—for example Bank Rate changed only half as often in the 1925–1931 period than it had been on average over the period 1890–1913. Initially, that may have reflected the need to keep a cap on the government's short-term borrowing costs. At the end of WW1, the national debt contained a large amount of Treasury bills and efforts were made to shift the maturity structure away from the floating rate debt so that debt service considerations did not interfere with domestic monetary policy when tightening was required. Between 1918 and 1929 the share of floating rate debt fell from around 20 to 10% of the total national debt. Overall, Eichengreen et al. (1985) also find evidence of an increased sensitivity of Bank Rate to domestic economic conditions which qualified the normal response to gold flows under the standard "rules of the game". They also find some evidence of asymmetry. The Bank was more inclined to raise rates in response to gold outflows but was less inclined to lower them when gold was flowing in and looked to sterilise the impact on the monetary base.

Short-term interest rates remained relatively high in the initial stages of the "Great Depression" in 1929–1931, largely as the result of having to maintain sterling's gold standard parity under mounting pressure of an arguably overvalued exchange rate. Nominal rates did fall following similar cuts overseas, but falling prices meant that real interest rates increased rapidly. The vulnerability of the Bank's position was emphasised during the sharp rise in US interest rates to check the boom on the New York stock market in 1929. Following the Wall Street Crash and the movement of the world economy into recession, the weak position of sterling was exposed. In the crisis of confidence of 1931, the Bank was fortunately able to suspend the gold standard and so avoided what was potentially a major financial crisis, which could have threatened the domestic banking system. Accominotti (2012) emphasises the vulnerability of the London merchant banks and documents the Bank's actions to support them. As a result British domestic finance emerged unscathed but at the expense of dropping out of the gold standard. In handling the 1931 crisis the Bank was arguably able to benefit from its experience in coping with the financial crisis in 1914 at the outbreak of WWI. The crisis of 1914 similarly threatened the solvency of the City's accepting houses (merchant banks) but did not damage the banking system.

When sterling came off the gold standard in 1931 Bank Rate was initially increased to 6% mitigate the degree of potential depreciation and caused a double-dip recession. But as soon as confidence returned Bank

Rate was reduced to 2%. This ushered in a period of cheap money and allowed the real exchange rate to depreciate. Despite sterling's depreciation, the recovery from 1933 was driven mainly by domestic demand with both consumption and investment growing strongly. The latter reflected an initial boom in housebuilding followed later by rising industrial investment and growing government spending on rearmament. Net trade made a muted contribution, largely because the limited recovery of world trade and the impact of foreign protectionism offset the benefits from sterling's depreciation and the imposition of import tariffs. So a major feature of the recovery of the 1930s is the dependence on the revival of domestic demand with only a weak contribution from exports. This outcome contrasts strongly with recoveries in the pre-1914 period which were typically led by exports.

The important role of domestic demand in the 1930s recovery during a policy of cheap money means that the 1930s have been the subject of much scrutiny by those interested in the transmission mechanism of monetary policy. One particular issue is the role of price expectations and their influence on real interest rates. The intention to return to gold at the pre-war parity in the early 1920s and the announcement in 1932 at the Ottawa British Empire conference of a desire to return the price level to 1929 levels were both public commitments to a path for prices that arguably had a strong effect on real interest rates and expected inflation (Broadberry 1986; Crafts 2013).

The other interesting development in the transmission of monetary policy is the increased role of mortgage borrowing and its impact on the housing market. The interwar period saw a rise in home ownership fuelled by increased lending by the building society sector.

During the interwar period, there was increasing public debate about the use of fiscal policy to alleviate unemployment. Keynes famously argued for a more expansive budgetary policy from the late 1920s onwards. However, his arguments did not have much impact on the views of the Treasury and the interwar Chancellors. Keynes and Henderson supported the arguments of the Liberal party in the 1929 election for fiscal expansion in a well-known pamphlet "Can Lloyd George Do It?". They argued that expenditure of 2% of GDP could raise employment by 200,000. This argument was not accepted by the Treasury or leading economists, but the case for public works to raise employment was greatly strengthened by

Kahn's innovation of the employment multiplier (1931). This enabled the relationship between primary and secondary employment to be analysed. Keynes drew on Kahn's work in restating the case for public expenditure to combat recession in both Britain and the United States in "The Means to Prosperity" articles that appeared in the Times newspaper in March 1933. He calculated the income multiplier to be about 2. He returned to the size of the multiplier in The General Theory (Keynes 1936) suggesting that the multiplier might be about 5 in a closed economy and 2–3 in an open economy, such as Britain. By the late 1930s it was accepted officially that budget deficits might be incurred to finance defence spending, but this did not imply official acceptance of countercyclical fiscal policy.

As a result, discretionary movements in underlying fiscal policy generally contributed little to the economic cycle during the late 1920s and for much of the 1930s (Turner 1991; Middleton 2010). Debate continues as to how effective fiscal might have been had it been used more actively (see Thomas 1983; Dimsdale and Horsewood 1995; Cloyne et al. 2018). However, managing the national debt was the major preoccupation of governments and the aim of not adding more to that debt by running deficits was the rule or "Treasury view" as it became known. Equally important was the need to take the opportunity of refinancing the national debt when interest rates were low, such as the conversion of the 5% War Loan into a 3.5% loan in 1932. The other notable fiscal development was the introduction of the General Tariff in 1932 although there is a debate about whether this materially aided the recovery (see for example Richardson 1967; Capie 1978; Kitson and Solomou 1990; Broadberry and Crafts 2011; Lloyd and Solomou 2019).

Given this background, we again embark on a more detailed narrative discussion of cycles in the interwar period and here we rely heavily on previous accounts such as Dimsdale (1981) and Broadberry (1986). But we also review that narrative in the light of more recent research.

6.4.2 WW1 and the 1921 Trough

The end of WWI culminated in a vigorous private sector boom which reached a peak early in 1920. However, overall GDP is estimated to have fallen in 1919 given the decline in government spending and public sector (military) output. Pigou (1947) attributed the private sector boom to the urgent worldwide need to rebuild stocks of manufactured goods which had been depleted in wartime. Once stocks had been restored to more normal levels, the demand for British exports declined steeply. So Pigou's analysis suggests there was a severe post-war inventory cycle and at a global level.

An alternative explanation emphasising monetary factors has been advanced by Hawtrey (1962) and Huffman and Lothian (1984). According to these writers, the boom could be explained by rapid monetary growth in 1918–1919, followed by a slowdown in 1920. However, since a decline in exports precipitated the downturn, Pigou's explanation in terms of an external demand shock appears to be more convincing. Where monetary factors come in is in aggravation of the subsequent recession by the enforcement of a tight monetary policy, leading to a reduction in investment in 1922.

Excess demand at the cyclical peak in 1919–1920 was aggravated by a supply-side shock in the form of a 13% reduction in normal working hours from 54 to 48 hours per week (Chart 6.51). Since the reduction in hours was not associated with a fall in weekly wage rates or an increase in labour productivity, it served to raise labour costs. The sudden increase in own product real wages aggravated the problem of unemployment in the 1920s noted earlier (Hatton and Thomas 2010).

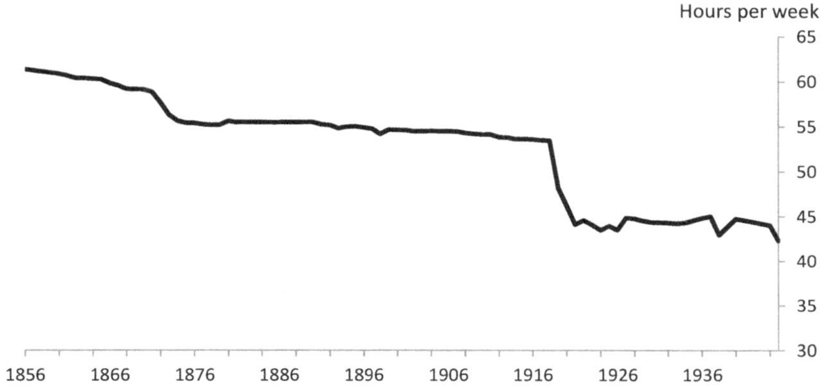

Chart 6.51 Average hours 1856–2017 (*Source* Thomas and Dimsdale [2017] and Boyer and Hatton [2002])

It is true that fiscal and monetary policy were both lax at the end of the war. In 1918–1919 public sector borrowing was a massive 25% of GDP and monetary financing had contributed to the strong money growth discussed earlier. The wartime peg of $4.76 to the £, which had been sustained by loans of more than $2 billion over the course of the war (see Moggridge 1969), was withdrawn and the sterling-dollar exchange rate fell to £3.40 in February 1920. This is despite the Cunliffe Committee's conclusion in 1919 that a return to the gold standard under the pre-war parity ($4.86 to the £) was imperative and should be achieved as soon as possible. As a result of these excess demand pressures and the ending of wartime price controls retail price inflation picked up to more than 20% per annum in 1920, so there was an urgent need to curb it.

Monetary and fiscal policies were tightened sharply in response. Bank Rate was initially raised from 5 to 6% in November 1919. Real government consumption fell by over 40% between 1919 and 1920, having fallen massively the year before as the war-related expenditures came to end. There were then fears that the Bank would not be able to finance the floating debt which had expanded in wartime and the government might have to resort to Ways and Means advances, which would boost money growth further. A further rise in Bank Rate to 7% came as the economy reached its cyclical peak and it was held at this rate for nearly a year. This counter-inflationary policy was continued despite signs the economy going into steep recession.

The sharp rise in nominal rates was passed through into borrowing and deposit rates and reduced consumption (Chart 6.52). Exports also declined as a result of a sharp fall in world activity. There then followed a period of severe deflation during which real interest rates rose to unprecedented levels. Overall private demand plunged in 1921 leading to a severe depression not seen since the end of the Napoleonic Wars. GDP fell by 10%, with a decline in exports of 21% and falls in consumers' expenditure and stockbuilding. Fixed investment continued to rise in 1921 and did not fall back until the following year. The fall in the GDP deflator was over 20% between 1920 and 1922 according to Feinstein (1972), making this the most severe deflation on record. Unemployment rose from 2.0% in 1920 to over 11% in 1921.

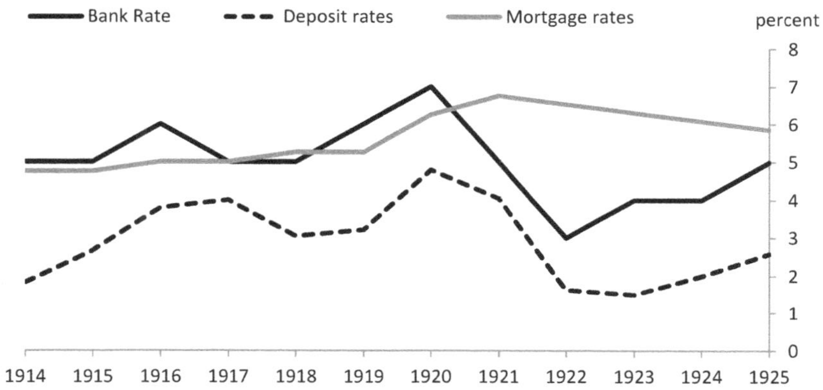

Chart 6.52 Loan and deposit rates 1914–1925 (*Source* Thomas and Dimsdale 2017)

6.4.3 The Return to Gold and the Great Depression 1921–1932

In response to the recession of 1921, Bank Rate was brought down to 3% by mid-1922 (Chart 6.53). But monetary policy was then steadily tightened following the decision to return to gold at a high (and possibly overvalued) parity in 1925. The severity of the monetary contraction, with M3 falling by 15.6% from 1921 to 1925 can be explained by the determination of the Bank to squeeze out inflationary expectations and to prepare the way for the restoration of the gold standard at the pre-war parity of $4.86/£. The heavy depreciation of sterling against the dollar which followed the floating of the pound in 1919 meant that a major appreciation would be needed to restore the pre-war parity. At its low point in February 1920 the pound had fallen to $3.40 (Chart 6.54), so that a return to the pre-war exchange would have necessitated a sterling appreciation of more than 40%. The Bank's target level for the exchange rate could only be achieved by a restrictive monetary policy which would strengthen sterling against the dollar and this was the main aim of monetary policy until the gold standard was restored in 1925. Rates were raised back to 4% in 1923 and to 5% in 1925.

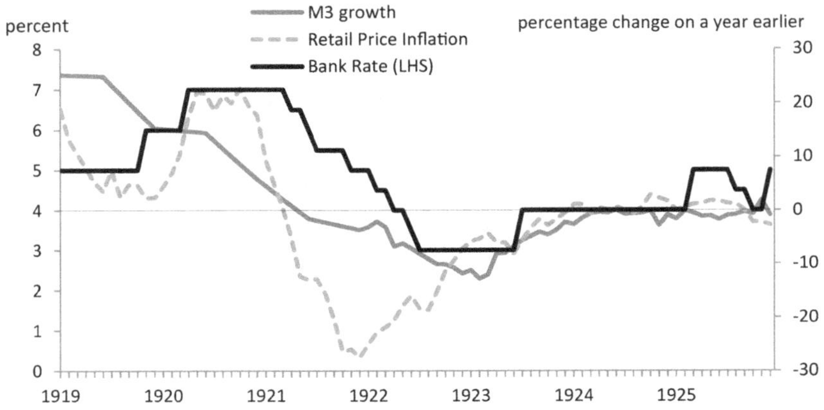

Chart 6.53 Money, interest and prices 1919–1925 (*Source* Thomas and Dimsdale [2017], M3 growth from Capie and Webber [1985])

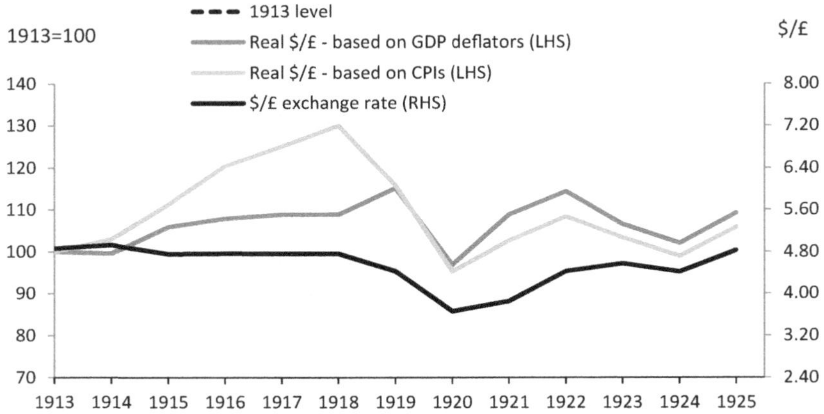

Chart 6.54 Dollar exchange rates 1913–1925 (*Source* Thomas and Dimsdale 2017)

The overvaluation of the exchange rate, which emerges more strongly from calculations of the sterling's effective exchange rate rather than the sterling-dollar exchange rate (see Chart 6.55), impeded recovery in the period 1925–1929. In 1925 the real effective rate based on the latest research by Catao and Solomou (2005) was between 10 and 15% higher than 1913 levels. It was reinforced by the high level of short-term and

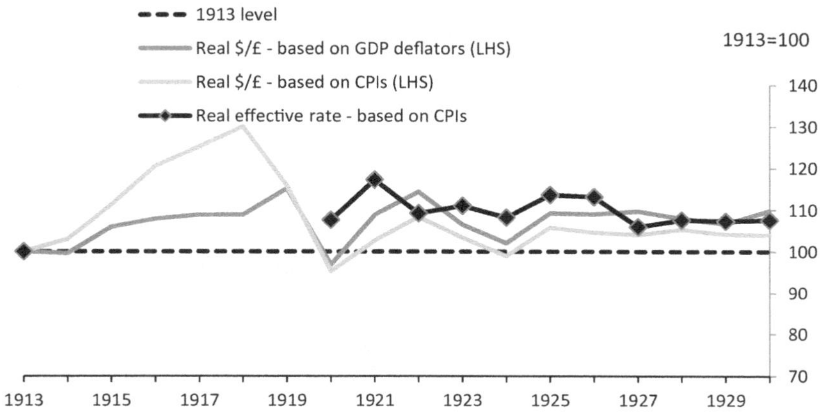

Chart 6.55 Real exchange rate measures 1913–1930 (*Source* Thomas and Dimsdale [2017], based on Catao and Solomou [2005])

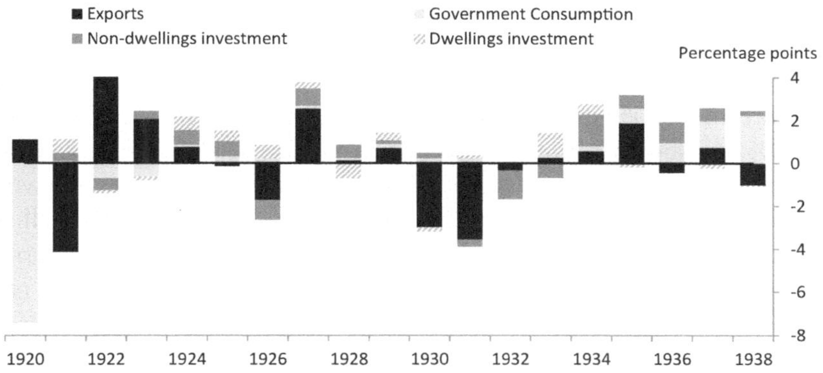

Chart 6.56 Contributions to GDP (*Source* Thomas and Dimsdale [2017] derived from Sefton and Weale [1995])

long-term interest rates which were more burdensome in real, ex-post terms on account of the downward trend in the price level. Despite the discouragement of a high exchange rate and a restrictive monetary policy, there was a gradual recovery of demand from 1921 to 1929. Both exports and fixed investment increased by 40–50% and, apart from the year of the General Strike, contributed positively to GDP (Chart 6.56). But as shown earlier the rate of unemployment remained stubbornly high.

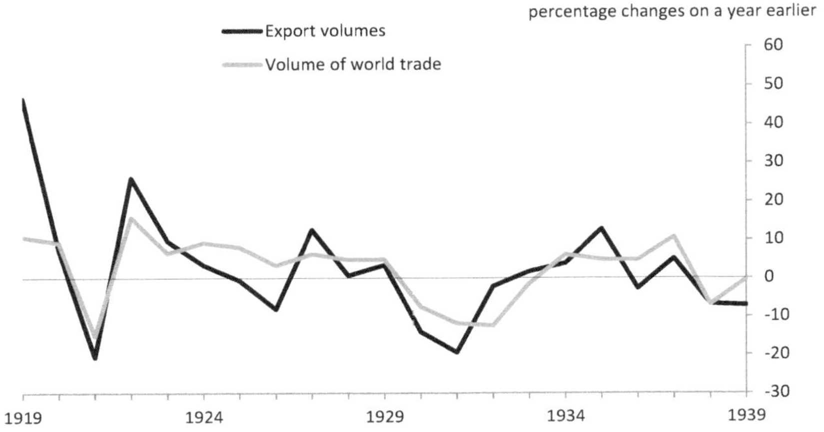

Chart 6.57 Export volumes and world trade 1919–1939 (*Source* Thomas and Dimsdale 2017)

The Great Depression of 1929–1932 came as an external and unwelcome demand shock to a gradually-recovering economy. Exports fell by more than 30% in response (Chart 6.57) and fixed investment fell by 14%. As shown earlier the decline in GDP was, however, relatively mild compared with the fall in 1920–1921 and also compared with leading economies such as the United States and Germany. The fall in real national income was moderated by the improvement in the terms of trade on account of a sharp fall in import prices. In this way real personal incomes were cushioned against the recession, enabling consumers' expenditure to rise by 2%. By contrast in, in the contraction of 1920–1921 both real personal income and consumers' expenditure declined and the terms of trade deteriorated. However, the decline in both exports and fixed investment was greater in 1932 than in 1919–1920. Interest rates were cut reaching a low of 2.5% in mid-1931.

Fiscal policy in this period was governed by the Treasury orthodoxy that the government should run a balanced budget. A variety of window dressing methods were employed to give this impression but underlying fiscal policy tightened as the government sought to finance increased payments on unemployment benefits and other automatic stabilisers by cutting spending and increasing taxes in other areas. In other words,

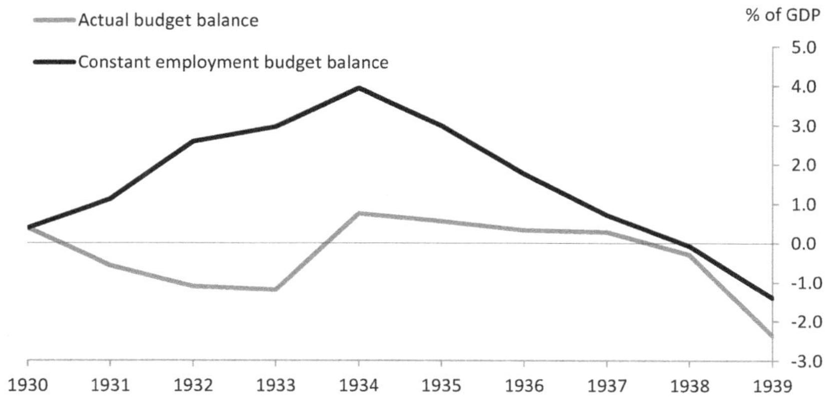

Chart 6.58 Fiscal stance based on central government revenue and expenditure (*Source* Middleton 1981)

the automatic stabilisers were effectively overridden. Middleton's (1981) estimates of the constant employment surplus—the fiscal stance that would have operated had employment stayed constant and the automatic stabilisers had not kicked in—suggests a tightening of around 4% of GDP by 1934 (Chart 6.58).

Middleton's estimates of the constant employment budget deficit have been disputed by Broadberry (1986). However, the major qualification to be made to the analysis of fiscal policy is, as pointed out in Middleton (2010), that the discussion has focussed on the central government's budget deficit, whereas the impact of fiscal measures should be assessed by using total public expenditure and revenue. This measure shows only a small deficit relative to the size of the output gap. The balance of total government spending was harder for the Treasury to control than the balance of central government spending, since it includes expenditure by local authorities. Middleton (2010) finds that the overriding of the built-in stabilisers when viewed from the perspective of total government expenditure is less than complete. So while there was some tightening of fiscal stance in the Great Depression, it appears to have been enough to restore confidence in the crisis of 1931 without providing a major obstacle to recovery.

6.4.4 The Recovery of the 1930s

Britain was forced to abandon the Gold Standard in September 1931 and the exchange rate fell from $4.86 to $3.69. The suspension of the gold standard in 1931 and the floating of sterling enabled the exchange rate fall to a more competitive level. In the short-term Bank Rate was actually raised back up to 6% from 2.5% to avoid too precipitous a fall in sterling and this led to a noticeable double-dip recession in 1932. Howson (1975) argues this reflected an interim period of uncertainty about the required policy framework in the absence of a sterling anchor. However, over the medium term the depreciation facilitated the reduction of both nominal short-term and long-term interest rates in the slump and a policy of "cheap money" was adopted (Chart 6.59). Bank Rate was reduced by stages from 6% in September 1931 to 2% in June 1932, while the yield on consols fell from an average of 4.4% in 1931 to 3.75% in 1932. The effective market rate based on Treasury bills fell to around 0.5%.

Although nominal rates fell, Crafts (2013) argues that real interest rates were also falling because of higher inflation expectations. He points to the announcement by the Chancellor Neville Chamberlain at

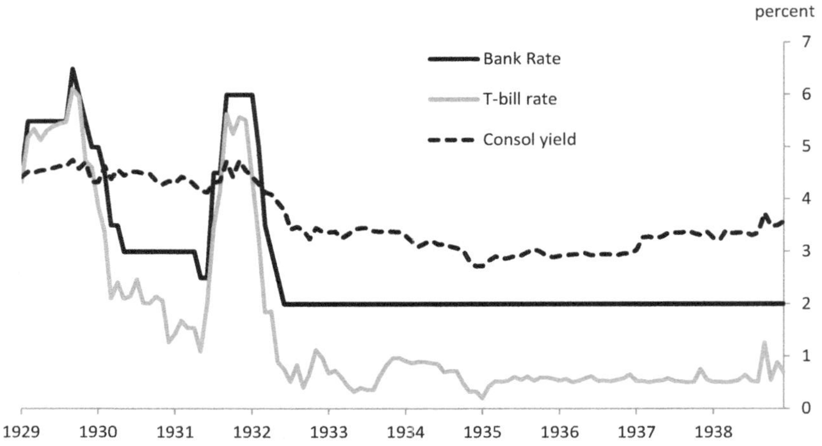

Chart 6.59 Cheap money in the 1930s (*Source* Thomas and Dimsdale 2017)

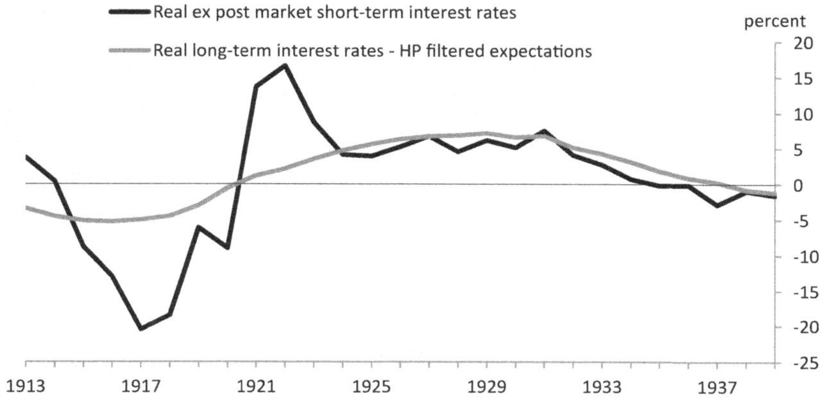

Chart 6.60 Real interest rates (*Source* Thomas and Dimsdale 2017)

the Ottawa British Empire conference in 1932 promising to return the price level to its 1929 level. Although expectations cannot be measured directly over this period this is backed up by simple estimates of real interest rates based on actual outturns or statistical filtered estimates of inflation (Chart 6.60). As testament to the effect of the policy of low nominal and real interest rates, broad money increased by around 25% during the recovery from 1932 to 1937.

This contributed to the revival of economic activity, first through stimulating a revival in private housebuilding, which contributed to the early stages of the upturn in 1933 and 1934. But the importance of this must not be overstated in terms of its overall contribution to GDP even if multiplier effects are built-in. Chart 6.56 shows this at best had a strong impact in 1933 and 1934, and that its contribution was if anything negative thereafter. It is also not clear this was driven by interest rates given that mortgage borrowing growth itself was slowing in 1933. Increased housing demand also did not push up on house prices according to Samy's (2015) hedonic price estimates (Chart 6.61).

The main component of demand contributing to the recovery was actually the rise in non-dwellings investment. It contributed to GDP substantially more than dwellings investment between 1935

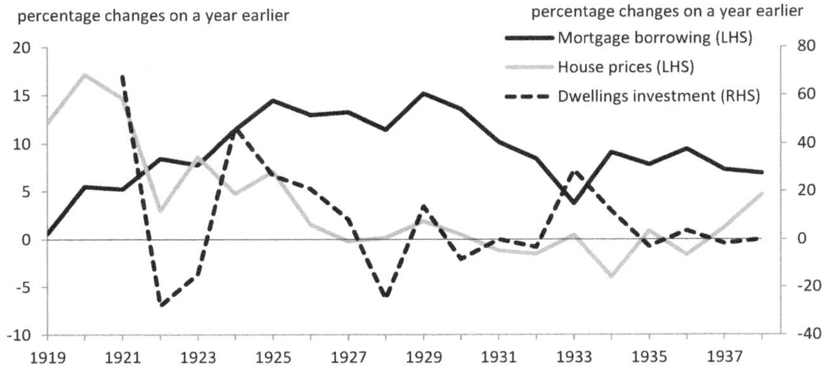

Chart 6.61 Mortgage borrowing, house prices and dwellings investment (*Source* Thomas and Dimsdale 2017)

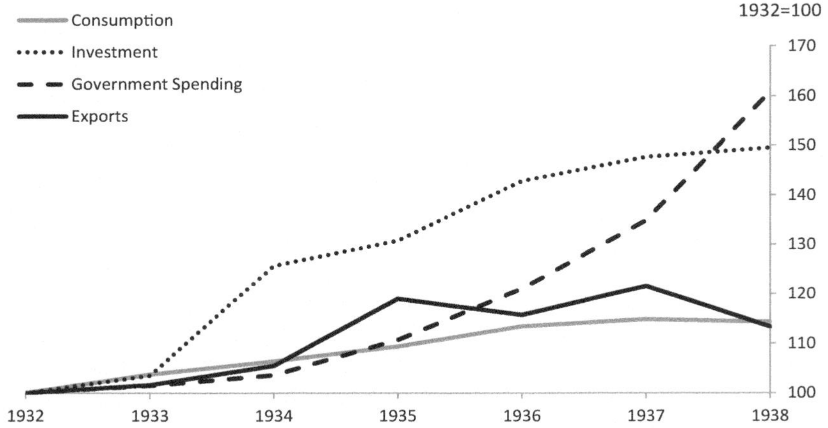

Chart 6.62 Components of final demand 1932–1938 (*Source* Thomas and Dimsdale 2017)

and 1938. The evidence suggests this was in response improved profits and higher capacity utilisation, rather than lower interest rates given the low-interest rate elasticity estimated by Broadberry (1986). During the recovery fixed investment rose by 50% (Chart 6.62). Consumers' expenditure appears to have made only a limited contribution to recovery. Consumer spending showed steady growth rising by 6% to 1934 and then by further 7% to 1938.

Exports increased by only 20% despite the improved competitiveness of the exchange rate and the limited revival of world trade. In part, this was because the advantage of a lower exchange rate was short-lived as other countries depreciated their exchange rates such as France following the Tripartite Agreement of 1936 (Chart 6.63).

In the later 1930s public expenditure rose rapidly after 1935 as defence spending gathered pace. When exports declined in 1938 under the impact of the US recession of 1937–1938, the fall in GDP was averted on account of the rapid growth of public expenditure. Crafts and Mills (2013) attempt to make this conclusion robust using the concept of "defence news" introduced by Ramey (2011) which deals with potential problems of endogeneity in estimating the government-expenditure multiplier. This approach involves looking at government announcements in the annual (and supplementary) defence estimates and commentaries on defence spending intentions in *The Economist*. Their estimates are also shown in Chart 6.64. This suggests public expenditure was the key driver of the recovery from 1936 onwards and

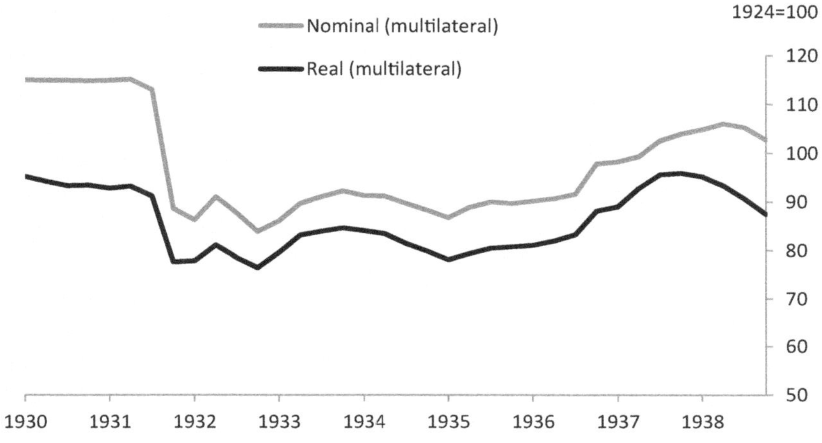

Chart 6.63 Real effective exchange rates in the recovery (*Source* Andrews 1987)

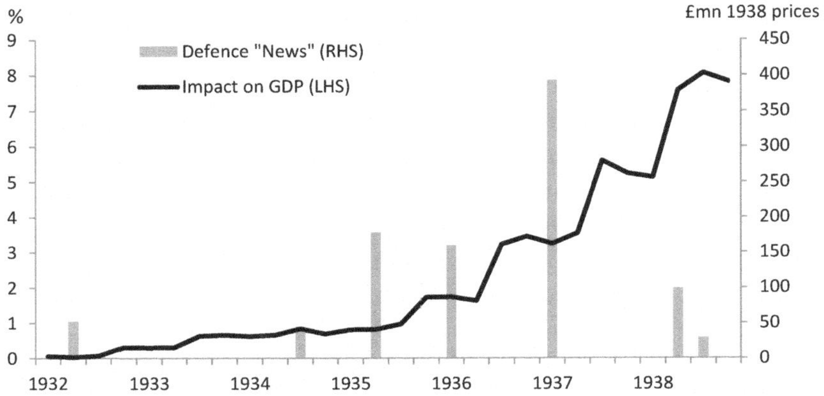

Chart 6.64 Crafts and Mills (2013) estimates of defence spending (*Source* Crafts and Mills 2013)

overall contributed around 8pp of the 24% increase in real GDP in the recovery period as a whole.

Beenstock et al. (1984) have challenged the view that shifts in demand largely account for the depression and recovery of the 1930s. In particular, they argue that moderation of real wages contributed to recovery. However, the evidence suggests the course of real wages reflected a response to demand shocks rather than an independent influence acting on the supply side of the economy as discussed in Dimsdale et al. (1989).

To conclude, each of the downturns in the interwar period resulted in part from external demand shocks. In 1920 there was also a large supply-side shock on account of a reduction in normal weekly hours of work. Restrictive monetary and exchange rate policies hindered recovery in the 1920s, while the flexible exchange rate and expansionary monetary policy promoted it in the 1930s. A major feature of the recovery of the 1930s was its dependence on the revival of domestic demand with only a weak contribution from exports. This outcome contrasts strongly with recoveries in the pre-1914 period in which recoveries were typically led by exports.

6.5 The Managed Economy 1945–1973

6.5.1 Overview—Institutional Factors and Key Drivers

The post-war period is often seen as a "golden age" of productivity growth. On the latest national accounts data the UK experienced the fastest rates of labour productivity growth in its history, peaking at around 4% in the late 1960s and 1970s based on ouptut per hour worked (Chart 6.65). Yet at the same time the UK lagged behind many of its competitors and was increasingly perceived as being in decline. By the 1970s the UK had become known as "the sick man of Europe". The UK's share of manufacturing trade continued to decline (see earlier Chart 6.39).

There was a marked change in cyclical fluctuations after WW2. In both the C19th and the interwar period there were regular classical fluctuations in the level of economic activity. By contrast in the 20 years after WW2 the classical trade cycle almost vanished and we see only growth cycles, with fluctuations in the growth rate rather than the level of GDP. Looking at the quarterly data for growth cycles in Chart 6.66 there are four clear growth cycles identified which have common characteristics. The cycle of 1968–1973 may be included in

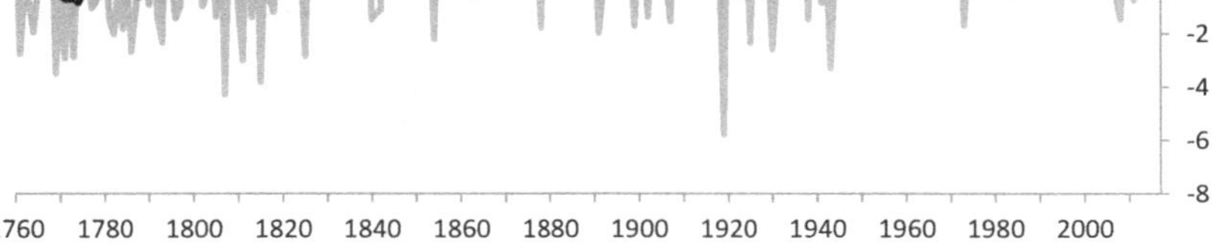

Chart 6.65 Labour productivity growth (output per hour) (*Source* Thomas and Dimsdale 2017)

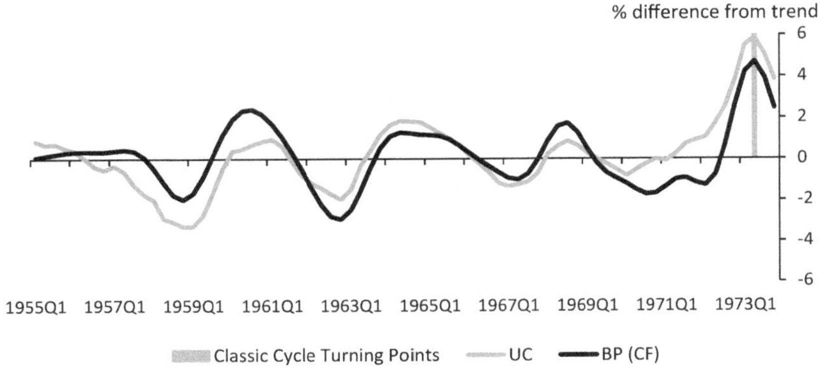

Chart 6.66 Cycles: quarterly basis 1955–1973 (*Source* Chapter 5)

this group, although it differed from its immediate predecessors on account of the impact of the devaluation of sterling in 1967 and the policy measures implemented to make it effective.

Unlike the period before 1938, fluctuations in the post-war economy became increasingly influenced by economic policy measures, as policymakers attempted to stabilise the economy. Post-war policy during the 1950s and 1960s has often been characterised as one of Keynesian demand management with an overall goal of full employment. There was a post-war consensus where governments, both Conservative and Labour, took a corporatist view and saw their role as planning and managing the economy together with trade unions and the bosses of key industries. This approach became known as "Butskellism" named after the Chancellor "Rab" Butler and Hugh Gaitskell who was shadow chancellor and, later, leader of the Labour party in the 1950s. These were also certainly the goals of two of the key Prime Ministers over this period Macmillan and Wilson, although on occasion their Chancellors and Treasury Ministers (most notably Thorneycroft and Enoch Powell who resigned in 1957) as well as the Bank of England often took a stand against excessive public spending.

Under the Bretton Woods system of fixed, but adjustable, exchange rates there was a persistent conflict between the objective of maintaining a high level of employment and correcting deficits in the balance of payments. This produced a succession of so-called "stop-go" or, perhaps more appropriately as Dow (1998) recommends, "go-stop" cycles in which expansionist periods of "go" led to balance of payments difficulties and deflationary measures were then implemented which checked economic growth. A pattern of post-war mini-cycles emerged from the tug of war between the objective of a high level of employment and the need to maintain external balance.

The 1950s and 1960s were very much the high watermark of the Keynesian approach to fiscal policy which came in to replace the system of war-time controls. Fiscal stance was a matter of government discretion but with an aim that fiscal instruments should be used to stabilise the economy. Policy was generally carried out by varying tax rates in the economy rather than by changes in public expenditure as advocated by Keynes in the interwar period. Cloyne (2013) provides an extremely useful taxonomy of tax changes over the post-WW2 period using a narrative approach pioneered by Romer and Romer (1989). The conventional wisdom is that there were expansionary budgets in 1955, 1959 and 1964, which were aimed to stimulate the economy and may have had some political motivation. But Cloyne (2013) notes that some tax changes were also made for the explicit purposes of improving the supply side of the economy such as Chancellor Peter Thorneycroft's tax cuts in 1957 and 1958. The use of tax cuts to improve the supply side would become an increasingly important issue during the 1970s and 1980s.

Monetary policy, as an active tool, was generally subordinated to fiscal policy over this period. But signing up to the Bretton Woods system of fixed exchange rates provided both a nominal anchor and also presented an external constraint on the full employment ambitions of successive governments. Following WW2, the government's control over monetary policy was rubber stamped when the Bank of England was nationalised in 1946. The Bank was now an officially an agent of government although it retained operational responsibilities. This was reflected in the ubiquitous use of the word "authorities" when referring to monetary and financial policy. In effect the authorities represented a tripartite relationship between the Bank, the Treasury and the Government. This was particularly so in the late 1940s and early 1950s during the debates about how post-war monetary and exchange rate policy should be conducted and the return to full convertibility of sterling. Sometimes the Treasury and the Bank would align to try and force a change in Government policy (e.g. in the early 1950s and the ROBOT scheme that would have meant in effect a floating exchange rate rather than joining Bretton Woods). At other times the Treasury and the Government were aligned against the Bank, such as in the mid-1950s when they were unhappy with the failure of monetary policy to rein in the Butler mini-boom of the early 1950s. That ultimately led to the appointment of the Radcliffe Committee to examine the workings of the monetary system. Discussions took place over the 1957–1959 period.

The Radcliffe Committee concluded that monetary policy should be concerned with the overall level of "liquidity" in the economy and that direct control of the quantity of credit and money should supplement control via interest rates. That tendency towards direct monetary controls had already started but was rubber stamped by Radcliffe. In particular, it recommended the use of Special Deposits, which were assets the banks would be required to held with the Bank of England but would not count towards their liquid asset ratios. These were supplemented by controls on hire purchase finance companies which were important in funding consumer durable purchases. Aikman et al. (2016) have recently examined the impact of direct controls and created an index summarising the different measures employed (see Chart 6.67).

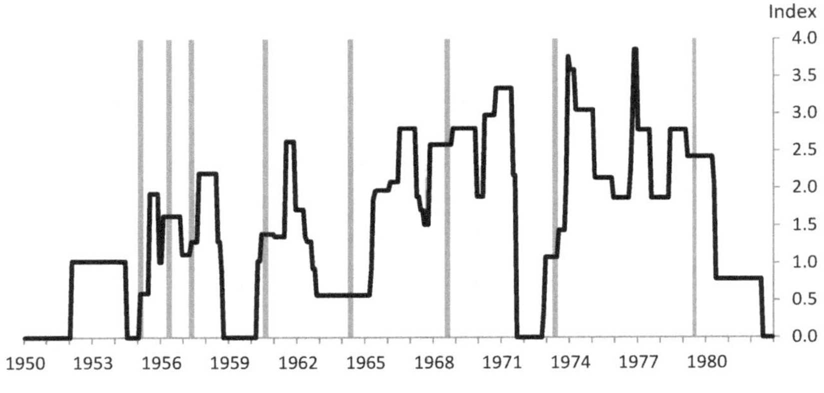

Chart 6.67 Aikman, Bush and Taylor—credit policy index and cyclical peaks (*Source* Aikman et al. 2016)

These were generally implemented at cyclical peaks in order to rein in consumer demand and improve the balance of payments.

Overall the monetary, credit and fiscal policy framework of the 1950s and 1960s had important implications for the nature of economic fluctuations over this period. Typically in the go-stop cycle, the "go" phase would be associated with a deterioration of the current balance of the balance of payments, which was then corrected during the subsequent recession. This pattern emerges strongly during cycles before 1967. It was characterised by a buoyancy of domestic demand during the upturn, and notably expenditure on consumer durables which were becoming ever more available in the post-war period and could be financed on hire purchase. This led to expenditure rising faster than the economy's productive potential, giving rise to higher imports and a deficit in the current account. Corrective monetary, credit and fiscal policies then pushed the economy into recession, consumer credit and imports would fall and the balance of payments would improve Chart 6.68.

This pattern differed from that observed before 1914 when the current account of the balance of payments was typically strong during the upswing because it was driven by the strong growth of exports combined with a higher level of overseas lending. In a recession, the balance of payments surplus declined with lower overseas lending and a check to the growth of exports. It was also different to the interwar period when recoveries were interrupted by external shocks which checked the growth

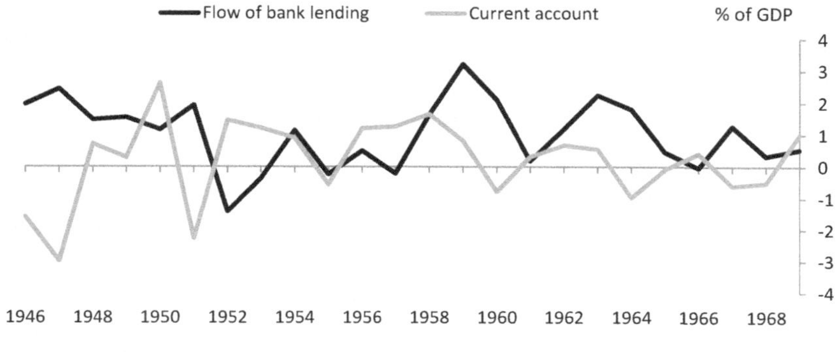

Chart 6.68 Current account deficits and bank lending (*Source* Thomas and Dimsdale 2017)

of exports as in 1921 and 1931. It was not the growth of imports that caused balance of payments problems unlike the the post-war period.

Balance of payments problems in the 1950s and 1960s were naturally aggravated by the adherence to a fixed exchange rate despite two devaluations in 1949 and 1967. Defence of the exchange rate forced the authorities to introduce restrictive policies which were necessary to correct the balance of payment deficit. Fiscal policy would tighten and credit controls and monetary policy were used to rein in the boom. Bank Rate was used relatively sparingly as an instrument particularly to avoid causing unhelpful movements in sterling away from parity. Typically the Bank of England would be asked to put pressure on the banks—"moral suasion"—to ration credit directly and cut back on their lending.

The key issue is whether demand management policies ended up stabilising or destablising the economy in practice. Originally Dow (1964) argued that government spending and taxes exacerbated rather than stabilised cyclical fluctuations due to the sluggish nature of fiscal policy responses and their lagged effect on the economy. In his 1998 book Dow (1998), he changes tack and prefers the interpretation that governments were simply too optimistic about supply potential and just overheated the economy beyond its limits. UK governments could see the growth rates being achieved by their competitors and were using fiscal policy to try to "force-feed" the economy with demand growth to try and achieve them. One argument underlying this was Verdoorn's law popularised by Kaldor (1966). This was based on the idea that rapid demand and output growth would cause economies of scale in manufacturing and improved productivity growth rather than high inflation.

Matthews' (1971) view is that the authorities just alternated myopically in their policy measures between concern about unemployment during slumps and the balance of payments during booms, without prejudging the issue of whether policy was the only factor generating fluctuations. The close connection between the post-war cycles and economic policy is also emphasised by Hicks (1982), who points to the role of economic policy at the key turning points of the post-war cycle. Another explanation for the stop-go cycle is the idea of the political business cycle. Politicians of the day would simply expand the economy just before an election in order to win popularity only to deflate the economy once the election was won and out of the way.

Whatever the reasons for the stop-go cycle the results were the same. Any attempt to stimulate the economy was thwarted by the balance of payments and the need to maintain the exchange rate. Governments would attempt to expand the economy through fiscal policy, inflation would pick up and the balance of payments would worsen.

In general, all components of demand contributed to the economic cycle during the 1950s and 1960s. Recoveries tended to be led by strong home demand—particularly through spending on consumer durables and an associated fall in the saving rate—with exports only tending to make a major contribution after exchange rate depreciations (Charts 6.69, 6.70).

Exports did not play such a leading role in initiating recovery or in pushing the economy into recession as in many of the cycles before 1938. Export growth was fairly well sustained during years of recession on account of the strong upward trend in world trade during the 1950s and 1960s. Investment showed less cyclical variation than in pre-1938 cycles and continued to grow in recessions, partly as a result of firms' belief that checks to the growth of output would be short-lived on account of the

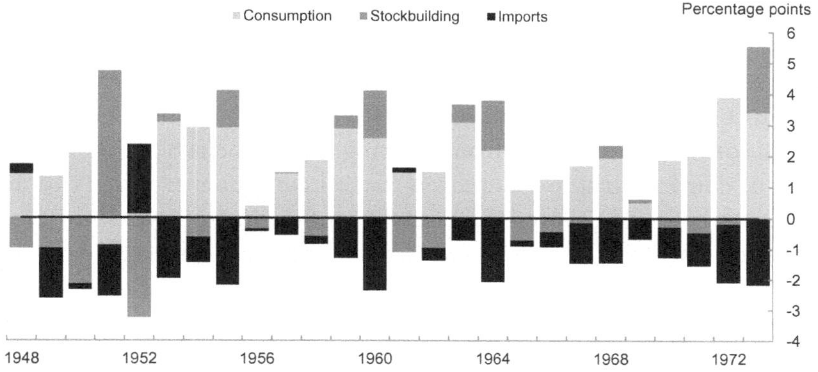

Chart 6.69 Contributions to GDP—endogenous components (*Source* Thomas and Dimsdale 2017)

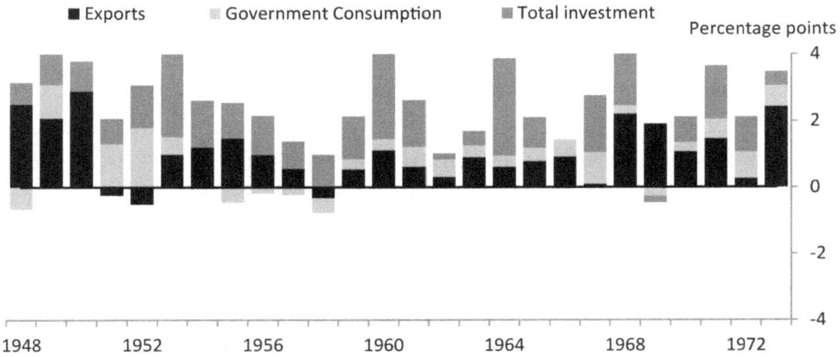

Chart 6.70 Contributions to GDP—driver components (*Source* Thomas and Dimsdale 2017)

vigorous growth of the world economy and the government's commitment to pursue full employment as a policy objective. Although it should be noted that the behaviour of government expenditure on goods and services does not immediately suggest an active countercyclical policy.

One major difference in the immediate post-war cycles from those before WW2 was the more active role of consumer spending. As noted earlier, increases in consumers' expenditure tended to lead the upturn from the recession on account of the larger role of expenditure on consumer durables. Expenditure on durables tended to fall away before the peak of the cycle, while fixed investment was strong near the upper turning point. Stockbuilding also varied widely over the post-war cycle, but comparison with pre-1938 behaviour is rather speculative on account of the poor quality of data on inventories in earlier periods. The conclusion which emerges from looking at the behaviour of components of demand in stop-go cycles is that all components varied over the cycle and there was no predominant element during the cycle.

During the first three post-war cycles, prices, as measured by the GDP deflator, rose as much in the downward phase of the cycle as in the upward phase and this applied also to cycles between 1967 and 1975. This outcome contrasts with the generally pro-cyclical movement of prices before 1938 and can be explained by the relatively steady rate of increase of money wages over the cycle combined with a check to productivity growth in recessions. Costs and prices tended to rise faster at the cyclical peak and in the downturn than during the upturn, when there was a strong rise in productivity. The countercyclical movement of prices tended to dampen post-war fluctuations in nominal income. There was also a noticeable lag of unemployment behind other variables over the cycle and smaller variations in employment than in previous cycles. Labour hoarding in recessions was characteristic of stop-go cycles and helps to explain the check to productivity in the downturn.

6.5.2 The After-Effects of WW2 and the "Go-Stop" Cycles in the 1950s and 1960s

In this secton we present a more detailed analysis of each cycle. The go-stop nature of cycles with see-sawing expansions and contractions is clear. As in previous wars, the end of conflict in 1945 brought a sharp slowdown in growth as government spending was reduced. In fact the annual data suggests wartime peak in production appears to have occurred in 1943 in preparation for the invasions of Southern and Western Europe in 1943 and 1944. The post-war trough appears to have occurred in around 1947–1948 as in Chart 6.71.

The recovery from the trough started with a revival in exports in part due to the expansion of world trade and was given added impetus by sterling's devaluation in 1949. The British economy was able to make a relatively smooth adjustment at the end of WW2, since the lessons arising from the end of WW1 had been thoroughly learned. As a result, there was no repeat of the severe boom and bust of 1919–1920. Thanks to reliance on physical controls combined with fiscal policy, the economy expanded from 1948 to 1950 with no sign of recession. In 1951 growth was disturbed by the impact of the Korean War which caused a sharp rise in commodity prices and a deterioration of the terms of trade. There was a balance of payments crisis and in November Bank Rate was reactivated as a policy tool and raised from 2 to 2.5%, which was the first peacetime increase since the introduction of the

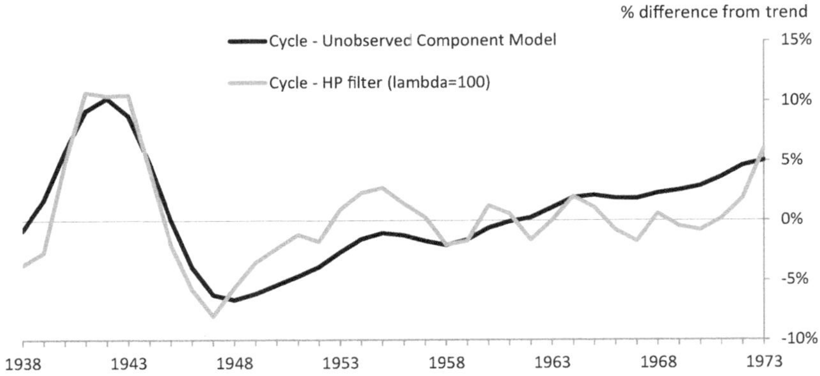

Chart 6.71 Cycles—annual basis 1938–1973 (*Source* Chapter 5)

Cheap Money Policy in 1932.[2] In March 1952 there was a further rise in Bank Rate to 4%, which was intended to curb inflationary pressures.

The movement of the economy into a mild recession in 1952, combined with an improvement in the balance of payments and reduction in inflation, was attributed by the Conservative government to the tightening of monetary policy. As demand pressures eased, market rates of interest declined and Bank Rate was reduced to 3.5% in September 1953 and 3% in May 1954. In March 1952 controls on hire purchase had been introduced and these were withdrawn in July 1954. This resulted in an upsurge in spending on consumer durables. The economy recovered vigorously as the increase in spending of consumer durables was followed by a boom in fixed investment. Bank advances to the personal and company sectors rose rapidly to which the Bank responded by raising Bank Rate in two stages to 4.5% in February 1955 and hire purchase (HP) controls were reintroduced to check the growth of demand. Two rises in Bank Rate in early 1955 did not prevent sales of gilts by the banks to facilitate an expansion in their advances. Demand continued to rise leading a to a balance of payments crisis in the autumn of 1955 as the current account moved into deficit.

[2]Bank Rate was increased temporarily to 4% just before the outbreak of World War 2.

In the general election held in May 1955 the Conservatives were re-elected, but the tax cuts introduced in the March 1955 Budget were substantially reversed in the Autumn Budget. In raising taxes in his second Budget, Chancellor Butler recognised that his expectations of the impact of monetary policy at the time of the March Budget had been excessive. Bank advances continued to rise in the summer of 1955. The Treasury argued for more pressure being put on the banks to restrict the growth of credit, while the Bank argued the case for tighter fiscal policy. Delay in securing agreement on this issue aggravated the exchange rate crisis in the autumn of 1955. The over-optimism of Butler's policies led to his replacement as Chancellor by Macmillan. Discussions between the Treasury and the Bank resulted in the introduction of a package of restrictive measures in February 1956, when the new Chancellor announced a rise in Bank rate of 1pp to 5.5% combined with a tightening of HP restrictions. Fiscal policy was also tightened by a reduction in investment incentives and cuts in public investment.

The easing of external pressures allowed Bank Rate to be reduced to 5% in February 1957. Such a relaxation in monetary policy proved to be premature in the face of a major crisis of confidence in sterling in the autumn of 1957. Pressure on the pound arose from a devaluation of the French franc in August 1957 and general expectations of an appreciation of the Deutsche Mark and a possible fall in sterling. There was therefore a decline in the reserves on account of short-term capital movements, since the current account was in surplus in the autumn of 1957. Bank Rate was raised by a full 2 percentage points to 7%. Although the crisis arose in the foreign exchange market, the major concern in the market was about the lack of resolution of the government in the face of powerful wage demands. Even though inflation was below 4%, there were fears that it would rise in the event of wage concessions to organised labour.

Chancellor Thorneycroft who had succeeded Macmillan argued that inflation should be checked by tight control over the money supply. The rise in Bank Rate to 7% was accompanied by a requirement that banks should hold their advances at the average level of the proceeding twelve months and HP restrictions were tightened.

The economy moved into recession in 1958, while a worldwide decline in commodity prices moderated the rate of inflation. In retrospect, the fears of inflation and overheating which had dominated the policy discussions in the second half of 1957 were largely misconceived. Under the new Chancellor, Derick Heathcoat-Amory, Bank Rate was reduced from 7 to 6% in March 1958, followed by a series of four reductions of ½ to 4% in November. In July 1958 restraints on bank advances were relaxed, following a two year period of controls since 1956.

Special Deposits were introduced in 1958. They were the result of extensive discussions on the need for a variable liquidity ratio. It was intended that Special Deposits should provide a way of discouraging banks from engaging in excessive expansion of advances and would reduce the need for official ceilings on bank lending. Banks were free to increase lending for the first time since WW2. There was a similar relaxation of higher purchase controls, when all restrictions were suspended in October 1958. They had been enforced continuously with varying terms from 1952 apart of a seven month period of suspension in 1954–1955. Relaxation of monetary controls was accompanied by an expansionary Budget in April 1959, which included measures to stimulate consumers' expenditure and investment.

The results of these expansionary measures was a rapid recovery of economic activity and a fall in unemployment. In the first half of 1960 it was becoming increasingly apparent that restrictive measures were needed, Bank Rate was therefore raised by 1pp to 5% and there was a first call for Special Deposits in April 1960. A second call for Special Deposits was made in June 1960, when Bank Rate was raised further to 6%. Fiscal policy had not been tightened in the 1960 Budget so the burden of restraining the boom fell on monetary measures.

The use of Special Deposits to check the rise was only partially successful. Advances grew less vigorously in 1961 than in the two previous years, but there was a tendency for banks to react to a call for Special Deposits by selling investments rather than reducing advances.

The authorities had not expected this reaction from the banks, but they were willing to see a fall in the price of gilts, since a rise in long-term interest rates would exert downward pressure on demand.

During the vigorous recovery from the recession of 1958 Bank Rate was raised to 6% in June 1960 which was followed by two reductions to 5% in December 1960. However pressures on sterling forced the Bank to raise Bank Rate to 7% in July 1961 which was accompanied by renewed restrictions on bank lending and a call for Special Deposits. This would become known as the "Selwyn Lloyd Squeeze" named after the Chancellor who would lose his job soon after in "the night of the long knives" when Harold Macmillan sacked a third of his cabinet. Following the restoration of confidence in sterling, there was a gradual reduction in Bank Rate to 4% in January 1963. Lending restrictions were lifted when it was clear that the economy was moving into recession and lending was encouraged by a reduction in the liquidity ratio from 30 to 28% in May 1963.

The economy stagnated in 1962, but revived strongly in 1963 and 1964, when there was a rapid expansion of bank lending. Fiscal policy was relaxed both before and in the 1964 Budget as a result of Chancellor Maudling's "Dash for Growth" policy which aspired to meet a growth target of 5% for real GDP. The recovery in the economy led to growing fears about the state of the balance of payments which prompted a rise in Bank Rate to 5% in February 1964. However despite growing evidence of overheating, no further action was taken in the run up to the October election in which the Conservative government was defeated leaving a difficult legacy for the incoming government.[3]

6.5.3 Devaluation and Deflation in the Late 1960s

The incoming Labour administration faced a severe balance of payments deficit and a high level of domestic demand. There was a re-introduction of restrictions on lending in May 1965. The regulations were stated in quantitative form and froze lending at 105% of the current level for the next twelve months and were to apply to all banks

[3]On arriving at the Treasury to take over as the Chancellor, Jim Callaghan passed Reggie Maudling on the stairs who said to Callaghan "Sorry to leave things in such a mess old cock" on his way out.

and to the larger finance houses. The ceiling applied to holdings of commercial bills as well as to bank lending. Bank Rate was temporary reduced to 6% in June 1965, but the continuing weakness of sterling forced a rise to 7% in July 1966, which was accompanied by a tightening of lending ceilings and HP restrictions combined with reduction in public spending. Some relaxation occurred in the first part of 1967 as Bank Rate came down to 5.5% in May following three reduction of ½%. There were also some relaxations of lending restrictions on the banks.

Renewed pressure on sterling, culminating in the devaluation crisis of November 1967 forced a rise in Bank Rate to 8% and re-imposition of lending ceilings. Bank Rate was maintained within a narrow range of 7–8% from November 1967 until April 1970. Lending ceilings were in continuous operation during the period. The need to correct the balance of payments deficit following the devaluation of sterling by 14.3% from $2.8 to $2.40 in November 1967 gave little scope for the relaxation of either interest rates or credit controls. It was only after the turnaround of the current account in 1970 that interest rates could be brought down and credit ceilings be relaxed. Bank Rate was reduced from 8 to 7.5% in March 1970 with a further three reductions to 5% in September 1971. Credit restrictions were relaxed in April 1971, having been in continuous operation since 1965.

Fiscal policy also presented a challenge following the devaluation of sterling in 1967. Devaluation had been preceded by balance of payments deficits since 1964 under the Wilson government. It was felt that contraction of fiscal policy was necessary to make way for the expansion of exports without causing inflationary pressure. The correction of the balance of payments following devaluation proved to be a slow process and was achieved by Chancellor Jenkins with some assistance from the IMF. He also sought to negotiate drawing rights from the IMF to support sterling. His Letter of Intent stated that the growth of the money supply in 1968 would be limited to its estimated rate of growth in 1967. There were discussions with the IMF about Domestic Credit Expansion (DCE)—a measure of the money supply adjusted for the balance of payments which was viewed as useful for assessing the monetary policy stance in a fixed exchange rate system. In his Second Letter of Intent of

May 1969, the Chancellor set a target for the growth of DCE of £400 million for 1969–1970. The implementation of the targets agreed with the IMF led to a sharp fiscal contraction which turned the Public Sector Borrowing Requirement (PSBR) of around 4.5% of GDP in 1967 into a surplus of around 1% of GDP in 1969.

Fiscal contraction was associated with a decline in the rate of growth of sterling M3 from around 10% in 1967 to 1.7% in 1969, while the current account moved from a deficit to surplus. In his Budget statement in April 1970 Chancellor Jenkins reported that DCE had turned out to be negative in 1969–1970 because of the swing of the current account into surplus. In April 1971 when the external position had been greatly strengthened, the Chancellor did not set a target for DCE and the concept was not revived until November 1976, when there was a renewed application for assistance from the IMF.

The cycle from 1967 to 1971 was distorted by the devaluation in November 1967 and by the restrictive measures taken to make the devaluation effective in the budgets of 1969 and 1970. The recovery from 1967 to 1969 was unusually weak and the recession which followed from 1969 to 1971 was marked by a rise in the rate of inflation and slow growth of output.

6.6 The Liberalised Economy 1971–2018

6.6.1 Overview—Institutional Factors and Key Drivers

Cyclical fluctuations asserted themselves more strongly from the 1970s onwards. The cycles of 1971–1975, 1975–1981 and 1981–1992 differed from the go-stop cycles which preceded them in the 1950s and 1960s. During slowdowns, the level of output declined and not merely its rate of growth. That reflected an increased incidence of large shocks, primarily to the supply side of the economy and world commodity prices. The increase in oil prices in the early 1970s came as a bolt from the blue against a background of an exceptionally high level of activity in the world economy, combined with a sharp rise in non-oil commodity prices. It also came at a time when the post-war monetary order based on the Bretton Woods gold standard was unravelling. Money and credit growth also both picked up in the early 1970s and 1980s as a result of moves towards financial liberalisation. As a result inflation was substantially higher over the 1970s, reaching well into double digits, and unemployment followed an upward trend leading to the use of the terms "Great Inflation" and "Stagflation" to describe this period. The early 1980s then ushered in a period of disinflation as successive Conservative governments attempted to bring down price inflation through various attempts at providing a new a nominal anchor for the economy. This led initially to a recession from 1979 until 1981. But it took until 1992 to squeeze inflation out of the system. The stilted recovery of the early 1980s turned into a boom in the late-1980s from an internally driven rise in domestic demand, which was stimulated by financial deregulation and a surge in asset prices. A further recession followed in the early 1990s once policy was tightened to deal with the building inflationary pressure. The early 1990s recession was followed by a period of sustained growth until the early 2000s, which was unparalleled in British macroeconomic history. The long period of steady growth, known alternatively as the "Great Stability", "the Great Moderation" and the "Long Expansion" was then severely interrupted by a major international financial crisis in 2007, leading to a severe contraction known as the Great Recession (Chart 6.72). In this section, we

Chart 6.72 Growth cycles 1973–2018 (*Source* Chapter 5)

discuss some of the key institutional changes over this period and how they affected the nature of economic fluctuations. Then, as in previous sections, we turn to a more detailed narrative of each of the cycles. Here we draw on previous accounts by Britton (1991) and Dimsdale (1991).

The years 1971–1972 in many ways mark a watershed in UK economic history. This is true across several dimensions.

First, it saw the introduction of Competition and Credit Control (CCC) in 1971, the first step in a rocky road to full financial liberalisation in the 1980s and 1990s (see Goodhart 1986, 2015). The apparatus of direct controls on money and credit was dismantled and the banking and building society cartels began to break up. Controls were reintroduced at various points in the 1970s such as via the supplementary special deposits scheme or "Corset" as it would become known.[4] But overall the emphasis switched irrevocably towards using interest rates to manage the economy and allowing banks and building societies to determine the amount of credit and money conditional on a given monetary policy stance. After the election of Mrs. Thatcher, financial liberalisation proceeded at an increased pace. Foreign exchange controls were removed in 1979 and the mid-1980s saw the Big Bang which introduced fundamental reforms to the stock exchange. The financial system became steadily de-compartmentalised and led to the break up of the banking and building society cartels. At the start of the 1980s controls on banks' balance sheets were relaxed allowing them to compete more effectively in the mortgage market. This broke down the traditional segmentation in the market. Mortgage rationing by the building societies is generally thought to have ended in the early 1980s. And they began to offer interest-bearing transactions accounts and entered wholesale funding markets in 1983, once they were allowed to pay interest gross rather than net of tax. However, building societies still found themselves at a competitive disadvantage to the banks, which could offer a wider variety of services. As a result the government decided to level the playing field and introduced the Building Societies Act in 1986, which freed the last constraints on societies from offering the whole range of products and services provided by banks. As a result of

[4]The Corset was a scheme to penalise banks whose interest-bearing eligible liabilities, essentially their interest-bearing sterling deposits, grew faster than a prescribed rate. See Bank of England (1982).

this banks entered the mortgage business and building societies became more like banks. Beginning in 1989 with Abbey National there was then a wave of demutualisations where building societies turned themselves into banks, and the banking system became the predominant provider of mortgages. The other development in the 1990s and early 2000s was the securitisation of mortgages where banks and were able to pool and package up mortgages and move them off-balance sheet to special purpose vehicles (SPVs) who would then issue securities to investors that were linked to the underlying mortgage repayments (Chart 6.73).

The second major change was the emergence of large global commodity price shocks which, after 1973, would have major effects on the supply side of the economy given they implied large adjustments in real wages which workers might potentially resist or take time to adjust to. The 1970s were associated with two large oil price increases in 1973/4 and 1979 which was then followed by a large oil price fall in the mid-1980s (see Chart 6.74). This presented trade-offs to policymakers that they, and the public at large, had not been used to dealing with in the 1950s and 1960s when living standards had generally improved and inflationary pressures had generally been benign or held in check by the fixed exchange rate system. Oil prices then began to pick up in the early 2000s and there were several large swings. The discovery of North Sea oil meant that the UK turned from a net oil importer in the early 1970s to a substantial net exporter by the mid-1980s, returning to being a net

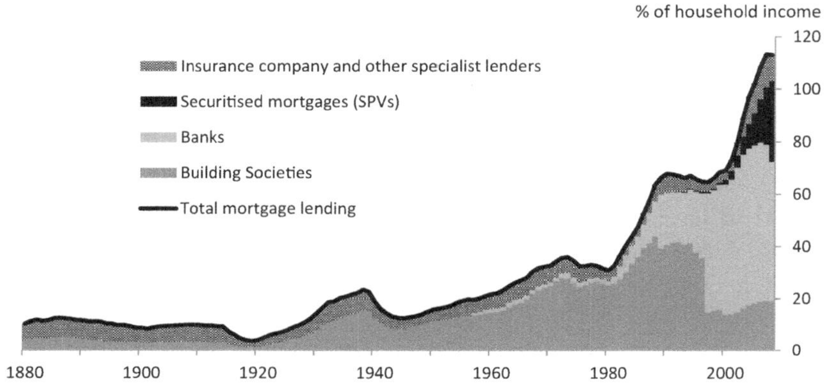

Chart 6.73 Mortgage providers 1880–2008 (*Source* Thomas and Dimsdale 2017)

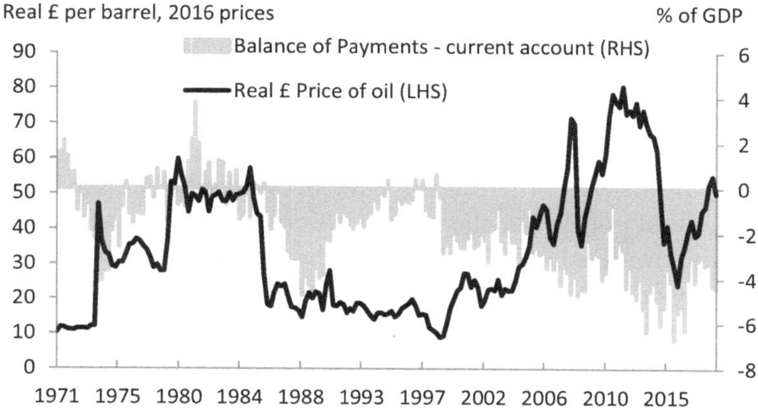

Chart 6.74 Oil prices and the current account 1971–2018 (*Source* Thomas and Dimsdale 2017)

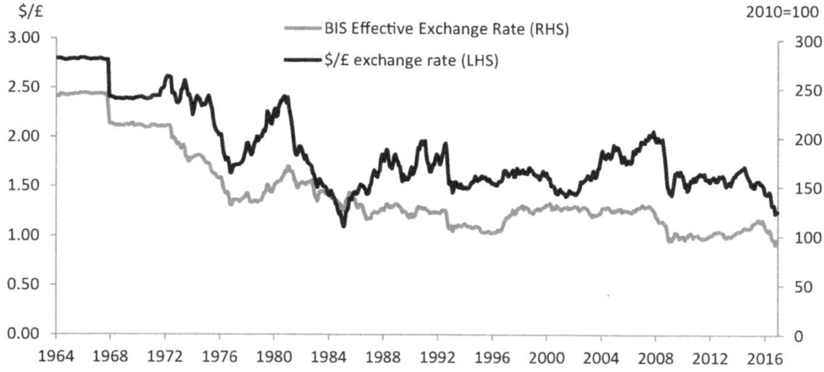

Chart 6.75 Exchange rates 1963–2016 (*Source* Thomas and Dimsdale 2017, BIS)

importer by the mid 2000s as fields were exploited and production fell off. That meant oil price shocks at different points in time would have different implications for the UK economy.

The third major paradigm shift was the collapse of Bretton Woods in 1971 which ushered in a period when the UK largely operated with floating exchange rates. Movements in the exchange rate after this point were often large and provided many challenges to policy makers (Chart 6.75). The subsequent search for an adequate nominal anchor to replace the Bretton Woods system took twenty years, and indeed some might argue the UK was on a managed float for much of the period up to 1992 despite the authorities' dalliance with monetary targeting during that period. From the late 1960s monetarist thinking had begun to influence policymaking circles. Monetary targets were insisted upon by the IMF in 1976 in return for assistance which *de facto* made them part of official policy. But the Labour government viewed these as necessary window dressing for assistance rather than any belief in the benefits of monetary targets. And the Bank itself took an eclectic approach to the use of monetary targets. Needham (2014) shows the Bank had experimented with unpublished monetary targets in the early 1970s but the introduction of Competition and Credit Control had fundamentally changed the relationship between money and nominal spending on which those targets had been based. As a result the Bank did not embrace all aspects of monetarism, particularly operational aspects such as monetary base control (Capie 2011).

Monetary targets did not explicitly form the centrepiece of counter-inflationary policy until the introduction of the Medium Term Financial Strategy (MTFS) by the Conservative Government following its election in 1979. Initially, the Conservative government retained the Labour government's use of one-year monetary targets, and ceased to employ an incomes policy. But the MTFS began to set medium-term intermediate targets for broad money growth, based on the £M3 measure, as the keystone of its counter-inflationary policy. Fiscal policy was now viewed as subordinate but supportive of monetary policy rather than vice versa. For example, control of government borrowing and the extent to which it was funded from the non-bank private sector were seen as key planks in the control of broad money (£M3) which was the chief monetary target of interest. This was a result of the use of the credit counterparts approach to the supply of money.[5]

At the same time, monetary targets were introduced the Conservative government revived the financial liberalisation that had been attempted

[5]See Goodhart and Needham (2017) for a discussion of why the British monetary authorities have traditionally focused on broader monetary aggregates and the use of the credit counterparts approach.

with CCC in 1971. Similar to the 1970s, this had the unfortunate side effect that monetary targets (which had been calibrated on data when controls had been in place) were missed and this undermined the credibility of counter-inflationary policy despite the fact that inflation was successfully brought down. As the 1980s wore on Nigel Lawson, as Chancellor, began to shift away from broad money targets, first by switching to narrower targets and then by looking for other alternatives as a nominal anchor.

In 1988 the Chancellor began to moot the idea of central bank independence. This rested on an intellectual case (e.g. Barro and Gordon [1983], Rogoff [1985] building on Kydland and Prescott [1977]) that independent central banks could offset the inherent inflation bias when governments would target a level of output or unemployment beyond what was feasible (i.e. below the natural rate). But it was also based on the evidence of the proven counter-inflationary records of the Bundesbank, Swiss National Bank and the Federal Reserve under Paul Volcker. But Lawson failed to persuade Mrs Thatcher who worried about the democratic accountability of central bank independence.

As an intermediate step Lawson attempted to import credibility by shadowing the Deutschmark in the late 1980s with a longer term aim of joining the Exchange Rate Mechanism (ERM) and moving towards central bank independence as part of a prospective European monetary union. But this brought up the age-old problem of a fixed rate regime. It could imply keeping interest rates at a level inconsistent with the domestic economy if the UK and German economies were out of synch. This was true in the late 1980s as the government had inadvertently stoked up a credit-driven boom, following a substantial loosening of policy following the stock market crash in 1987. Shadowing the Deutschmark was argued to have kept interest rates lower than they otherwise would have been. Lawson was forced to abandon this policy following intellectual opposition from Mrs Thatcher (and her adviser Sir Alan Walters) and the need to raise rates to counter a pick up inflation. This tightening of policy ultimately led to the early 1990s recession.

Following Lawson's resignation in late 1989, John Major became Chancellor and he pushed through full ERM membership in October 1990. Initially this allowed interest rates to fall a little in a bid to stem the recession, but ultimately pressure soon built up on sterling (which was viewed by many as overvalued as in the return to gold in 1925) and interest rates remained in double digits to defend sterling despite the ongoing recession. In September 1992 the UK was forced to suspend its membership of the ERM when ongoing speculation put enormous pressure on sterling and at one point during the day had forced the government to raise interest rates to 15%.

Following ERM exit, the government and the Bank now had to find a new nominal anchor and fast. Various intermediate targets had failed and there was an intellectual shift towards directly targeting the goal of monetary policy—inflation. The Reserve Bank of New Zealand (RBNZ) had moved to inflation targeting in 1989/1990 and this was soon adopted by Canada in 1991. This appeared to provide a ready-made solution for the UK and under Bank advice was adopted.

As part of this, the Bank's advisory role was enhanced and made more transparent as a disciplining device and pointed towards a move to central bank independence. It was committed to produce a Quarterly Inflation Report in which it would give its view on inflationary prospects. The Governor and Chancellor would meet monthly (the' Ken and Eddie' show as it became known) where the Governor would give the Bank's advice on policy (formalised in the monthly "Burns letter") and the minutes of those meetings would be published. The initial results of the new framework were very promising as the economy began to recover and inflation began to settle to around its new target of 2.5% based on the RPIX index of prices.

The incoming Labour government in 1997 surprised everyone by announcing operational independence for the Bank as one of its first acts. Government would still set the goal for monetary policy—the inflation target—but the setting of policy would be now be undertaken by a Monetary Policy Committee consisting of both internal and external members, each individually accountable to parliament for their vote. Major breaches of the target would oblige the Governor to write a letter to the Chancellor explaining how the MPC would attempt to bring inflation back to target. But the remit for monetary policy also allowed for a degree of "constrained discretion" by instructing the MPC to support the Government's economic policy, including its objectives for growth and employment. In general, the period after the introduction of inflation targeting ushered in a period of relative stability for the UK with, at the most, a modest growth cycle apparent in the data. This period became known as the Great Moderation. This may have been good luck with the absence of the large oil price shocks seen in the 1970s and 1980s but is likely to have been helped by improved policy performance under inflation targeting and the introduction of the MPC. However, it is true that even after the introduction of inflation targeting in 1992 large movements in sterling would continue to dominate the attention of the MPC given the policy trade-offs they implied. The Great Stability period came to an end with the financial crisis of 2007 that led to the largest recession since the Great Depression.

The shift of focus towards monetary policy from the mid-1970s onwards also had profound implications for fiscal policy. In the early 1970s, fiscal policy was still used for demand management. However, the failure of the Labour government to control inflation in the 1970s while unemployment rose inevitably led to the abandonment of the post-war Keynesian consensus. The emphasis placed on monetary policy by the Thatcher government meant that fiscal policy at best played a supporting role, as noted earlier. Under the Medium Term Financial Strategy (MTFS), the achievement of monetary targets was viewed through a credit counterparts approach where public sector deficits and the degree to which it was funded from the non-bank sector could be used to influence broad money growth. In the mid-1980s, for example, the government decided to "overfund" the deficit by selling more gilts to the non-bank private sector than was necessary to fund the deficit which in itself pushed down on broad money growth in a bid to reclaw some of the overshoot of the £M3 target. There was also a renewed emphasis by the Thatcher government on the supply-side benefits of lower direct taxes on incomes and profits. As a result there was a shift between indirect and direct taxation, initiated by an immediate rise in Value Added Tax (VAT) from 8% to 15% in 1979, followed by series of cuts in direct taxation. The basic rate of income tax was reduced from 30% in 1983 to 25% in 1988 while the top rate of tax also came down from 60% to 40%. Under the Labour government in 1997 there was a further shift to explicit fiscal rules which were brought in to manage the current deficit over the cycle, but also to support public sector investment and ensure sustainability of

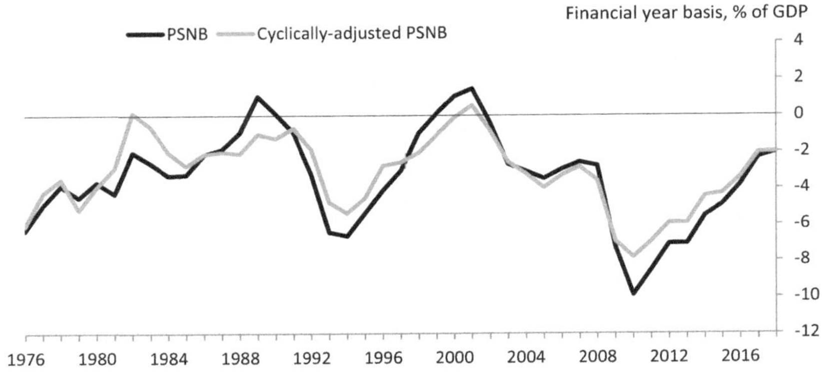

Chart 6.76 Public sector net borrowing (*Source* Office for Budget Responsibility, Public Sector Finances Databank)

the public sector debt. Overall, this meant that fiscal policy played less of an explicit role in demand management after 1979 but it did not mean shifts in fiscal policy played no role in cycles. There were significant fiscal tightenings in the early 1980s and late 1990s and loosenings in the mid-1980s, early 1990s and early 2000s (Chart 6.76). Following the Great Financial Crisis however, there was a period where fiscal policy was used to try and mitigate the effect of the crisis on GDP with a temporary cut in VAT. But the incoming coalition government in 2010 then embarked on a programme of cutting the deficit with a plan to ensure the ultimate stabilisation of public sector debt which peaked at around 85% of GDP in 2016/17.

6.6.2 The Great Inflation and a Search for a Nominal Anchor 1971–1992

As in previous sections we now consider each cycle in more detail. In 1971, growing unemployment led the Heath government, which had succeeded the previous Labour administration in 1970, to relax its restrictive policies. The basic rate of income tax was reduced in 1971 but this did not reverse the downturn, and unemployment rose to more than

1 million in 1972. Chancellor Anthony Barber then adopted a more expansionary fiscal stance to reduce the level of unemployment. In the March 1972 budget he introduced tax cuts and increased public expenditure with an aim of achieving a rate of growth of GDP of 5% per annum, which was barely sustainable even if, after the floating of sterling in June 1972, any weakness in the trade balance would now just cause a depreciation in sterling rather than causing a "go-stop" balance of payments crisis. There was a strong recovery in domestic demand as a result of these measures. Public Sector Borrowing increased to 6% of GDP, which was larger than the deficits of the 1950s and 1960s which had generally averaged 2–3% of GDP. The loosening of fiscal policy coincided with an international boom and a severe shock from the first major oil price increase in 1973/4. The government had also entered into threshold wage agreements with the Trade Unions which locked in real wage rigidity at the worst possible time and ensured wage settlements would rise with prices. "Stage 3" of the Heath Government's pay policy was designed to limit wage increases to £2.25 a head or 7% (whichever was greater) but it also contained provisions for extra "threshold payments" which would be triggered once the Retail Price Index (RPI) rose 7% above the level at the start of the policy. Heath announced this policy on 3rd October. Literally, a fortnight later Arab oil producers would cut oil production by 5% following the start of the Yom Kippur war, prompting the surge in oil prices and ensured the thresholds would be triggered.

The result of these developments was a vigorous recovery in 1971–1973 which became known as the "Barber Boom" with strong growth in both consumers' expenditure and exports. Monetary policy was expansionary with M3 rising by 56% between 1971 and 1973 as the banking system responded to the new monetary arrangements under Competition and Credit Control and property prices increased as borrowing expanded. Imports also grew more rapidly than exports and the current account of the balance of payments swung from a surplus of 1.6% of GDP in 1971 to a deficit of about the same size in 1973. And, as noted, sterling was floated in June 1972 and started to depreciate as the domestic boom gathered pace.

The Barber boom of 1973 was checked by the quadrupling of oil prices in 1973/4, which raised inflation and reduced output given the stance of monetary and fiscal policy. The triggering of the Stage 3 threshold payments meant that the required adjustment in real consumption wages to the oil price shock was inhibited and pushed up the natural rate of unemployment, at least in the short run. Private domestic expenditure declined in the face of higher interest rates, the upsurge in import prices and the squeeze in real incomes, but some cushioning was provided by higher public expenditure and the continued growth of exports despite the ending of the world boom of the early 1970s. During the recession of 1973–1975 GDP declined by 3.7%, the GDP deflator rose by almost 50% and import prices rose steeply as sterling depreciated. Monetary growth slowed from the peak rates recorded in the preceding recovery, but the stability of the financial system was threatened by a crisis among secondary banks, that were exposed to the bursting of the property price bubble in 1974 and which was averted by the timely intervention of the Bank. This episode naturally invites comparison with previous financial crises such as the Barings in 1890 which was saved by a similar 'lifeboat' operation.

Policymakers responded to the crisis of high inflation and unemployment by tightening monetary and fiscal policy. Monetary conditions were tightened under the Heath government with a rise in interest rates and introduction of the Corset, which implied moving away from the experiment in deregulation of the banking system introduced by the Bank under CCC. Minimum Lending Rate (MLR), which had replaced Bank Rate as the instrument of monetary policy, went up from 7.5% in June 1973 to 13% in November. The Heath government fell following the confrontation with the miners and Harold Wilson formed a Labour government in February 1974. The new administration placed an increased emphasis on an incomes policy—the "Social Contract"—as a way of restraining inflation. The new government's fiscal policy followed an uncertain course, since rising inflation was now accompanied by rising unemployment. This was a combination which was not expected to occur and created severe challenges for policymakers used to the post-war consensus and a Keynesian approach to demand management. As a result, the government's fiscal policy consisted of announcing deflationary measures in March 1974 and April 1975 and expansionary measures in July 1974. By 1976, the Labour government decided that priority should be given to controlling inflation, even if this involved a rise in unemployment. It abandoned, at least temporarily, the post-war economic objective of full employment. In 1976 unemployment picked up and reached 5% (on the modern Labour Force Survey-based measure), while the Labour government introduced deflationary measures, which were reinforced by an approach for financial assistance to the IMF later in the year. That approach was necessary given the weakness of sterling that emerged in 1976. Despite tighter fiscal policy, the PSBR remained obstinately high at around 6% of GDP in 1976 (Chart 6.76). There was nevertheless a marked strengthening of the balance of payments. The current account deficit fell from nearly 4% of GDP in 1974 to under 1% in 1976 (Chart 6.74). But this improvement in the current account did not translate into a stronger pound. There was a sharp decline in sterling as the Sterling-Dollar exchange rate fell from \$ 2.22 in 1975 to \$1.80 in 1976 (Chart 6.75). This occurred because of fears about an impending financial crisis on account of the high level of the PSBR and fears about renewed monetary growth (Chart 6.77). The Prime Minister Jim Callaghan gave a famous speech at the 1976 Labour Party Conference where he effectively announced the end of the post-war consensus with the words "We used to think you could spend your way out of a recession and increase employment by cutting taxes and boosting government spending. I tell you in all candour, that option no longer exists". Chancellor Healey wrote a letter

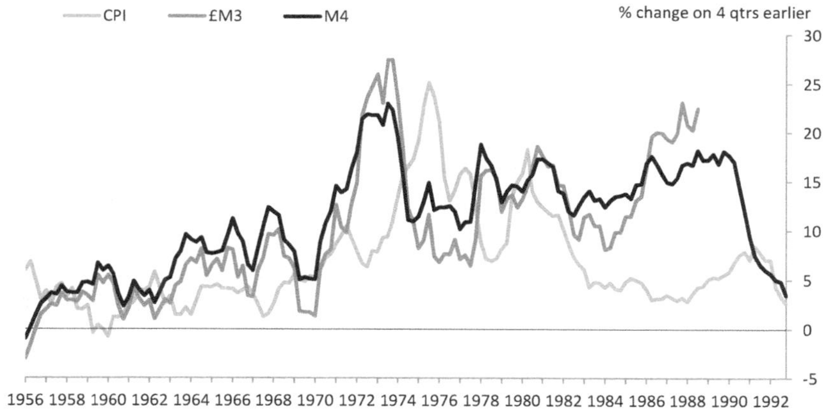

Chart 6.77 Broad money growth and inflation (*Source* Thomas and Dimsdale 2017)

to the IMF undertaking further tightening of fiscal policy in exchange for a loan to help repay a previous swap facility from the G10 central banks, organised through the Bank for International Settlements (BIS) that had been required to try and stabilise sterling earlier in the year (Schenk 2010). Healey's restrictive policies continued in 1977, when unemployment reached 6–7%, but there was some relief in the 1978 budget.

Despite the turmoil during this period, there was a recovery from 1975 to 1979 marked by a revival in both consumer spending and exports given the depreciation of sterling. In fact, so quickly did the situation improve in 1977 that the Bank of England was intervening to keep sterling down in order to lock in the improved competitiveness from sterling's depreciation in the previous year. However, the impact of the upswing on unemployment was slight. Attempts by the government to keep a cap on wage growth via a 5% limit on pay increases in the public sector failed however, and led to the Winter of Discontent in 1978/9. The Labour government, which by this time was in a minority in Parliament, fell after a confidence vote and was replaced by Mrs Thatcher's Conservative government following an election in May 1979.

The new government came to power at the same time as a second large increase in world oil prices, which pushed the world economy into severe depression. In 1979, unlike 1974, the rise in oil prices was associated with an appreciation of the sterling exchange rate. This reflected the fact that Britain was no longer a net importer of oil. But it also reflected more restrictive monetary and fiscal policies. In the early 1980s, a determined attempt was made to reduce the rate of inflation. Policy was geared towards meeting targets for money supply growth, but the measure of broad money chosen, £M3, remained stubbornly resilient. This was largely due to the suspension of the Corset, following the abolition of exchange controls in 1979. The removal of exchange controls made the Corset ineffective since it could now readily be by-passed by offshore intermediation. However, the abolition of the Corset opened the way for a new round of re-intermediation of the traditional banking system which was now able to lend freely and no longer faced a penalty for accumulating excessive interest bearing liabilities. The result was that broad money grew more rapidly than envisaged in the MTFS even though this did not signify a loose monetary policy stance in the conventional sense and this would be borne out by a subsequent fall in inflation (Chart 6.77). In addition, banks started to move into the mortgage market providing extra impetus to credit and money growth. MLR was increased sharply in 1980 as a result of the need to try and meet the £M3 target and the yield on Treasury bills averaged 15.1%, the highest ever recorded. Indeed, nominal short rates remained within a range of 10–15% until the mid-1980s in order to restrain credit and money growth. During the 1980s, both the targets for the growth of broad money and the PSBR (Public Sector Borrowing Requirement) were exceeded. The high level of interest rates and strong appreciation of sterling made the prospect of further tightening monetary policy unattractive. So in the 1981 Budget Chancellor Howe decided to tighten fiscal policy despite the severity of the recession. This prompted an infamous letter by 365 economists in protest. Fiscal contraction was judged to be necessary to achieve the money target set out in the MTFS. In the Budget, taxes were effectively raised through the non-indexation of allowances. In 1981, actual public sector borrowing was about 3% of GDP, but because of the depressed state of the economy, this implied that at full employment there would have been a fiscal surplus on a cyclically-adjusted basis.

The high level of British interest rates relative to those prevailing internationally also led to a sharp appreciation of the exchange rate. Both the growing perception that Britain's balance of payments was underpinned by its role as an oil producer and its high level of interest rates strengthened sterling which appreciated by 15% in 1980 and caused great difficulty for the manufacturing sector. The impact of monetary and fiscal tightening on the level of activity was severe although real incomes were not squeezed as much under the first oil price shock given there was not a worsening of the terms of trade. Unemployment on a Labour Force Survey basis increased from 5.4% in 1979 to 9.7% in 1981. It was to continue to rise, reaching a peak of 11.8% in 1984 (Chart 6.78). The recession which followed the second oil price shock was therefore severe and was concentrated in the tradable goods sector. While the Conservative government was not successful in achieving the stated targets of the MTFS, it had greater success in checking inflation which fell from nearly 20% in 1980 to around 5% in 1983.

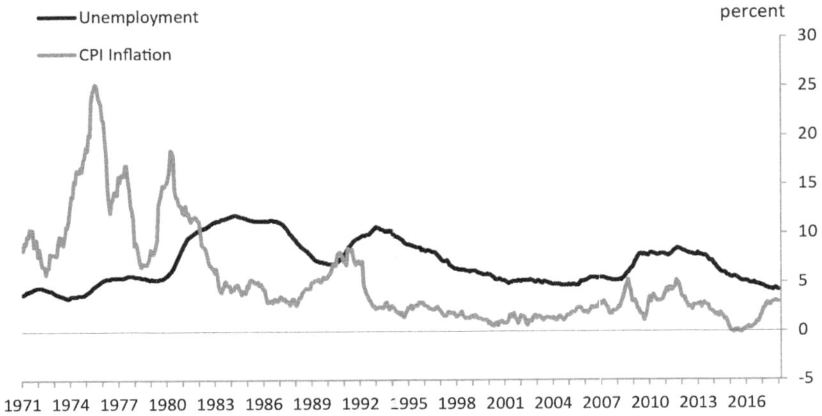

Chart 6.78 Unemployment and inflation 1971–2018 (*Source* Thomas and Dimsdale 2017)

The recovery, which started in 1981, was initially gradual, but investment grew more rapidly than in any recovery since the early 1960s. In 1982 there were signs of a fall in inflation and the government, concerned about the persistence of high unemployment, made some reductions in taxes to promote the recovery. The lagged effect of the overvalued exchange rate severely restricted the growth of exports and encouraged the growth of imports, resulting in a major reduction in the current account surplus (see above in Chart 6.74). Inflation was lower than in the two previous upturns as a result of the restrictive stance of the Conservative government's MTFS (Chart 6.79) and the reduction in the world rate of inflation in part helped by a fall in oil prices. The rise in output did not lead to a reduction in the rate of unemployment, which continued to rise until 1984. This contrasts with all previous recoveries since 1870, which have been accompanied by falling unemployment with the possible exception of the limited recovery of 1967–1969.

The failure of monetary targeting led to shifts in the policy framework that would sow the seeds of the next boom. Attempts to revise the definition of money used for the monetary target met with only limited success. Overfunding of the PSBR was another device which was used in the mid-1980s to contain the growth of broad money, but this was abandoned on

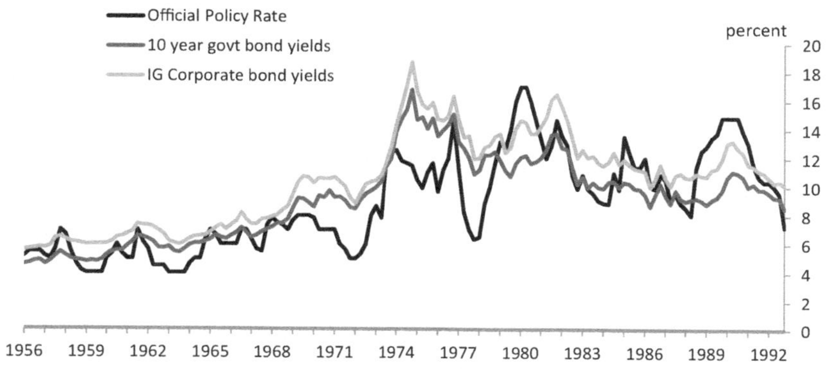

Chart 6.79 Interest rates (*Source* Thomas and Dimsdale 2017)

account of its supposed distortionary effects. The result was the suspension of monetary targeting. Chancellor Lawson claimed that although the record of achieving monetary targets had been disappointing, the record of inflation was much better. He then began to turn back to the exchange rate as a nominal anchor and began shadowing the Deutschemark as a means of importing the low inflation credentials of the Bundesbank but also with a view to joining the European Exchange Rate Mechanism or ERM. As sterling began to recover in the mid-1980s, interest rates would be set lower than otherwise to keep the level of the pound at just under a 3DM/£ rate against the Deutschemark. The other complicating factor was the stock market crash, also known as, "Black Monday" in 1987. Fearing a repeat of the Great Depression that followed the Wall Street Crash of 1929, there was a co-ordinated attempt to loosen policy. A similar response in 2008 would be lauded as an example of policymakers learning the lessons of the Great Depression, but in this case such a loosening proved misconceived as the stock market fall did not lead to or reflect any fall in underlying consumer condfidence or aggregate demand. Indeed underlying demand pressures had been building up in the mid-1980s in part due to financial liberalisation.

As noted above, the abolition of the Corset had relaxed restrictive conditions on bank lending through removing restrictions on the growth of interest-bearing deposits. Once banks were free from restrictions on either side of their balance sheets, they could attract funds and expand their loan portfolios. Particularly significant was the decision of banks to enter the mortgage market. Building societies which had previously dominated the market for housing finance took steps to make their activity more commercial and following the Building Societies Act of 1986 were put on a level playing field with the banks. They abandoned their previous practice of rationing mortgages and were now able to access wholesale funding markets and enter the market for unsecured credit. The result was an increased access to unsecured borrowing and the potential for households to withdraw equity from their homes via mortgage borrowing both of which they could use to increase spending.

Starting in 1985 there appears to have been an upsurge of confidence among households, who were now willing to take on large mortgage commitments to finance house purchase and were less contrained in taking out unsecured credit. The personal sector saving ratio declined as households increased their expenditure in part financed by drawing down the equity in their homes (Chart 6.80). Rising house prices encouraged this process through increasing the value of the collateral households could use to secure home equity loans. A similar degree of optimism increased the commercial and industrial demand for loans. The strong sense of optimism resulted in a house price boom with strong growth in both consumption and investment. Overall domestic demand was the key driver of the recovery during the mid-to-late 1980s.

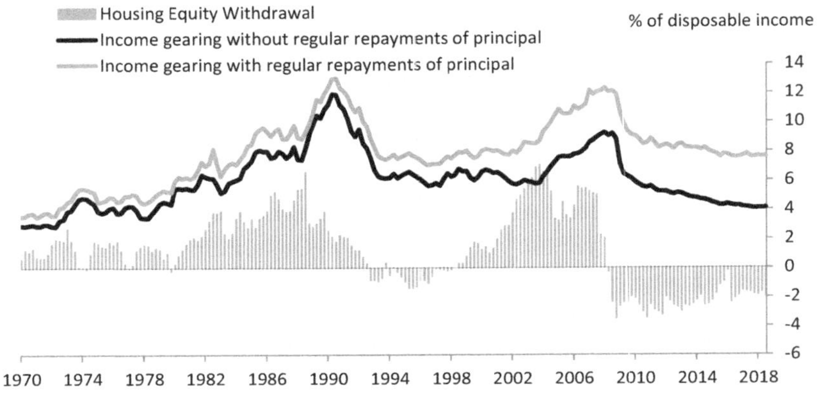

Chart 6.80 Household income gearing and housing equity withdrawal 1970–2018 (*Source* ONS)

The strength of sterling and the fall in manufacturing capacity meant (non-oil) exports played little role.

Despite the emerging boom both monetary and fiscal policies remained relatively loose. Chancellor Lawson made major reductions in income tax in the 1986, 1987 and 1988 budgets, while at the same time reducing public sector borrowing by sales of public sector assets under government privatisations schemes. The expansionary effects of a booming private sector combined with the relaxed stance of economic policy led to renewed inflation and a growth rate of GDP of around 5% per annum that ultimately proved unsustainable. This unsustainable position was not recognised at the time despite a significant current account deficit emerging in the balance of payments (shown earlier in Chart 6.74). The deficit was viewed as the natural counterpart to improved productivity in the UK and increased foreign direct investment in an increasingly competitive UK economy. In particular, the government's supply-side reforms were argued to have increased the underlying performance of the economy. Similarly the public sector finances looked sound. The unadjusted public sector borrowing requirement (PSBR) looked comfortable in 1987 and 1988, as tax receipts were boosted by the strong recovery. However, the level of activity in 1988–9 was in fact in excess of the potential capacity of the economy. While tax receipts increased and the accounts showed a surplus, the sustainable level of output was well below actual GDP. In other words, although there appeared to be a budget surplus, there was in fact an underlying budget deficit (as shown earlier in Chart 6.76).

The strength of output growth began to put upward pressure on inflation which increased to around 8%. There was a tightening of short term interest rates, in part to rein in demand but also to match European interest rates leading up to Britain's entry into the ERM in October 1990. Household income gearing (debt service payments as a % of household income) reached unprecedented levels given high itnerest rates and the build up of debt in the boom(Chart 6.80), even higher than those observed at the peak of the Great Financial Crisis in 2008. This tightening of monetary policy ultimately led to a significant recession in the early 1990s. The economy which had become accustomed to the ready availability of credit went into sharp reverse and led to a recession starting in 1990Q3. To prevent the decline in activity proceeding too far, there was a large relaxation of fiscal policy. From 1990 to 1993 the cyclically-adjusted public sector deficit increased to 6.3% of GDP. As discussed in Clark and Dilnot (2004) this was a degree of discretionary expansion unmatched at any point in the post-war era except during the mid-1970s but was not fully appreciated at the time.

6.6.3 The Great Stability 1992–2007

The United Kingdom's exit from the ERM in 1992 was associated with a reduction in nominal short-term interest rates and a depreciation of the exchange rate. From that point on, exports contributed to the recovery. From the introduction of inflation targeting in 1992, both nominal and real short term rates remained relatively low and stable compared to the high levels seen in the 1980s and early 1990s (Chart 6.81).

This outcome, and the stability in growth it engendered, reflected not only the impact of inflation targeting (and from 1997, the operational independence of the Bank of England). But the shocks hitting the economy over this period were also relatively benign, at least until the onset of the financial crisis in mid-2007. Overall the 14 years following the ERM exit were a "NICE" (non-inflationary continuous expansion)

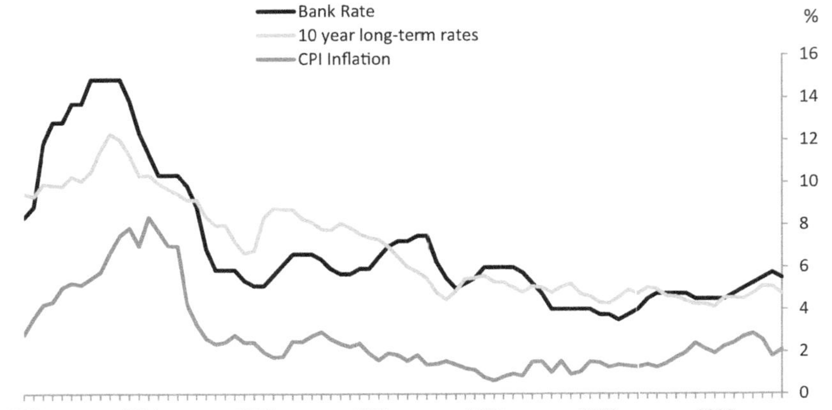

Chart 6.81 Interest rates 1988–2007 (*Source* Thomas and Dimsdale 2017)

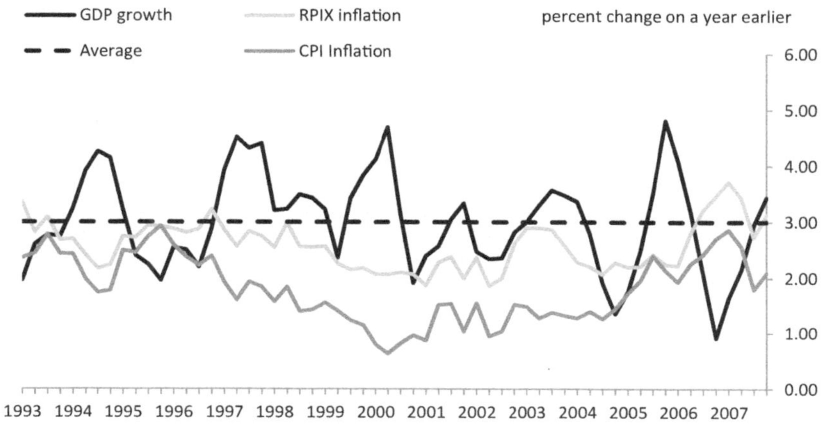

Chart 6.82 NICE outcomes 1993–2007 (*Source* Thomas and Dimsdale 2017)

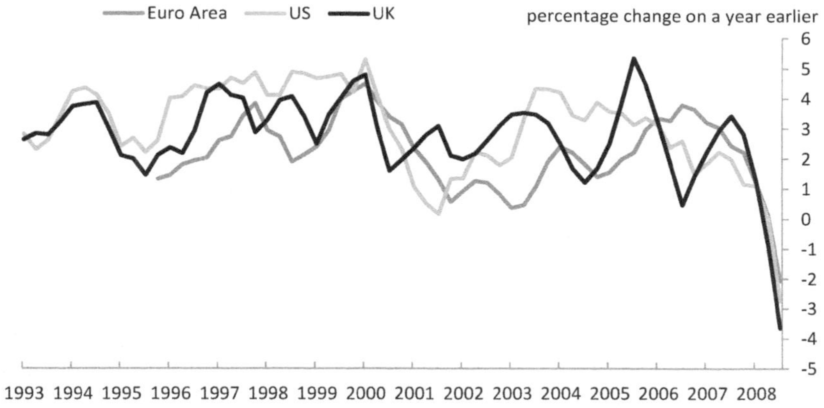

Chart 6.83 Growth in the UK, US and Euro area (*Source* Thomas and Dimsdale 2017)

decade (and almost a half) as defined by the then Governor of the Bank Mervyn King.[6] Growth averaged 3% per annum of over this period (Chart 6.82) and inflation remained close to target.

Growth however was not completely stable over this period. After an initial recovery in output growth slowed somewhat in 1995, reflecting a similar slowdown in the United States (Charts 6.83) and the fact

[6]See King (2003).

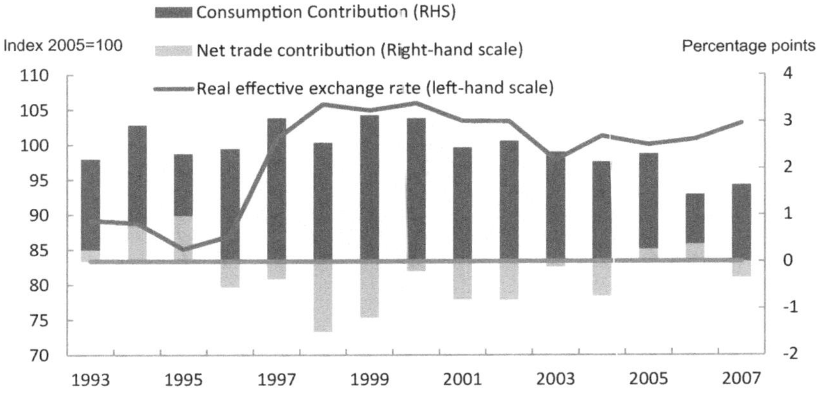

Chart 6.84 Imbalances and the real exchange rate (*Source* Thomas and Dimsdale 2017)

that investment was subdued due to the ongoing need for companies to repair their balance sheets after the early 1990s recession.

However demand recovered in 1996 and 1997. A feature of this period was the appreciation of sterling after the large depreciation following the ERM exit in 1992. This had the effect of boosting real incomes and consumption at the expense of net trade and marked the start of growing imbalances in the economy that would signal the impending financial crisis in 2007. Consumption spending was also affected by windfalls associated with building society demutualisation, and this meant the strong positive contributions to growth from consumption persisted, especially from durable consumption during the mid-1990s. Demutualisations may have contributed around £6–12 billion, equivalent to 1–2% to on the level of consumption, between 1997 and 1999 (Bank of England 1997) (Chart 6.84).

The general stability of output was punctured by slowdowns in growth in 1998 in the wake of the Asian financial crisis and especially in 2001 reflecting the bursting of the dotcom bubble. Following these international shocks UK growth appears well correlated with US and Euro-area GDP of this period and reflected the increasing globalisation of the world economy.

Related to this real import prices were also declining, in part as a result of the re-entry of China into the global market and its strategy

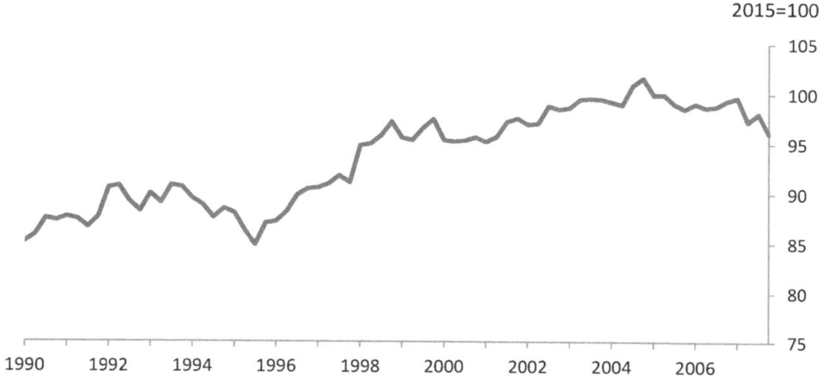

Chart 6.85 The UK Terms of trade: 1990–2007 (*Source* Thomas and Dimsdale 2017)

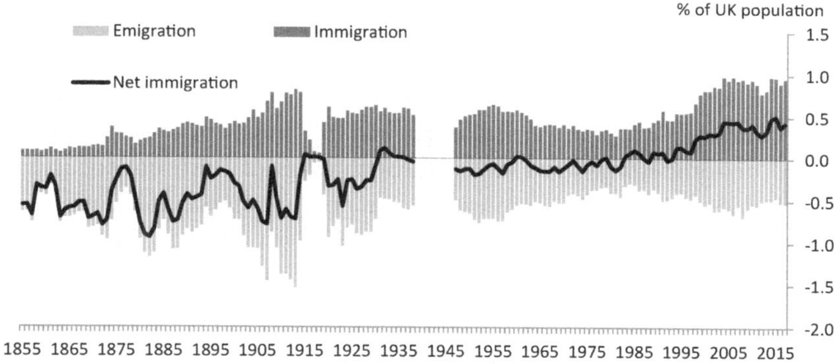

Chart 6.86 Net UK immigration since 1855 (*Source* Thomas and Dimsdale 2017)

of export-led growth. This resulted in a 15% boost to the UK terms of trade (export prices relative to import prices) which helped support living standards and consumption (Chart 6.85). However, the early 2000s saw a return to higher oil and commodity prices beginning in 2004. This pushed down on real incomes and growth in 2005.

The other feature of the Great Stability was emergence of a sustained positive rate of net immigration for the first time in 150 years (Chart 6.86). While there were several reasons for this it suggsted that

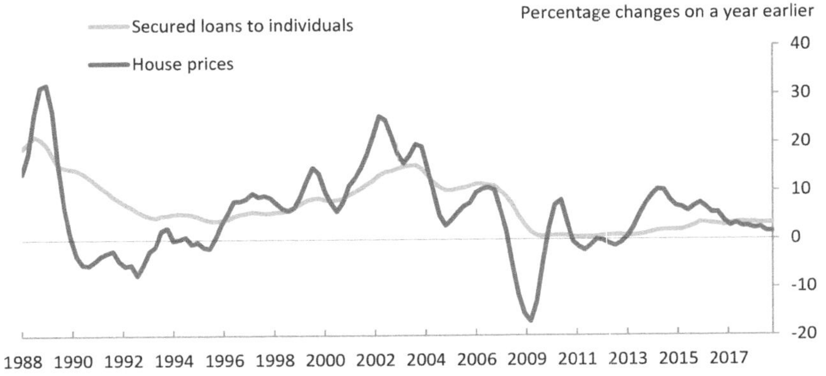

Chart 6.87 House prices and secured lending (*Source* Thomas and Dimsdale 2017)

fluctuations in demand in the UK relative to overseas were likely to be met with a more elastic supply of overseas labour, compared with the past, and with less upward pressure on real wages.

The other feature of the Great Stability period both in the UK and other countries was the relentless growth of house prices and lending secured on property (Chart 6.87). Growth rates of both ended up well into double figures and represented a major imbalance building up in the economy despite the stability of GDP growth. In part, this reflected increased competition in the mortgage market and the move to securitisation which allowed banks and building societies to move loans off balance sheet and relax capital constraints on lending. However problems in the global financial system began to emerge with the sub-prime crisis in the United States in 2007, followed by the collapse of Lehman Brothers in late 2008. This conflagrated into what would become the the Great Financial Crisis and led to what would be called the Great Recession.

6.6.4 Epilogue—The Great Financial Crisis and Recession of 2008 and the Productivity Puzzle

Analysis of the Great Financial Crisis and the Great Recession that followed is still in its infancy in terms of assessing its place in a historical context. Moreover recent official data revisions have rewritten the story in terms of the timing of the impact on UK GDP compared to earlier vintages of data. So here we treat the period since 2008 as a short epilogue, and give a very brief outline of events since 2008 and highlight some of the broad issues that arise for an analysis of business cycles over this period. Following the Great Financial Crisis, UK output fell sharply from early 2008. The speed and severity of the recession was a shock compared to the Great Stability that had come before. The global financial crisis led to a general collapse in world trade, similar to other C20th recessions, amounting to over 10% and this hit UK exports (Chart 6.88) in a similar way to many other episodes already discussed in earlier periods. Given the importance of financial service exports to the UK tradable sector, sterling depreciated by over 20% in order to mitigate the impact on the UK's long-term current account position. Domestically money and credit growth slowed to rates not seen since the Selwyn Lloyd Squeeze in the early 1960s (Chart 6.89), driven by a decline in credit supply by the commercial banks in their efforts to recapitalise and stabilise their balance sheets (Bridges et al. 2011; Butt et al. 2012).

A key difference relative to previous recessions was the rapid loosening of monetary policy. In earlier episodes in the C20th, the policy response was often delayed (or even of the opposite sign). Those earlier responses typically reflected monetary policy attempting to respond to intermediate targets such as maintaining a particular exchange rate

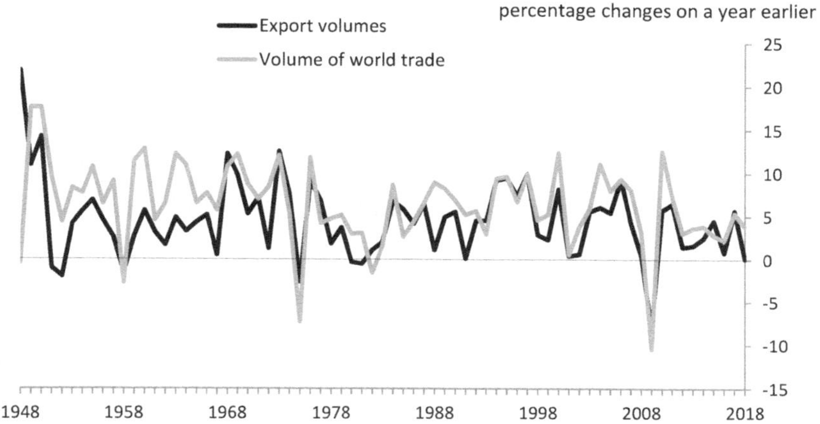

Chart 6.88 Exports and world trade (*Source* Thomas and Dimsdale 2017)

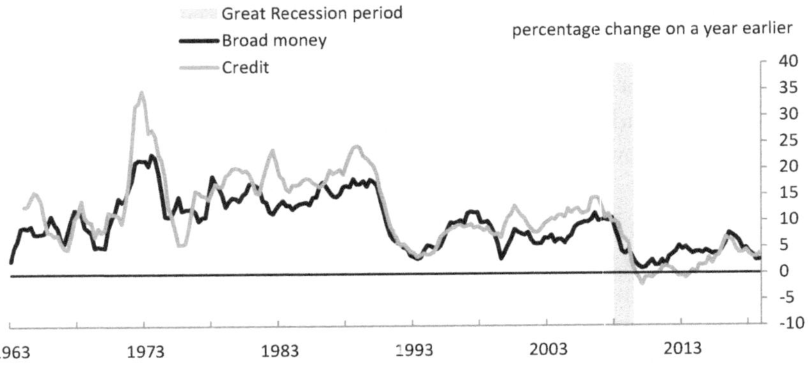

Chart 6.89 Money and credit growth (*Source* Bank of England: (a) Credit measured as M4 lending 1963–1998, M4 lending excluding intermediate 'other financial corporations' [IOFCs] 1998–2018. Data are adjusted to exclude the impact of securitisations and loan transfers; (b) Broad money measured as M4 1963–1998, M4 excluding intermediate 'other financial corporations' [IOFCs] 1998–2018)

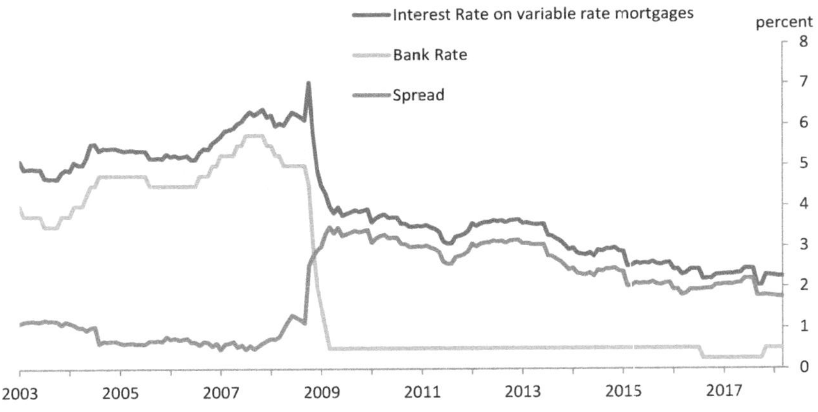

Chart 6.90 Variable rate mortgage spreads (*Source* Thomas and Dimsdale 2017)

or money supply objective rather than a final objective like inflation. In the case of 2009 interest rates were cut rapidly until the effective lower bound constraint became binding on the UK and other major economies. As a result, the rise in credit spreads arising from the shock to credit supply was mitigated by lower risk-free rates so that actual lending rates in the UK fell in absolute terms (see Chart 6.90 for mortgages).

Central banks around the world then resorted to various methods to try and escape the possible deflationary implications of this constraint. Various forms of quantitative easing ("QE") were introduced. In the UK this took a very traditional form, purchases of government debt designed to boost broad money and lower longer term yields in the economy. From 2009 the MPC undertook £435 billion of asset purchases in several stages. However this was backed up with measures designed to improve bank liquidity and funding conditions (the Special Liquidity Scheme or "SLS" in 2008, the Funding for Lending scheme or "FLS" in 2012 and the Term funding scheme or "TFS" in 2016). Various forms of forward guidance (open-ended, time contingent and state-contingent) were introduced by central banks. In the UK the aim of forward guidance was designed to reduce uncertainty about the reaction function to try and ensure market expectations of rates moved in a way consistent with meeting the inflation target in the medium term.

Further shocks hit the UK economy over this period most notably the rise in oil prices in 2008, the Euro-area crisis in 2011 and 2012 and the impact of the Brexit referendum, each of which required additional policy responses by the Monetary Policy Committee. Despite the support of monetary policy the recovery after 2008 was the longest of those seen in the previous hundred years (Chart 6.91) and productivity

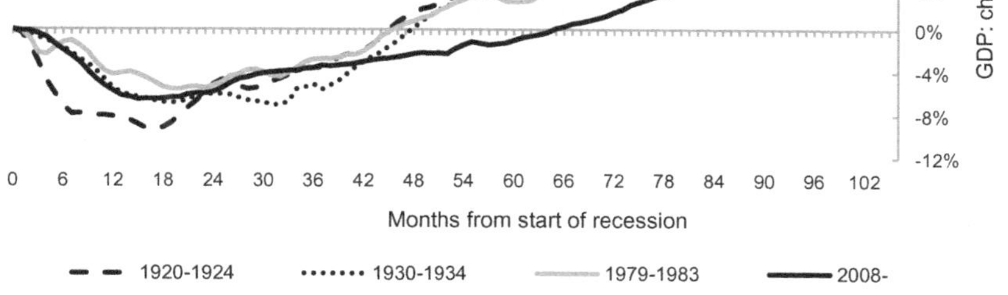

Chart 6.91 Recoveries in the C20th and C21st (*Source* Thomas and Dimsdale [2017] and NIESR and Mitchell et al. [2012])

growth has remained weak relative to historic trends (Chart 6.65). But the fluctuations around a low growth path have in general been modest compared to previous cycles, and unemployment has returned to levels not seen since the early 1970s (Chart 6.78). It remains to be seen whether a strong cyclical pattern of growth emerges.

References

Accominotti, O. (2012). London Merchant Banks, the Central European Panic and the Sterling Crisis of 1931. *Journal of Economic History, 72*(2012), 1–43.

Aikman, D., Bush, O., & Taylor, A. (2016). *Monetary Versus Macroprudential Policies: Causal Impacts of Interest Rates and Credit Controls in the Era of the UK Radcliffe Report* (NBER Working Paper 22380).

Andrews, B. P. A. (1987). *Exchange Rate Appreciation, Competitiveness and Export Performance: The UK Experience in the Inter-War Period.* Oxford University DPhil Thesis. http://ora.ox.ac.uk/objects/uuid:69b9bcfe-a2fa-4f02-8d49-2f847fa6dc32.

Anson, M., Bholat, D., Kang, M., & Thomas, R. (2017). *The Bank of England as Lender of Last Resort: New Historical Evidence from Daily Transactional Data* (Bank of England Working Paper 691).

Ashton, T. (1949). *The Industrial Revolution, 1760–1830.* Oxford: Oxford University Press.

Ashton, T. (1959). *Economic Fluctuations in England 1700–1800.* Oxford: Clarendon Press.

Bagehot, W. (1873). *Lombard Street: A Description of the London Money Market.* London: Henry S. King & Co.

Bank of England. (1982). The Supplementary Special Deposits Scheme. *Quarterly Bulletin, Q1,* 74–85.

Bank of England. (1997, November 20). *Inflation Report.*

Barro, R. (1987). Government Spending, Interest Rates, Prices and Budget Deficits in the United Kingdom, 1701–1918. *Journal of Monetary Economics, 20*(2), 221–247.

Barro, R., & Gordon, R. (1983). Rules, Discretion and Reputation in a Model of Monetary Policy. *Journal of Monetary Economics, 12*(1), 101–121.

Beenstock, M., Capie F., & Griffiths, B. (1984). *Economic Recovery in the United Kingdom in the 1930s* (Bank of England Panel Paper 23).

Benjamin, D., & Kochin, L. (1979). Searching for an Explanation of Unemployment in Interwar Britain. *Journal of Political Economy, 87*(3), 441–478.

Bordo, M. (1985). *Some Historical Evidence 1870–1933 on the Impact and International Transmission of Financial Crises* (NBER Working Paper 1606).

Boyer, G., & Hatton, T. (2002). New Estimates of British Unemployment, 1870–1913. *The Journal of Economic History, 62*(3), 643–675.

Bridges, J., Rossiter, N., & Thomas, R. (2011). Understanding the Recent Weakness in Broad Money Growth. *Bank of England Quarterly Bulletin, 51*(1), 22–35.

Britton, A. (1991). *Macroeconomic Policy in Britain 1974–1987*. Cambridge: Cambridge University Press.

Broadberry, S. (1986). *The British Economy Between the Wars: A Macroeconomic Survey*. Oxford: Blackwell.

Broadberry, S. (1990). The Emergence of Mass Unemployment: Explaining Macroeconomic Trends in Britain During the Trans-World War I Period. *The Economic History Review, 43*(2), 271–282.

Broadberry, S., Campbell, B., Klein, A., Overton, M., & van Leeuwen, B. (2015). *British Economic Growth 1270–1870*. Cambridge: Cambridge University Press.

Broadberry, S., & Crafts, N. (2011). Openness, Protectionism and Britain's Productivity Performance Over the Long-Run. In G. Wood, T. Mills, & N. Crafts (Eds.), *Monetary and Banking History: Essays in Honour of Forrest Capie*. Abingdon: Routledge International Studies in Money and Banking.

Butt, N., Domit, S., McLeay, M., Thomas, R., & Kirkham, L. (2012). What Can the Money Data Tell Us About the Impact of QE? *Bank of England Quarterly Bulletin, 52*(4), 321–331.

Cairncross, A. (1953). *Home and Foreign Investment 1870–1913. Studies in Capital Accumulation*. Cambridge: Cambridge University Press.

Campbell, G. (2014). Government Policy During the British Railway Mania and the 1847 Commercial Crisis. In N. Dimsdale & A. Hotson (Eds.), *British Financial Crises Since 1825* (pp. 58–75). Croydon: Oxford University Press.

Capie, F. (1978). The British Tariff and Industrial Protection in the 1930's. *The Economic History Review, 31*(3), 399–409.

Capie, F. (2007). The Emergence of the Bank of England as a Mature Central Bank. In F. Capie & G. Wood (Eds.), *The Lender of Last Resort*. Abingdon: Routledge.

Capie, F. (2011). *The Bank of England 1950 s to 1979*. Cambridge: Cambridge University Press.
Capie, F., & Webber, A. (1985). *A Monetary History of the United Kingdom, 1870–1982* (Vol. 1). London: Routledge.
Capie, F., & Wood, G. (1996). Money Demand and Supply Under the International Gold Standard: The United Kingdom 1870–1914. In T. Bayoumi, B. Eichengreen, & M. P. Taylor (Eds.), *Modern Perspectives on the Gold Standard* (pp. 261–283). Cambridge: Cambridge University Press.
Capie, F. H., & Mills, T. C. (1991). Money and Business Cycles in the US and UK, 1870–1913. *The Manchester School, 59*(S1), 38–56.
Catao, L., & Solomou, S. (2005). Effective Exchange Rates and the Classical Gold Standard Adjustment. *American Economic Review, 95*(4), 1259–1275.
Chadha, J., & Newby, E. (2013). *Midas, Transmuting All, Into Paper: The Bank of England and the Banque de France During the Revolutionary and Napoleonic Wars* (Research Discussion Papers 20/2013), Bank of Finland.
Checkland, S. (1975). *Scottish Banking: A History, 1695–1973*. London: Collins.
Clapham, J. (1944). The Bank of England: A History (2 Volumes). Cambridge: Cambridge University Press.
Clark, T., & Dilnot, A. (2004). British Fiscal Policy Since 1939. In R. Floud & P. Johnson (Eds.), *The Cambridge Economic History of Modern Britain* (pp. 368–398). Cambridge: Cambridge University Press.
Cloyne, J. (2013). Discretionary Tax Changes and the Macroeconomy: New Narrative Evidence from the United Kingdom. *American Economic Review, 103*(4), 1507–1528.
Cloyne, J., Dimsdale, N., & Postel-Vinay, N. (2018). *Taxes and Growth: New Narrative Evidence from Interwar Britain* (NBER Working Paper 24659).
Coffman, D., Stephenson, J., & Sussman, N. (2019). *Financing the Rebuilding of the City of London After the Great Fire of 1666*. Mimeo.
Collins, M. (1988). English Banks and Business Cycles. In P. Cottrell & D. Moggridge (Eds.), *Money and Power: Essays in Honour of L.S. Pressnell*. London: Macmillan.
Collins, M. (1989). The Banking Crisis of 1878. *The Economic History Review, 42*(4), 504–527.
Crafts, N. (2013). *Returning to Growth: Lessons from the 1930s* (Economic History Society Working Paper 13010).
Crafts, N., & Mills, T. (2013). Rearmament to the Rescue? New Estimates of the Impact of "Keynesian" Policies in 1930s' Britain. *The Journal of Economic History, 73*(4), 1077–1104.

Crafts, N., & Mills, T. (2017). Six Centuries of British Economic Growth: A Time-Series Perspective. *European Review of Economic History, 21*(2), 141–158.

Davis, R. (1954). English Foreign Trade, 1660–1700. *The Economic History Review, 7*(2), 150–166.

Deane, P. (1968). New Estimates of Gross National Product for the United Kingdom 1830–1914. *Review of Income and Wealth, 14*(2), 95–112.

Dickson, P. (1967). *The Financial Revolution in England: A Study in the Development of Public Credit, 1688–1756*. London: Macmillan.

Dimsdale, N. (1981). British Monetary Policy and the Exchange Rate 1920–1938. In W. Eltis & P. Sinclair (Eds.), *The Money Supply and the Exchange Rate*. Oxford: Oxford University Press.

Dimsdale, N. (1990). Money, Interest and Cycles in Britain Since 1830. *Greek Economic Review, 12*(Supplement), 153–196.

Dimsdale, N. (1991). British Monetary Policy Since 1945. In N. Crafts & N. Woodward (Eds.), *The British Economy Since 1945*. Oxford: Clarendon.

Dimsdale, N. (2013a). *The Dynamics of Consumption and Investment in the Victorian Economy* (University of Oxford Discussion Papers in Economic and Social History 122).

Dimsdale, N. (2013b). *The Bank of England and the British Economy 1890–1913* (University of Oxford Discussion Papers in Economic and Social History 123).

Dimsdale N. (2015). Monetary Trends in the UK Since 1870. In M. Allen & D. Coffman (Eds.), *Money, Wages and Prices: Essays in Honour of Professor Nicholas Mayhew* (pp. 228–249). Basingstoke: Palgrave Macmillan.

Dimsdale, N. H., & Horsewood, N. (1995). Fiscal Policy and Employment in Interwar Britain: Some Evidence from a New Model. *Oxford Economic Papers, 47*, 369–396.

Dimsdale, N., Nickell, S., & Horsewood, N. (1989). Real Wages and Unemployment in Britain During the 1930s. *The Economic Journal, 99*(396), 271–292.

Dow, J. (1964). *The Management of the British Economy*. Cambridge: Cambridge University Press.

Dow, J. (1998). *Major Recessions, Britain and the World, 1920–1995*. Oxford: Oxford University Press.

Dowie, J. (1975). 1919–20 is in Need of Attention. *The Economic History Review, 28*(3), 429–450.

Duffy, I. P. H. (1982). The Discount Policy of the Bank of England During the Suspension of Cash Payments, 1797–1821. *The Economic History Review, 35*(1), 67.

Dutton, J. (1984). The Bank of England and the "Rules of the Game" Under the International Gold Standard: New Evidence. In M. Bordo & A. Schwartz (Eds.), *A Retrospective on The Classical Gold Standard*. Chicago: University of Chicago Press.

Edelstein, M. (1981). Foreign Investment and Empire 1860–1914. In R. Floud & D. McCloskey (Eds.), *The Economic History of Britain Since 1700* (Vol. 2). Cambridge: Cambridge University Press.

Edelstein, M. (1982). *Overseas Investment in the Age of High Imperialism*. New York: Columbia University Press.

Eichengreen, B., Watson, M., & Grossman, R. (1985). Bank Rate Policy Under the Interwar Gold Standard: A Dynamic Probit Model. *The Economic Journal, 95*, 725–745.

Federico, G., & Tena-Junguito, A. (2019). World Trade, 1800–1938: A New Synthesis. *Revista de Historia Económica/Journal of Iberian and Latin American Economic History, 37*(1), 9–41. https://doi.org/10.1017/S0212610918000216.

Feinstein, C. (1972). *National Income Expenditure and Output of the United Kingdom 1855–1965*. Cambridge: Cambridge University Press.

Ford, A. (1962). *The Gold Standard 1880–1914: Britain and Argentina*. Oxford: Oxford University Press.

Ford, A. (1969). British Economic Fluctuations, 1870–1914. *The Manchester School, 37*(2), 99–130.

Ford, A. (1981). The Trade Cycle in Britain 1860–1914. In R. Floud & D. McCloskey (Eds.), *The Economic History of Britain Since 1700* (Vol. 2). Cambridge: Cambridge University Press.

Friedman, M., & Schwartz, A. (1963). *A Monetary History of the United States,1867–1960*. Princeton: Princeton University Press.

Gayer, A., Rostow, W., & Schwartz, A. (1953). *The Growth and Fluctuation of the British Economy, 1790–1850*. Oxford: Clarendon Press.

Gent, J. (2016). *Abundance and Scarcity: Classical Theories of Money, Bank Balance Sheets and Business Models, and the British Restriction of 1797–1818* (PhD thesis). London School of Economics.

Ginarlis, J., & Pollard, S. (1988). *Roads and Waterways 1750–1850*. In Feinstein and Pollard (1988) op. cit.

Goodhart, C. (1972). *The Business of Banking 1891–1914*. London: Weidenfeld & Nicolson.

Goodhart, C. (1986). Financial Innovation and Monetary Control. *Oxford Review of Economic Policy, 2*(4), 79–102.
Goodhart, C. A. E. (2015). Competition and Credit Control: Some Personal Reflections. *Financial History Review, 22*(2), 235–246.
Goodhart, C. A. E., & Needham, D. J. (2017). Historical Reasons for the Focus on Broad Monetary Aggregates in Post-World War II Britain and the 'Seven Years War' with the IMF. *Financial History Review, 24*(3), 331–356.
Green, G. (2018). *Monetary Policy Spillovers in the First Age of Financial Globalisation: A Narrative VAR Approach 1884–1913* (Bank of England Working Papers 718). Bank of England.
Hatton, T., & Thomas, M. (2010). Labour Markets in the Interwar Period and Economic Recovery in the UK and the USA. *Oxford Review of Economic Policy, 26*(3), 463–485.
Hawtrey, R. (1919). *Currency and Credit.* London: Longmans.
Hawtrey, R. (1928). *Trade and Credit.* London: Longmans.
Hawtrey, R. (1962). *A Century of Bank Rate* (2nd ed.). London: Frank Cass.
Hayek, F. (1962). *Introduction to an enquiry into the Nature and Effects of the Paper Credit of Great Britain by Henry Thornton.* London: George Allen & Unwin.
Hicks, J. (1967). *Critical Essays in Monetary Theory.* Oxford: Clarendon Press.
Hicks, J. (1977). *Economic Perspectives: Further Further Essays on Money and Growth.* Oxford: Clarendon Press.
Hicks, J. (1982). *Are There Economic Cycles?* In J. R. Hicks (Ed.), *Money Interest and Wages: Collected Essays on Economic Theory* (Vol. II). Oxford: Basil Blackwell.
Hoppit, J. (1986). Financial Crises in Eighteenth-Century England. *The Economic History Review, 39*(1), 39–58.
Hoppit, J. (1987). *Risk and Failure in English Business.* Cambridge: Cambridge University Press.
Hoskins, W. (1968). Harvest Fluctuations and English Economic History, 1620–1759. *The Agricultural History Review, 16*(1), 15–31.
Howson, S. (1975). *Domestic Monetary Management in Britain, 1919–38.* Cambridge: Cambridge University Press.
Huffman, W., & Lothian, J. (1984). The Gold Standard and the Transmission of Business Cycles, 1833–1932. In M. Bordo & A. Schwartz (Eds.), *A Retrospective on The Classical Gold Standard.* Chicago: University of Chicago Press.
Hughes, J. (1960). *Fluctuations in Trade, Industry, and Finance: A Study of British Economic Development, 1850–1860.* Oxford: Clarendon Press.

Jones, D. (1988). *War and Economy in the Age of William III and Marlborough*. Oxford: Basil Blackwell.
Kahn, R. F. (1931). The Relation of Home Investment to Unemployment. *The Economic Journal, 41*, 173–198.
Kaldor, N. (1966). *Causes of the Slow Rate of Growth of the United Kingdom: An Inaugural Lecture*. Cambridge: Cambridge University Press.
Keynes, J. M. (1936). *The General Theory of Employment, Interest and Money*. London: Macmillan.
King, M. (2003, October). *Speech Given at East Midlands Development Agency/Bank of England Dinner*. Leicester.
King, W. (1936). *A History of the London Discount Market*. London: Cass.
Kitson, M., & Solomou, S. (1990). *Protectionism and Economic Revival: The British Inter-War Economy*. Cambridge: Cambridge University Press.
Kosmetatos, P. (2018). *The 1772–73 British Credit Crisis*. London: Palgrave Macmillan.
Kydland, F., & Prescott, E. (1977). Rules Rather Than Discretion: The Inconsistency of Optimal Plans. *Journal of Political Economy, 85*(3), 473–492.
Lennard, J. (2018). Did Monetary Policy Matter? Narrative Evidence from the Classical Gold Standard. *Explorations in Economic History, 68*, 16–36.
Lévy-Leboyer, M. (1982). Central Banking and Foreign Trade: The Anglo-American Cycle in the 1830s. In C. P. Kindleberger & J.-P. Laffargue (Eds.), *Financial Crises: Theory, History and Policy*. Cambridge: Cambridge University Press.
Lewis, W. A. (1978). *Growth and Fluctuations, 1870–1913*. London: Allen and Unwin.
Lloyd, S., & Solomou, S. (2019). *The Impact of the 1932 General Tariff: A Difference-in-Difference Approach*. Cliometrica.
Lovell, M. (1957). The Role of the Bank of England as Lender of Last Resort in the Crises of the Eighteenth Century. *Explorations in Entrepreneurial History, 10*, 8–21.
Matthews, R. (1954). *A Study in Trade-Cycle History: Economic Fluctuations in Great Britain 1833–1842*. Cambridge: Cambridge University Press.
Matthews, R. (1971). The Role of Demand Management. In A. Cairncross (Ed.), *Britain's Economic Prospects Reconsidered*. London: Allen and Unwin.
Matthews, R., Feinstein, C., & Odling-Smee, J. (1982). *British Economic Growth, 1856–1973*. Oxford: Oxford University Press.

Melton, F. (2002). *Sir Robert Clayton and the Origins of English Deposit Banking 1658–1685*. Cambridge: Cambridge University Press.

Michie, R. (2016). *British Banking: Continuity and Change 1694 to the Present*. Oxford: Oxford University Press.

Middleton, R. (1981). The Constant Employment Budget Balance and British Budgetary Policy, 1929–39. *The Economic History Review, 34*(2), 266–286.

Middleton, R. (2010). British Monetary and Fiscal Policy in the 1930s. *Oxford Review of Economic Policy, 26*(3), 414–441.

Mirowski, P. (1981). The Rise (and Retreat) of a Market: English Joint Stock Shares in the Eighteenth Century. *The Journal of Economic History, 41*(3), 559–577.

Mirowski, P. (1985 [2015]). *The Birth of the Business Cycle*. London: Routledge.

Mitchell, B. (1988). *British Historical Statistics*. Cambridge: Cambridge University Press.

Mitchell, J., Solomou, S., & Weale, M. (2012). Monthly GDP Estimates for Inter-War Britain. *Explorations in Economic History, 49*(4), 543–556.

Moggridge, D. (1969). *The Return to Gold, 1925: The Formulation of Economic Policy and Its Critics* (Occasional Papers 19). Department of Applied Economics, University of Cambridge.

Muellbauer, J., & Murphy, A. (1990). Is the UK Balance of Payments Sustainable? *Economic Policy, 5*(11), 347.

Neal, L. (1998). The Financial Crisis of 1825 and the Restructuring of the British Financial System. *Federal Reserve Bank of St. Louis Review, 80*(3).

Neal, L., & Weidenmier, M. (2002). *Crises in the Global Economy from Tulips to Today: Contagion and Consequences* (NBER Working Paper 9147).

Needham, D. (2014). *UK Monetary Policy from Devaluation to Thatcher, 1967–82*. London: Palgrave.

O'Brien, P. (1988). The Political Economy of British Taxation, 1660–1815. *The Economic History Review, 41*(1), 1–32.

O'Brien, P., & Hunt, P. (1999). England 1485–1815. In R. Bonney (Ed.), *The Rise of the Fiscal State in Europe, c. 1200–1815*. Oxford.

O'Brien, P., & Palma, N. (2017). *Danger to the Old Lady of Threadneedle Street? The Bank Restriction Act and the Regime Shift to Paper Money, 1797–1821* (Economic History Society Working Paper 17001).

Palma, N. (2018). Reconstruction of Money Supply Over the Long Run: The Case of England, 1270–1870. *The Economic History Review, 71*(2), 373–392.

Pigou, A. (1947). *Aspects of British Economic History 1918–1925*. London: Macmillan.

Pippenger, J. (1984). Bank of England Operations. In M. Bordo & A. Schwartz (Eds.), *A Retrospective on the Classical Gold Standard* (pp. 1893–1913). Chicago: University of Chicago Press.

Pressnell, L. (1956). *Country Banking in the Industrial Revolution*. Oxford: Oxford University Press.

Price, J. (1992). The Bank of England's Discount Activity and the Merchants of London, 1694–1773. In I. Blanchard, A. Goodman, & J. Newman (Eds.), *Industry and Finance in Early Modern History—Essays Presented to George Hammersley on the Occasion of His 74th Birthday* (pp. 92–114). Stuttgart: Franz Steiner Verlag.

Ramey, V. (2011). Can Government Purchases Stimulate the Economy? *Journal of Economic Literature, 49*(3), 673–685.

Richardson, H. (1967). *Economic Recovery in Britain 1932–39*. London: Weidenfeld & Nicolson.

Rockoff, H. (1971). *Monetary Statistics of the United States: Estimates, Sources, Methods*. By Milton Friedman and Anna Jacobson Schwartz. New York, Columbia University Press, 1970. *Business History Review, 45*(3): 377–379.

Rogoff, K. (1985). The Optimal Degree of Commitment to an Intermediate Monetary Target. *Quarterly Journal of Economics, 100,* 1169–1189.

Romer, C. D., & Romer, D. H. (1989). Does Monetary Policy Matter? A New Test in the Spirit of Friedman and Schwartz. *NBER Macroeconomics Annual, 4*, 121–170.

Samy, L. (2015). *Indices of House Prices and Rent Prices of Residential Property in London, 1895–1939* (University of Oxford Discussion Papers in Economic and Social History 134).

Sayers, R. (1976). *The Bank of England 1891–1944*. Cambridge: Cambridge University Press.

Schenk, C. (2010). *The Decline of Sterling: Managing the Retreat of an International Currency, 1945–1992*. Cambridge: Cambridge University Press.

Sefton, J., & Weale, M. (1995). *Reconciliation of National Income and Expenditure: Balanced Estimates of National Income for the United Kingdom, 1920–1990*. Cambridge: Cambridge University Press.

Silberling, N. J. (1924). Financial and Monetary Policy of Great Britain During the Napoleonic Wars. *The Quarterly Journal of Economics, 38*(3), 397.

Sowerbutts, R., Schneebalg, M., & Hubert, F. (2016). The Demise of Overend Gurney. *Bank of England Quarterly Bulletin, 56*(2), 94–106.

Stratton, J. (1978). *Agricultural Records, A.D. 220–1977*. London: Baker.

Temin, P. (1974). The Anglo-American Business Cycle, 1820–60. *The Economic History Review, 27*(2), 207–221.

Temin, P., & Voth, H. (2013). *Prometheus Shackled: Goldsmith Banks and England's Financial Revolution After 1700*. Oxford: Oxford University Press.

Thomas, B. (1954). *Migration and Economic Growth: A Study of Great Britain and the Atlantic Economy*. Cambridge: Cambridge University Press.

Thomas, M. (1983). Rearmament and Recovery in the Late 1930s. *Economic History Review, 36*(4), 552–579.

Thomas, R., & Dimsdale, N. (2017). *A Millennium of UK Macroeconomic Data*. Bank of England OBRA Dataset.

Tooke, T., & Newmarch, W. (1838). *A History of Prices, and of the State of the Circulation, from 1793 to 1837; Preceded by a Brief Sketch of the State of Corn Trade in the Last Two Centuries*. London: Longman, Orme, Brown, Green, and Longmans.

Turner, P. (1991). Wealth Effects and Fiscal Policy in the 1930s. *The Economic History Review, 44*(3), 515.

Turner, M. (1992). Output and Prices in UK Agriculture, 1867–1914, and the Great Agricultural Depression Reconsidered. *Agricultural History Review, 40*, 38–51.

Turner, J. (2014). *Banking in Crisis: The Rise and Fall of British Banking Stability, 1800 to the Present*. Cambridge: Cambridge University Press.

Turner, M., Beckett, J., & Afton, B. (2001). *Farm Production in England 1700–1914*. Oxford: Oxford University Press.

Ugolini, S. (2016). *Liquidity Management and Central Bank Strength: Bank of England Operations Reloaded, 1889–1910* (Norges Bank Working Paper 10/16).

Ward-Perkins, C. (1962). The Commercial Crisis of 1847. In E. Carus-Wilson (Ed.), *Essays in Economic History* (Vol. 3, pp. 263–279). London: Arnold.

Wrigley, E., & Schofield, R. (1989). *The Population History of England 1541–1871* (2nd ed.). Cambridge: Cambridge University Press.

7

Conclusions

Evaluating the nature of business cycles in the UK over the past three and a half centuries remains a challenge. Many theories still compete as viable explanations for the existence of cycles and a huge range of statistical techniques exist to dissect and interpret those cycles. This volume has attempted to summarise the state of play on many of the issues although there are various issues we have not been able to cover.

It is clear that a wide variety of different metrics can be constructed to date and evaluate UK business cycles with the range methods available. In each case however a substantial amount of judgement is involved in establishing turning points precisely and a narrative history to go alongside such business cycle dating is essential. The narrative supplied in this volume makes a start but more can be done especially at a higher frequency than has been attempted here. But the unavoidable idiosyncratic nature of any one narrative is not a substitute for the collective wisdom and expert knowledge of many economists and economic historians. For this reason we would support the formation of a UK business cycle dating committee that has a similar role to that performed by the NBER business cycle dating committee for the United States.

N. Dimsdale and R. Thomas,
UK Business and Financial Cycles Since 1660,
https://doi.org/10.1007/978-3-030-26346-1_7

It is also clear from the narrative that financial cycles and business cycles in the UK are related. The evidence suggests financial cycles are longer than standard business cycles but turning points in those cycles, such as those that reflect major banking and financial crises, do appear to have played a role in episodes of output contraction. As Eichengreen and Mitchener (2003) suggest many recessions may reflect credit booms that simply went wrong. The summary of the univariate approach to business cycles adopted here is not sufficient to shed light on that statistically. In part that is due to the fact that data on quantities of bank money and credit in the UK are only readily available from the late C19th onwards, although an increasing body of work is pointing the way to pushing the estimates back to the C18th. That work will ultimately make it possible to evaluate the linkages between business and financial cycles more precisely using the range of multivariate methods available. We intend to explore this further in a future volume.

The new GDP data by Broadberry et al. (2015) has also helped to sharpen the historical narrative for the C18th and C19th especially by outlining the respective roles for agriculture, industry and services. For example, it has shed light on the nature of growth in the 1780s showing that what was seen as an expansionary period in between the War of Independence and the start of the French wars was more muted when agricultural output is taken into account.

More should also be done to integrate both World Wars into the UK business cycle narrative. The contractions that occurred towards the end of both conflicts and in their immediate aftermath were among the largest on record and it took many years to recover the peak level of GDP attained during the war. Even after accounting for the effects of lower government spending and demobilisation the 1920–1921 recession stands out as the largest contraction in UK economic history. And the decline in output between 1943 and 1947 is rarely mentioned. These may be the natural result of demobilisation and post-war reduction of effort and labour participation but more needs to be done to evaluate them in terms of the traditional UK business cycle narrative.

Overall the three and a half-century history of business cycles in the UK represents the longest continuous record of economic fluctuations.

It should remain at the heart of research into the causes and nature of business cycles and the policy responses that may be necessary to offset the inefficiencies—if any—that arise from them.

References

Broadberry, S., Campbell, B., Klein, A., Overton, M., & van Leeuwen, B. (2015). *British Economic Growth 1270–1870*. Cambridge: Cambridge University Press.

Eichengreen, B., & Mitchener, K. (2003). *The Great Depression as a Credit Boom Gone Wrong* (BIS Working Paper 137).

Correction to: UK Business and Financial Cycles Since 1660

Correction to:
N. Dimsdale and R. Thomas,
UK Business and Financial Cycles Since 1660,
https://doi.org/10.1007/978-3-030-26346-1

The original version of the book unfortunately had some chapter-wise corrections post publication. The corrections have been incorporated in the book.

The updated versions of the chapters can be found at
https://doi.org/10.1007/978-3-030-26346-1_2
https://doi.org/10.1007/978-3-030-26346-1_3
https://doi.org/10.1007/978-3-030-26346-1_4
https://doi.org/10.1007/978-3-030-26346-1_6
https://doi.org/10.1007/978-3-030-26346-1

N. Dimsdale and R. Thomas,
UK Business and Financial Cycles Since 1660,
https://doi.org/10.1007/978-3-030-26346-1_8

References

Accominotti, O. (2012). London Merchant Banks, the Central European Panic and the Sterling Crisis of 1931. *Journal of Economic History, 72*(2012), 1–43.

Aikman, D., Haldane, A., & Nelson, B. (2013). Curbing the Credit Cycle. *Economic Journal, 125*(585), 1072–1109.

Aikman, D., Bush, O., & Taylor, A. (2016). *Monetary Versus Macroprudential Policies: Causal Impacts of Interest Rates and Credit Controls in the Era of the UK Radcliffe Report* (NBER Working Paper 22380).

Aldcroft, D., & Fearon, P. (1972). *British Economic Fluctuations, 1790–1939.* Basingstoke: Macmillan.

Andersson, F., & Lennard, J. (2019). Irish GDP Between the Famine and the First World War: Estimates Based on a Dynamic Factor Model. *European Review of Economic History, 23*(1), 50–71.

Andrews, B. P. A. (1987). *Exchange Rate Appreciation, Competitiveness and Export Performance: The UK Experience in the Inter-War Period.* Oxford University DPhil Thesis. http://ora.ox.ac.uk/objects/uuid:69b9bcfe-a2fa-4f02-8d49-2f847fa6dc32.

Anson, M., Bholat, D., Kang, M., & Thomas, R. (2017). *The Bank of England as Lender of Last Resort: New Historical Evidence from Daily Transactional Data* (Bank of England Working Paper 691).

N. Dimsdale and R. Thomas,
UK Business and Financial Cycles Since 1660,
https://doi.org/10.1007/978-3-030-26346-1

Ashton, T. (1949). *The Industrial Revolution, 1760–1830*. Oxford: Oxford University Press.
Ashton, T. (1959). *Economic Fluctuations in England 1700–1800*. Oxford: Clarendon Press.
Bagehot, W. (1873). *Lombard Street: A Description of the London Money Market*. London: Henry S. King & Co.
Bank of England. (1982). The Supplementary Special Deposits Scheme. *Quarterly Bulletin, Q1*, 74–85.
Bank of England. (1997, November 20). *Inflation Report*.
Barro, R. (1987). Government Spending, Interest Rates, Prices and Budget Deficits in the United Kingdom, 1701–1918. *Journal of Monetary Economics, 20*(2), 221–247.
Barro, R., & Gordon, R. (1983). Rules, Discretion and Reputation in a Model of Monetary Policy. *Journal of Monetary Economics, 12*(1), 101–121.
Baxter, M., & King, R. (1995). *Measuring Business Cycles: Approximate Band-Pass Filters for Economic Time Series* (NBER Working Paper 5022).
Beenstock, M., Capie F., & Griffiths, B. (1984). *Economic Recovery in the United Kingdom in the 1930s* (Bank of England Panel Paper 23).
Benati, L. (2001). *Band-Pass Filtering, Cointegration, and Business Cycle Analysis* (Bank of England Working Paper 142).
Benjamin, D., & Kochin, L. (1979). Searching for an Explanation of Unemployment in Interwar Britain. *Journal of Political Economy, 87*(3), 441–478.
Berge, T., & Jorda, O. (2013). A Chronology of Turning Points in Economic Activity: Spain, 1850–2011. *SERIEs, Journal of the Spanish Economic Association, 4*(1), 1–34.
Beveridge, S., & Nelson, C. (1981). A New Approach to Decomposition of Economic Time Series into Permanent and Transitory Components with Particular Attention to Measurement of the 'Business Cycle'. *Journal of Monetary Economics, 7*(2), 151–174.
Blanchard, O., & Summers, L. (1986). Hysteresis and the European Unemployment Problem. *NBER Macroeconomics Annual, 1*, 15–90.
Bohlmann, G. (1899). Ein ausgleichungsproblem. *Nachrichten Gesellschaft Wissenschaften Gottingen. Mathematisch-Physikalische Klasse, 1899*, 260–271.
Bordo, M. (1985). *Some Historical Evidence 1870–1933 on the Impact and International Transmission of Financial Crises* (NBER Working Paper 1606).
Boyer, G., & Hatton, T. (2002). New Estimates of British Unemployment, 1870–1913. *The Journal of Economic History, 62*(3), 643–675.

Bridges, J., Rossiter, N., & Thomas, R. (2011). Understanding the Recent Weakness in Broad Money Growth. *Bank of England Quarterly Bulletin, 51*(1), 22–35.

Britton, A. (1991). *Macroeconomic Policy in Britain 1974–1987*. Cambridge: Cambridge University Press.

Broadberry, S. (1986). *The British Economy Between the Wars: A Macroeconomic Survey*. Oxford: Blackwell.

Broadberry, S. (1990). The Emergence of Mass Unemployment: Explaining Macroeconomic Trends in Britain During the Trans-World War I Period. *The Economic History Review, 43*(2), 271–282.

Broadberry, S., Campbell, B., Klein, A., Overton, M., & van Leeuwen, B. (2015). *British Economic Growth 1270–1870*. Cambridge: Cambridge University Press.

Broadberry, S., & Crafts, N. (2011). Openness, Protectionism and Britain's Productivity Performance Over the Long-Run. In G. Wood, T. Mills, & N. Crafts (Eds.), *Monetary and Banking History: Essays in Honour of Forrest Capie*. Abingdon: Routledge International Studies in Money and Banking.

Broadberry, S., & van Leeuwen, B. (2010). *British Economic Growth and the Business Cycle, 1700–1870: Annual Estimates* (CAGE Online Working Paper Series 20).

Bry, G., & Boschan, C. (1971). *Cyclical Analysis of Time Series: Selected Procedures and Computer Programs*. New York: NBER.

Burns, A., & Mitchell, W. (1946). *Measuring Business Cycles*. New York: NBER.

Butt, N., Domit, S., McLeay, M., Thomas, R., & Kirkham, L. (2012). What Can the Money Data Tell Us About the Impact of QE? *Bank of England Quarterly Bulletin, 52*(4), 321–331.

Cainrcross, A. (1953). *Home and Foreign Investment 1870–1913. Studies in Capital Accumulation*. Cambridge: Cambridge University Press.

Campbell, G. (2014). Government Policy During the British Railway Mania and the 1847 Commercial Crisis. In N. Dimsdale & A. Hotson (Eds.), *British Financial Crises Since 1825* (pp. 58–75). Croydon: Oxford University Press.

Capie, F. (1978). The British Tariff and Industrial Protection in the 1930's. *The Economic History Review, 31*(3), 399–409.

Capie, F. (2011). *The Bank of England 1950s to 1979*. Cambridge: Cambridge University Press.

Capie, F. (2007). The Emergence of the Bank of England as a Mature Central Bank. In F. Capie & G. Wood (Eds.), *The Lender of Last Resort*. Abingdon: Routledge.

Capie, F., & Webber, A. (1985). *A Monetary History of the United Kingdom, 1870–1982* (Vol. 1). London: Routledge.

Capie, F., & Wood, G. (1996). Money Demand and Supply Under the International Gold Standard: The United Kingdom 1870–1914. In T. Bayoumi, B. Eichengreen, & M. P. Taylor (Eds.), *Modern Perspectives on the Gold Standard* (pp. 261–283). Cambridge: Cambridge University Press.

Capie, F. H., & Mills, T. C. (1991). Money and Business Cycles in the US and UK, 1870–1913. *The Manchester School, 59*(S1), 38–56.

Catao, L., & Solomou, S. (2005). Effective Exchange Rates and the Classical Gold Standard Adjustment. *American Economic Review, 95*(4), 1259–1275.

Centre for Economic Policy Research. (2019). *Euro Area Business Cycle Dating Committee*. CEPR.

Central Statistical Office. (1993). A Review of CSO Cyclical Indicators. *Economic Trends, 477*, 99–107.

Chadha, J., & Newby, E. (2013). *Midas, Transmuting All, Into Paper: The Bank of England and the Banque de France During the Revolutionary and Napoleonic Wars* (Research Discussion Papers 20/2013). Bank of Finland.

Chadha, J., & Nolan, C. (2002). A Long View of the UK Business Cycle. *National Institute Economic Review, 182*(1), 72–89.

Chadha, J., Lennard, J., & Thomas, R. (2019a). *Dating Business Cycles in the United Kingdom, 1700–2010*. Mimeo.

Chadha, J., Lennard, J., Tchuente, G., & Thomas, R. (2019b). *Quarterly GDP Estimates for the United Kingdom, 1938–55*. Mimeo.

Checkland, S. (1975). *Scottish Banking: A History, 1695–1973*. London: Collins.

Chow, G., & Lin, A. (1971). Best Linear Unbiased Interpolation, Distribution, and Extrapolation of Time Series by Related Series. *The Review of Economics and Statistics, 53*(4), 372–375.

Christiano, L., & Fitzgerald, T. (1999). *The Band Pass Filter* (NBER Working Paper 7257).

Clapham, J. (1944). The Bank of England: A History. (2 Volumes). Cambridge: Cambridge University Press.

Clark, T., & Dilnot, A. (2004). British Fiscal Policy Since 1939. In R. Floud & P. Johnson (Eds.), *The Cambridge Economic History of Modern Britain* (pp. 368–398). Cambridge: Cambridge University Press.

Cloyne, J. (2013). Discretionary Tax Changes and the Macroeconomy: New Narrative Evidence from the United Kingdom. *American Economic Review, 103*(4), 1507–1528.

Cloyne, J., Dimsdale, N., & Postel-Vinay, N. (2018). *Taxes and Growth: New Narrative Evidence from Interwar Britain* (NBER Working Paper 24659).

Coffman, D., Stephenson, J., & Sussman, N. (2019). *Financing the Rebuilding of the City of London After the Great Fire of 1666*. Mimeo.

Collins, M. (1988). English Banks and Business Cycles. In P. Cottrell & D. Moggridge (Eds.), *Money and Power: Essays in Honour of L.S. Pressnell*. London: Macmillan.

Collins, M. (1989). The Banking Crisis of 1878. *The Economic History Review, 42*(4), 504–527.

Congdon, T. (1992). *Reflections on Monetarism*. Oxford: Clarendon Press.

Congdon, T. (2005). *Money and Asset Prices in Boom and Bust* (IEA Hobart Paper No. 153). London.

Crafts, N. (2013). *Returning to Growth: Lessons from the 1930s* (Economic History Society Working Paper 13010).

Crafts, N. F. R., & Harley, C. K. (1992). Output Growth and the British Industrial Revolution: A Restatement of the Crafts-Harley View. *The Economic History Review, 45*(4), 703–730.

Crafts, N., & Mills, T. (2013). Rearmament to the Rescue? New Estimates of the Impact of "Keynesian" Policies in 1930s' Britain. *The Journal of Economic History, 73*(4), 1077–1104.

Crafts, N., & Mills, T. (2017). Six Centuries of British Economic Growth: A Time-Series Perspective. *European Review of Economic History, 21*(2), 141–158.

David, P. (1990). The Dynamo and the Computer: An Historical Perspective on the Productivity Paradox. *American Economic Review, 80*(2), 355–361.

Davis, R. (1954). English Foreign Trade, 1660–1700. *The Economic History Review, 7*(2), 150–166.

Davis, R. (1960). English Foreign Trade, 1700–1774. *The Economic History Review, 15*(2), 285–303.

Davis, J. (2006). An Improved Annual Chronology of U.S. Business Cycles Since the 1790s. *American Economic Review, 66*(1): 103–121.

Deane, P. (1968). New Estimates of Gross National Product for the United Kingdom, 1830–1914. *Review of Income and Wealth, 14*(2), 95–112.

Deane, P. (1979). *The First Industrial Revolution* (2nd ed.). Cambridge: Cambridge University Press.

Deane, P., & Cole, W. (1962). *British Economic Growth, 1688–1959: Trends and Structure*. Cambridge: Cambridge University Press.

Denley, H. (2016). *National Accounts Historic Dataset Developments Since Blue Book 2011* (Office for National Statistics Article).

Dickson, P. (1967). *The Financial Revolution in England: A Study in the Development of Public Credit, 1688–1756*. London: Macmillan.

Dimsdale, N. (1981). British Monetary Policy and the Exchange Rate 1920–1938. In W. Eltis & P. Sinclair (Eds.), *The Money Supply and the Exchange Rate*. Oxford: Oxford University Press.

Dimsdale, N. (1990). Money, Interest and Cycles in Britain Since 1830. *Greek Economic Review, 12*(Supplement), 153–196.

Dimsdale, N. (1991). British Monetary Policy Since 1945. In N. Crafts & N. Woodward (Eds.), *The British Economy Since 1945*. Oxford: Clarendon.

Dimsdale, N. (2013a). *The Dynamics of Consumption and Investment in the Victorian Economy* (University of Oxford Discussion Papers in Economic and Social History 122).

Dimsdale, N. (2013b). *The Bank of England and the British Economy 1890–1913* (University of Oxford Discussion Papers in Economic and Social History 123).

Dimsdale N. (2015). Monetary Trends in the UK Since 1870. In M. Allen & D. Coffman (Eds.), *Money, Wages and Prices: Essays in Honour of Professor Nicholas Mayhew* (pp. 228–249). Basingstoke: Palgrave Macmillan.

Dimsdale, N. H., & Horsewood, N. (1995). Fiscal Policy and Employment in Interwar Britain: Some Evidence from a New Model. *Oxford Economic Papers, 47*, 369–396.

Dimsdale, N. H., Nickell, S., & Horsewood, N. (1989). Real Wages and Unemployment in Britain During the 1930s. *The Economic Journal, 99*(396), 271–292.

Dow, J. (1964). *The Management of the British Economy*. Cambridge: Cambridge University Press.

Dow, J. (1998). *Major Recessions, Britain and the World, 1920–1995*. Oxford: Oxford University Press.

Dowie, J. (1975). 1919–20 is in Need of Attention. *The Economic History Review, 28*(3), 429–450.

Drehman, M., Borio, C., & Tsatsaronis, K. (2012). *Characterising the Financial Cycle: Don't Lose Sight of the Medium Term* (BIS Working Paper 380).

Duffy, I. P. H. (1982). The Discount Policy of the Bank of England During the Suspension of Cash Payments, 1797–1821. *The Economic History Review, 35*(1), 67.

Dutton, J. (1984). The Bank of England and the "Rules of the Game" Under the International Gold Standard: New Evidence. In M. Bordo & A. Schwartz (Eds.), *A Retrospective on The Classical Gold Standard*. Chicago: University of Chicago Press.

Edelstein, M. (1982). *Overseas Investment in the Age of High Imperialism*. New York: Columbia University Press.

Edelstein, M. (1981). Foreign Investment and Empire 1860–1914. In R. Floud & D. McCloskey (Eds.), *The Economic History of Britain Since 1700* (Vol. 2). Cambridge: Cambridge University Press.

Eichengreen, B., Watson, M., & Grossman, R. (1985). Bank Rate Policy Under the Interwar Gold Standard: A Dynamic Probit Model. *The Economic Journal, 95*, 725–745.

Eichengreen, B., & Mitchener, K. (2003). *The Great Depression as a Credit Boom Gone Wrong* (BIS Working Paper 137).

Everett, G. (2011). *Historic National Accounts*. Office for National Statistics Article.

Federico, G., & Tena-Junguito, A. (2019). World Trade, 1800–1938: A New Synthesis. *Revista de Historia Económica/Journal of Iberian and Latin American Economic History, 37*(1), 9–41. https://doi.org/10.1017/S0212610918000216.

Feinstein, C. (1972). *National Income Expenditure and Output of the United Kingdom 1855–1965*. Cambridge: Cambridge University Press.

Feinstein, C. (1990). What Really Happened to Real Wages? Trends in Wages, Prices, and Productivity in the United Kingdom, 1880–1913. *The Economic History Review, 43*(3), 329–355.

Feinstein, C., & Pollard, S. (1988). *Studies in Capital Formation in the United Kingdom 1750–1920*. Oxford: Oxford University Press.

Ford, A. (1962). *The Gold Standard 1880–1914: Britain and Argentina*. Oxford: Oxford University Press.

Ford, A. (1969). British Economic Fluctuations, 1870–1914. *The Manchester School, 37*(2), 99–130.

Ford, A. (1981). The Trade Cycle in Britain 1860–1914. In R. Floud & D. McCloskey (Eds.), *The Economic History of Britain Since 1700* (Vol. 2). Cambridge: Cambridge University Press.

Friedman, M., & Schwartz, A. (1963). *A Monetary History of the United States, 1867–1960*. Princeton: Princeton University Press.

Friedman, M., & Schwartz, A. (1982). *Monetary Trends in the United States and the United Kingdom*. Chicago: University of Chicago Press for the NBER.

Friedman, M. (1968). The Role of Monetary Policy: Presidential Address Delivered at the 80th Annual Meeting of the American Economic Association. *American Economic Review, 58*(1): 1–17.

Frisch, R. (1933). Propagation Problems and Impulse Problems in Dynamic Economics. In K. Koch (Ed.), *Economic Essays in Honour of Gustav Cassel*. London: Allen & Unwin.

Gayer, A., Rostow, W., & Schwartz, A. (1953). *The Growth and Fluctuation of the British Economy, 1790–1850*. Oxford: Clarendon Press.

Geary, F., & Stark, T. (2004). Trends in Real Wages During the Industrial Revolution: A View from Across the Irish Sea. *The Economic History Review, 57*(2), 362–395.

Geary, F., & Stark, T. (2015). Regional GDP in the UK, 1861–1911: New Estimates. *The Economic History Review, 68*(1), 123–144.

Geary, F., & Stark, T. (2018). 150 Years of Regional GDP: United Kingdom and Ireland. In J. Rosés & N. Wolf (Eds.), *The Economic Development of Europe's Regions: A Quantitative History Since 1900*. London: Routledge.

Gent, J. (2016). *Abundance and Scarcity: Classical Theories of Money, Bank Balance Sheets and Business Models, and the British Restriction of 1797–1818* (PhD thesis). London School of Economics.

Ginarlis, J., & Pollard, S. (1988). *Roads and Waterways 1750–1850*. In Feinstein and Pollard (1988) op. cit..

Goodhart, C. (1972). *The Business of Banking 1891–1914*. London: Weidenfeld & Nicolson.

Goodhart, C. (1986). Financial Innovation and Monetary Control. *Oxford Review of Economic Policy, 2*(4), 79–102.

Goodhart, C. A. E. (2015). Competition and Credit Control: Some Personal Reflections. *Financial History Review, 22*(2), 235–246.

Goodhart, C. A. E., & Needham, D. J. (2017). Historical Reasons for the Focus on Broad Monetary Aggregates in Post-World War II Britain and the 'Seven Years War' with the IMF. *Financial History Review, 24*(3), 331–356.

Grant, A., & Chan, J. (2017). Reconciling Output Gaps: Unobserved Components Model and Hodrick-Prescott Filter. *Journal of Economic Dynamics and Control, 75*, 114–121.

Green, G. (2018). *Monetary Policy Spillovers in the First Age of Financial Globalisation: A Narrative VAR Approach 1884–1913* (Bank of England Working Papers 718). Bank of England.

Hamilton, J. (1989). A New Approach to the Economic Analysis of Nonstationary Time Series and the Business Cycle. *Econometrica, 57*(2), 357–384.

Harding, D., & Pagan, A. (2002). Dissecting the Cycle: A Methodological Investigation. *Journal of Monetary Economics, 49*(2), 365–381.

Harding, D., & Pagan, A. (2006). A Suggested Framework for Classifying the Modes of Cycle Research. *Journal of Applied Econometrics, 20*(2), 151–159.

Harrison, M. (1990). A Volume Index of the Total Munitions Output of the United Kingdom, 1939–1944. *Economic History Review, 43*(2), 659–668.

Harvey, A. (1989). *Forecasting, Structural Time Series Models and the Kalman Filter*. Cambridge: Cambridge University Press.

Harvey, A., & Jaeger, A. (1993). Detrending, Stylized Facts and the Business Cycle. *Journal of Applied Econometrics, 8*(3), 231–247.

Hatton, T., & Thomas, M. (2010). Labour Markets in the Interwar Period and Economic Recovery in the UK and the USA. *Oxford Review of Economic Policy, 26*(3), 463–485.

Hawtrey, R. (1919). *Currency and Credit*. London: Longmans.

Hawtrey, R. (1928). *Trade and Credit*. London: Longmans.

Hawtrey, R. (1962). *A Century of Bank Rate* (2nd ed.). London: Frank Cass.

Hayek, F. (1962). *Introduction to an Enquiry into the Nature and Effects of the Paper Credit of Great Britain by Henry Thornton*. London: George Allen & Unwin.

Hayek, F. (1929 [1933]). *Monetary Theory and the Trade Cycle*. New York: Harcourt Brace.

Hicks, J. (1967). *Critical Essays in Monetary Theory*. Oxford: Clarendon Press.

Hicks, J. (1977). *Economic Perspectives: Further Further Essays on Money and Growth*. Oxford: Clarendon Press.

Hicks, J. (1982). *Are There Economic Cycles?* In J. R. Hicks (Ed.), *Money Interest and Wages: Collected Essays on Economic Theory* (Vol. II). Oxford: Basil Blackwell.

Hodrick, R., & Prescott, E. (1980). *Postwar U.S. Business Cycles: An Empirical Investigation* (Carnegie-Mellon University Discussion Paper 451).

Hodrick, R., & Prescott, E. (1997). Postwar U.S. Business Cycles: An Empirical Investigation. *Journal of Money, Credit and Banking, 29*(1): 1–16.

Hoffmann, W. (1955). *British Industry 1700–1950*. Oxford: Basil Blackwell.

Hoover, K. (1988). *The New Classcical Macroeconomics*. Oxford: Basil Blackwell.

Hoppit, J. (1986). Financial Crises in Eighteenth-Century England. *The Economic History Review, 39*(1), 39–58.

Hoppit, J. (1987). *Risk and Failure in English Business*. Cambridge: Cambridge University Press.

Horell, S., Humphries, J., & Weale, M. (1994). An Input-Output Table for 1841. *The Economic History Review, 47*(3), 545–566.

Hoskins, W. (1968). Harvest Fluctuations and English Economic History, 1620–1759. *The Agricultural History Review, 16*(1), 15–31.

Howlett, P. (1995). *Fighting with Figures: A Statistical Digest of the Second World War*. London: Central Statistical Office.

Howson, S. (1975). *Domestic Monetary Management in Britain, 1919–38*. Cambridge: Cambridge University Press.

Huffman, W., & Lothian, J. (1984). The Gold Standard and the Transmission of Business Cycles, 1833–1932. In M. Bordo & A. Schwartz (Eds.), *A Retrospective on The Classical Gold Standard*. Chicago: University of Chicago Press.

Hughes, J. (1960). *Fluctuations in Trade, Industry, and Finance: A Study of British Economic Development, 1850–1860*. Oxford: Clarendon Press.

Jakab, Z., & Kumhof, M. (2018). *Banks are Not Intermediaries of Loanable Funds—Facts, Theory and Evidence* (Bank of England Working Paper No. 761).

Jones, D. (1988). *War and Economy in the Age of William III and Marlborough*. Oxford: Basil Blackwell.

Jordà, Ò., Schularick, M., & Taylor, A. (2013). When Credit Bites Back. *Journal of Money, Credit and Banking, 45*(s2), 3–28.

Jordà, Ò., Schularick, M., & Taylor, A. (2016). The Great Mortgaging: Housing Finance, Crises, and Business Cycles. *Economic Policy, 31*(85), 107–115.

Juglar, C. (1862). *Des Crises commerciales et leur retour periodique en France, en Angleterre, et aux Etats-Unis*. Paris: Guillaumin.

Kahn, R. F. (1931). The Relation of Home Investment to Unemployment. *The Economic Journal, 41*, 173–198.

Kaldor, N. (1966). *Causes of the Slow Rate of Growth of the United Kingdom: An Inaugural Lecture*. Cambridge: Cambridge University Press.

Keen, S. (2013). A Monetary Minsky Model of the Great Moderation and the Great Recession. *Journal of Economic Behavior & Organization, 86*, 221–235.

Keynes, J. M. (1936). *The General Theory of Employment, Interest and Money*. London: Macmillan.

Kindleberger, C. (1978). *Manias, Panics, and Crashes: A History of Financial Crises*. New York: Basic Books.

King, M. (2003, October). *Speech Given at East Midlands Development Agency/Bank of England Dinner*. Leicester.

King, W. (1936). *A History of the London Discount Market*. London: Cass.

King, R., & Plosser, C. (1984). Money, Credit, and Prices in a Real Business Cycle. *The American Economic Review, 74*(3), 363–380.

Kitchin, J. (1923). Cycles and Trends in Economic Factors. *Review of Economics and Statistics, 5*(1), 10–16.

Kitson, M., & Solomou, S. (1990). *Protectionism and Economic Revival: The British Inter-War Economy*. Cambridge: Cambridge University Press.

Knoll, K., Schularick, M., & Steger, T. (2017). No Price Like Home: Global House Prices, 1870–2012. *The American Economic Review, 107*(2), 331–353.

Kondratieff, N. D., & Stolper, W. F. (1935). The Long Waves in Economic Life. *The Review of Economics and Statistics, 17*(6),105.

Kosmetatos, P. (2018). *The 1772–73 British Credit Crisis*. London: Palgrave Macmillan.

Kuznets, S. (1930). *Secular Movements in Production and Prices: Their Nature and Their Bearing Upon Cyclical Fluctuations*. Boston: Houghton Mifflin.

Kydland, F., & Prescott, E. (1977). Rules Rather Than Discretion: The Inconsistency of Optimal Plans. *Journal of Political Economy, 85*(3), 473–492.

Kydland, F., & Prescott, E. (1982). Time to Build and Aggregate Fluctuations. *Econometrica, 50*(6), 1345–1370.

Lachmann, L. (1956). *Capital and Its Structure*. London: Bell & Sons.

Lavoie, M. (2014). *Post-Keynesian Economics: New Foundations*. Cheltenham: Edward Elgar.

Layard, R., & Nicekll, S. (1986). Unemployment in Britain. *Economica, 53* (210(S)): S121–S169.

Lennard, J. (2018). Did Monetary Policy Matter? Narrative Evidence from the Classical Gold Standard. *Explorations in Economic History, 68*, 16–36.

Lévy-Leboyer, M. (1982). Central Banking and Foreign Trade: The Anglo-American Cycle in the 1830s. In C. P. Kindleberger & J.-P. Laffargue (Eds.), *Financial Crises: Theory, History and Policy*. Cambridge: Cambridge University Press.

Lewis, W. A. (1978). *Growth and Fluctuations, 1870–1913*. London: Allen and Unwin.

Lloyd, S., & Solomou, S. (2019). *The Impact of the 1932 General Tariff: A Difference-in-Difference Approach*. Cliometrica.

Long, J., & Plosser, C. (1983). Real Business Cycles. *Journal of Political Economy, 91*(1), 39–69.

Lovell, M. (1957). The Role of the Bank of England as Lender of Last Resort in the Crises of the Eighteenth Century. *Explorations in Entrepreneurial History, 10*, 8–21.

Lucas, R. (1973). Some International Evidence on Output-Inflation Tradeoffs. *American Economic Review, 63*(3), 326–334.

Lucas, R. (1975). An Equilibrium Model of the Business Cycle. *Journal of Political Economy, 83*(6), 1113–1144.

Martin, B. (2009). Resurrecting the UK Historic Sector National Accounts. *Review of Income and Wealth, 55*(3), 737–751.

Matthews, R. (1954). *A Study in Trade-Cycle History: Economic Fluctuations in Great Britain 1833–1842*. Cambridge: Cambridge University Press.

Matthews, R. (1971). The Role of Demand Management. In A. Cairncross (Ed.), *Britain's Economic Prospects Reconsidered*. London: Allen and Unwin.

Matthews, R., Feinstein, C., & Odling-Smee, J. (1982). *British Economic Growth, 1856–1973*. Oxford: Oxford University Press.

McLeay, M., Radia, A., & Thomas, R. (2014). Money Creation in the Modern Economy. *Bank of England Quarterly Bulletin, 54*(1), 14–27.

Melton, F. (2002). *Sir Robert Clayton and the Origins of English Deposit Banking 1658–1685*. Cambridge: Cambridge University Press.

Mensch, G. (1979). *Stalemate in Technology: Innovations Overcome the Depression*. Cambridge, MA: Ballinger Publishing.

Mian, A., & Sufi, A. (2014). *House of Debt*. Chicago: Chicago University Press.

Michie, R. (2016). *British Banking: Continuity and Change 1694 to the Present*. Oxford: Oxford University Press.

Middleton, R. (1981). The Constant Employment Budget Balance and British Budgetary Policy, 1929–39. *The Economic History Review, 34*(2), 266–286.

Middleton, R. (2010). British Monetary and Fiscal Policy in the 1930s. *Oxford Review of Economic Policy, 26*(3), 414–441.

Minsky, H. (1986). *Stabilizing an Unstable Economy*. London: Yale University Press.

Mirowski, P. (1981). The Rise (and Retreat) of a Market: English Joint Stock Shares in the Eighteenth Century. *The Journal of Economic History, 41*(3), 559–577.

Mirowski, P. (1985 [2015]). *The Birth of the Business Cycle*. London: Routledge.

Mitchell, B. (1988). *British Historical Statistics*. Cambridge: Cambridge University Press.

Mitchell, J., Solomou, S., & Weale, M. (2012). Monthly GDP Estimates for Inter-War Britain. *Explorations in Economic History, 49*(4), 543–556.

Moggridge, D. (1969). *The Return to Gold, 1925: The Formulation of Economic Policy and Its Critics* (Occasional Papers 19). Department of Applied Economics, University of Cambridge.

Morley, J., Nelson, C., & Zivot, E. (2003). Why Are the Beveridge-Nelson and Unobserved-Components Decompositions of GDP So Different? *The Review of Economics and Statistics, 85*(2), 235–243.

Morys, M. (2014). Cycles and Depressions. In R. Floud, J. Humphries, & P. Johnson (Eds.), *The Cambridge Economic History of Modern Britain: Volume II. 1870 to the Present*. Cambridge: Cambridge University Press.

Muellbauer, J., & Murphy, A. (1990). Is the UK Balance of Payments Sustainable? *Economic Policy, 5*(11), 347.

National Bureau of Economic Research. (2019). *US Business Cycle Expansions and Contractions*.

Neal, L. (1998). The Financial Crisis of 1825 and the Restructuring of the British Financial System. *Federal Reserve Bank of St. Louis Review, 80*(3).

Neal, L., & Weidenmier, M. (2002). *Crises in the Global Economy from Tulips to Today: Contagion and Consequences* (NBER Working Paper 9147).

Needham, D. (2014). *UK Monetary Policy from Devaluation to Thatcher, 1967–82*. London: Palgrave.

Neftci, S. (1982). Optimal Prediction of Cyclical Downturns. *Journal of Economic Dynamics and Control, 4*, 225–241.

Nelson, E. (2018). Seven Fallacies Concerning Milton Friedman's "The Role of Monetary Policy". *Journal of Money, Credit and Banking*. Early View.

O'Brien, P. (1988). The Political Economy of British Taxation, 1660–1815. *The Economic History Review, 41*(1), 1–32.

O'Brien, P., & Hunt, P. (1999). England 1485–1815. In R. Bonney (Ed.), *The Rise of the Fiscal State in Europe, c. 1200–1815*. Oxford.

O'Brien, P., & Palma, N. (2017). *Danger to the Old Lady of Threadneedle Street? The Bank Restriction Act and the Regime Shift to Paper Money, 1797–1821* (Economic History Society Working Paper 17001).

OECD. (2019). *OECD Composite Leading Indicators: Reference Turning Points and Component Series*. Paris: OECD.

Palma, N. (2018). Reconstruction of Money Supply Over the Long Run: The Case of England, 1270–1870. *The Economic History Review, 71*(2), 373–392.

Perron, P., & Wada, T. (2009). Let's Take a Break: Trends and Cycles in US Real GDP. *Journal of Monetary Economics, 56*(6), 749–765.

Pigou, A. (1947). *Aspects of British Economic History 1918–1925*. London: Macmillan.

Pippenger, J. (1984). Bank of England Operations. In M. Bordo & A. Schwartz (Eds.), *A Retrospective on the Classical Gold Standard* (pp. 1893–1913). Chicago: University of Chicago Press.

Pressnell, L. (1956). *Country Banking in the Industrial Revolution*. Oxford: Oxford University Press.

Price, J. (1992). The Bank of England's Discount Activity and the Merchants of London, 1694–1773. In I. Blanchard, A. Goodman, & J. Newman (Eds.), *Industry and Finance in Early Modern History—Essays Presented to George Hammersley on the Occasion of His 74th Birthday* (pp. 92–114). Stuttgart: Franz Steiner Verlag.

Ramey, V. (2011). Can Government Purchases Stimulate the Economy? *Journal of Economic Literature, 49*(3), 673–685.

Richardson, H. (1967). *Economic Recovery in Britain 1932–39*. London: Weidenfeld & Nicolson.

Rockoff, H. (1971). *Monetary Statistics of the United States: Estimates, Sources, Methods*. By Milton Friedman and Anna Jacobson Schwartz. New York, Columbia University Press, 1970. *Business History Review, 45*(3): 377–379.

Rogoff, K. (1985). The Optimal Degree of Commitment to an Intermediate Monetary Target. *Quarterly Journal of Economics, 100,* 1169–1189.

Romer, C. (1994). Remeasuring Business Cycles. *The Journal of Economic History, 54*(3), 573–609.

Romer, C. D., & Romer, D. H. (1989). Does Monetary Policy Matter? A New Test in the Spirit of Friedman and Schwartz. *NBER Macroeconomics Annual, 4*, 121–170.

Rostow, W. (1972). Cycles in the British Economy: 1790–1914. In D. Aldcroft & P. Fearon (Eds.), *British Economic Fluctuations, 1790–1939*. Basingstoke: Macmillan.

Samy, L. (2015). *Indices of House Prices and Rent Prices of Residential Property in London, 1895–1939* (University of Oxford Discussion Papers in Economic and Social History 134).

Sayers, R. (1976). *The Bank of England 1891–1944*. Cambridge: Cambridge University Press.

Schenk, C. (2010). *The Decline of Sterling: Managing the Retreat of an International Currency, 1945–1992*. Cambridge: Cambridge University Press.

Schumpeter, J. (1939). *Business Cycles: A Theoretical, Historical, and Statistical Analysis of the Capitalist Process*. New York: McGraw-Hill.

Sefton, J., & Weale, M. (1995). *Reconciliation of National Income and Expenditure: Balanced Estimates of National Income for the United Kingdom, 1920–1990*. Cambridge: Cambridge University Press.

Silberling, N. J. (1924). Financial and Monetary Policy of Great Britain During the Napoleonic Wars. *The Quarterly Journal of Economics, 38*(3), 397.

Solomou, S. (1994). Economic Fluctuations. In R. Floud & D. McCloskey (Eds.), *The Economic History of Britain Since 1700 Volume 2: 1860–1939* (pp. 1870–1913). Cambridge: Cambridge University Press.

Solomou, S., & Weale, M. (1991). Balanced Estimates of UK GDP 1870–1913. *Explorations in Economic History, 28*(1), 54–63.

Solomou, S., & Thomas, R. (2019). *Feinstein Fulfilled: GDP from the Income Side 1841–1920* (ESCoE Technical Report 04).

Solow, R. (1957). Technical Change and the Aggregate Production Function. *The Review of Economics and Statistics, 39*(3), 312–320.

Sowerbutts, R., Schneebalg, M., & Hubert, F. (2016). The Demise of Overend Gurney. *Bank of England Quarterly Bulletin, 56*(2), 94–106.

Stratton, J. (1978). *Agricultural Records, A.D. 220–1977*. London: Baker.

Temin, P. (1974). The Anglo-American Business Cycle, 1820–60. *The Economic History Review, 27*(2), 207–221.

Temin, P., & Voth, H. (2013). *Prometheus Shackled: Goldsmith Banks and England's Financial Revolution After 1700*. Oxford: Oxford University Press.

Thomas, B. (1954). *Migration and Economic Growth: A Study of Great Britain and the Atlantic Economy*. Cambridge: Cambridge University Press.

Thomas, M. (1983). Rearmament and Recovery in the Late 1930s. *Economic History Review, 36*(4), 552–579.

Thomas, R., & Dimsdale, N. (2017). *A Millennium of UK Macroeconomic Data: Bank of England OBRA Dataset*. London, UK: Bank of England. https://www.bankofengland.co.uk/-/media/boe/files/statistics/research-datasets/a-millennium-of-macroeconomic-data-for-the-uk.xlsx.

Tooke, T., & Newmarch, W. (1838). *A History of Prices, and of the State of the Circulation, from 1793 to 1837; Preceded by a Brief Sketch of the State of Corn Trade in the Last Two Centuries*. London: Longman, Orme, Brown, Green, and Longmans.

Turner, P. (1991). Wealth Effects and Fiscal Policy in the 1930s. *The Economic History Review, 44*(3), 515.

Turner, M. (1992). Output and Prices in UK Agriculture, 1867–1914, and the Great Agricultural Depression Reconsidered. *Agricultural History Review, 40*, 38–51.

Turner, J. (2014). *Banking in Crisis: The Rise and Fall of British Banking Stability, 1800 to the Present*. Cambridge: Cambridge University Press.

Turner, M., Beckett, J., & Afton, B. (2001). *Farm Production in England 1700–1914*. Oxford: Oxford University Press.

von Mises, L. (1934). *The Theory of Money and Credit*. London: Jonathan Cape.

Ugolini, S. (2016). *Liquidity Management and Central Bank Strength: Bank of England Operations Reloaded, 1889–1910* (Norges Bank Working Paper 10/16).

Ward-Perkins, C. (1962). The Commercial Crisis of 1847. In E. Carus-Wilson (Ed.), *Essays in Economic History* (Vol. 3, pp. 263–279). London: Arnold.

Whittaker, E. (1923). On a New Method of Graduation. *Proceedings of the Edinburgh Mathematical Association, 41*, 63–75.

Wicksell, K. (1898). *Interest and Prices*, Reprinted 1965. New York: Augustus Kelley.

Wrigley, E., & Schofield, R. (1989). *The Population History of England 1541–1871* (2nd ed.). Cambridge: Cambridge University Press.

Zarnowitz, V. (1985). Recent Work on Business Cycles in Historical Perspective: A Review of Theories and Evidence. *Journal of Economic Literature, 23*(2), 523–580.

Index

N. Dimsdale and R. Thomas,
UK Business and Financial Cycles Since 1660,
https://doi.org/10.1007/978-3-030-26346-1

The manufacturer's authorised representative in the EU is Springer Nature Customer Service Centre GmbH, Europaplatz 3, 69115 Heidelberg, Germany. If you have any concerns regarding our products, please contact ProductSafety@springernature.com

Printed and bound by CPI Group (UK) Ltd, Croydon, CR0 4YY

30/09/2026

02225656-0008